SIR EDWARD COLEBROOKE
OF ABINGTON AND OTTERSHAW
BARONET AND MEMBER OF PARLIAMENT

THE FOUR LIVES OF AN EXTRAORDINARY VICTORIAN

To Liz and Doug

All best wishes

Sheila Binns

Sheila Binns

**Grosvenor House
Publishing Limited**

This book is published by
Grosvenor House Publishing Ltd
28-30 High Street, Guildford, Surrey, GU1 3EL.
www.grosvenorhousepublishing.co.uk

A CIP record for this book
is available from the British Library

ISBN 978-1-78148-694-8

Sir Edward Colebrooke
of Abington and Ottershaw
Baronet and Member of Parliament

The four lives of an extraordinary Victorian

Listings of the baronetage give Sir Edward Colebrooke's seats as Abington House, Lanark, Scotland and Ottershaw Park, Chertsey, Surrey, England while his 'town house' was 37 South Street, Park Lane, London. He sat in the House of Commons as a Liberal for 38 years, was an excellent landlord and very popular among all classes in Lanarkshire, where he took an active part in county business for nearly half a century. In Ottershaw, he is remembered as a generous benefactor.

Supported by
The National Lottery®
through the Heritage Lottery Fund

heritage
lottery fund

Acknowledgements for front cover images

Abington House, early 1860s
From *The Upper Ward of Lanarkshire*, Volume 1,
by G V Irving and A Murray, 1864

Ottershaw Park by John Hassell, 1824
Reproduced by permission of Surrey History Centre

Sir Edward Colebrooke by George Richmond, 1877
From the collection at Wrotham Park

Sir Thomas Edward Colebrooke by Richard James Lane, after George Richmond, lithograph, 1860
© National Portrait Gallery, London

Contents

Foreword

This book is a very timely and fitting tribute to a significant but largely unknown Victorian aristocrat whose legacy is very evident in two very different locations; the Surrey village of Ottershaw and Lanarkshire in the Lowlands of Scotland. The information, uncovered by the recent research, about Sir Edward (1813-1890) is of particular interest to us in Ottershaw as 2014 marks the 150th anniversary of consecration of our lovely church that Sir Edward had built and which we still enjoy today. It is also in our churchyard that he was laid to rest along with his wife.

I am delighted that Sheila Binns was able to find the material which will help us understand and learn about Sir Edward. The project, involving the research and publication of this book, was made possible by Heritage Lottery funding under the 'All our Stories' programme to mark not only the 150th anniversary of the church but also to contribute to celebrations of Sir Edward's 200th birthday in 2013.

He effectively founded the village of Ottershaw through his provision of the church and by being instrumental in the establishment of three other buildings (the original vicarage, the original school and the working men's club (social club)) for the benefit of local people. Ottershaw is greatly indebted to this benefactor. He was someone who took his Christian duty, his obligations as a landlord and MP and the nurture of his family very seriously and this book has brought all this to light. Some of the conclusions reached about him will also challenge our preconceived ideas and accepted assumptions about him.

Rev Dr Sandra Faccini
Vicar of Ottershaw

Preface

The starting point for this book about Sir Edward Colebrooke was moving to the lovely Surrey village of Ottershaw and noticing immediately that it had a particularly attractive church but that it was in an odd location – on the top of a hill on the very edge of the village. Its odd location always niggled. Why was it not in the village? Why was it up there on the hill?

The opportunity to try to answer my own questions came during a university course, taken as a mature student, when, as an exercise in using archival material, I tried to find out about the church and the man behind the building of it and about whom, at that stage, I knew little more than his name. The essay I produced turned out to be no more than a toe in the water and I realised that much more was waiting to be found out – and so began a journey of discovery.

To my great pleasure, Christ Church was very keen to know more about their patron, especially as two celebrations approached: the patron's 200th birthday in 2013 and the 150th anniversary of the consecration of the church in 2014. The church was fortunate in securing Heritage Lottery funding to help progress research and this book is the major product of that research.

Several archives and museums have provided items that have helped me to piece together Sir Edward's life, including the archive of Christ Church Ottershaw, Surrey History Centre,

Chertsey Museum, the Wrotham Park archive, the National Archives, Biggar Museum Trust, Lanark Local History Library and the Victorian Society. An unexpected and extraordinarily rich source of information was the nineteenth century newspapers available online. Many of the reports were from Scottish newspapers, even for activities in London, as Scotland was where, as it turned out, newspaper readers had the greatest interest in Sir Edward Colebrooke. An unexpected collection of letters in the Surrey History Centre collection -*The Colebrooke Letters* - provided unique insight into the lives of the Colebrooke family. These are typescript copies of letters written between 1870 and 1888 to Mr W F Rawnsley, who was employed by Sir Edward and Lady Colebrooke as a tutor. They had turned up among a bookseller's reject stock and were presented to the Surrey History Centre in 2003 by a Guildford bookbinder.

In using material from the nineteenth century newspapers, it was recognised that only certain newspapers have survived and that what can be obtained from these newspapers does not necessarily give a full picture. However, in the case of this research project, a picture richer in detail than was ever anticipated gradually emerged. It was evident that the syndication of news items, as was common at the time, meant that a surviving report sometimes came from an unexpected source such as a regional paper from an area with no known connection to the subject matter.

In considering *The Colebrooke Letters*, I originally had some doubt as to their authenticity. It is not known whether the copies were made for Mr Rawnsley or whether the originals still exist. However, there are so many references that correspond exactly to information given in newspapers, that there can be no doubt that they are genuine – if unusual – transcriptions from original letters.

Some of the words, phrases and grammar used in Victorian times have now fallen out of use or changed meaning. Original text has been retained in quotations, with an explanation, if necessary. Otherwise, current terminology has normally been preferred. In particular, the term 'Scottish' has generally been adopted as 'Scotch', which was almost universally preferred in Victorian times, is now almost never used for people and things in Scotland.

Without the assistance of many people, the project could never have gained the unexpected depth that has been achieved. I should like to express my sincere thanks to Pam Brush, the archivist at Christ Church, Ottershaw, who found relevant documents and images for me; Charles Dace, archivist at Wrotham Park, Barnet, who provided me with a copy of *Sola Bona Quae Honesta: The Colebrooke Family, 1650-1950* and gave me access to the Wrotham Park archive, the repository of the remaining Colebrooke papers; Brian Lambie of the Biggar Museum Trust for his great help and encouragement and for providing several images; John Lindsay for introducing me to Brian Lambie and for information on the Caledonian Railway; Hannah Lane for much useful information; Geoff Bourne for census and electoral registers material and the staff of the various museums, archives and libraries I have visited. Without exception, everyone has been helpful and generous with their time. Most particularly, though, I want to thank Peter, my husband, who has put up with this 'other man' in my life, for his untiring support, interest and ideas.

As I gathered information on Sir Edward, it became increasingly apparent to me that he lived his life in four different spheres and his contacts in each sphere knew little or nothing about those in the others. He effectively lived four lives in one lifetime and any of these could have been a full life for an aristocrat of his time. The book is subtitled and structured to reflect this compartmentalised life. There is inevitably some repetition but it is hoped that there is no more than is necessary to allow understanding. The views and conclusions given in the book, unless attributed, are mine. I have done my best to check facts and sources but if there are any errors or omissions, I apologise - they are my fault alone.

I am delighted to have been able to produce this biography to coincide with the 150th anniversary in May 2014 of the consecration of Christ Church Ottershaw, the church that Sir Edward Colebrooke had built in Ottershaw, Surrey.

Sheila Binns
Ottershaw
February 2014

Introduction

Two small communities, more than 350 miles apart, know the name of Sir Edward Colebrooke but know very little about him. Both have at least one road named after him. One has a pub bearing his name with pictures inside showing parts of what was his estate. In the other, a portrait of him keeps an eye on drinkers in the Social Club, where he was the first president. Despite this, it is difficult to find anyone who knows much about who he was and what he did.

He was born the third son of an untitled father and seemingly unexceptional. His working life began with an administrative job in India, at which point he thought his career was to be in the Indian Administration with the East India Company. Wealth and a title came his way unexpectedly and whilst enjoying the lifestyle that riches provided, he determined to use his gifts of fortune wisely and spent most of his life working for the betterment of his fellow men.

His name was Thomas Edward Colebrooke but he was always known as Sir Edward and signed himself Edward Colebrooke. This book seeks to show what an extraordinary man this ordinary Victorian turned out to be.

Chapter 1

Prologue

The Colebrookes were one of the many families that rose through enterprise from humble origins to form the growing middle classes becoming wealthy, buying land and often marrying into the aristocracy. They were a family of dynastic proportions whose origins can be traced back to the early seventeenth century.[1] With wealth came a higher social standing and influence: political power accompanied high social standing and several of the Colebrookes became Members of Parliament. For around three hundred years, the Colebrooke family enjoyed wealth, power and influence, including an important role in the governance of India. Sir Edward Colebrooke furthered the dynastic objectives of the family but he was a product not only of his background but also of the rapid changes of the nineteenth century. He had his own focus on a better future both for society and for his family.

---

[1] Malcolm Sutherland describes the history of the Colebrooke dynasty from the first record to its extinction in the male line in *Sola Bona Quae Honesta: The Colebrooke Family 1650-1950*, Sawd Books,1998. Much of the information in this chapter on the early Colebrooke family is drawn from his account.

Sir Edward's ancestors

The first record[2] of the Colebrookes is of a James Colebrooke,[3] a farmer near Arundel, Sussex, in the early seventeenth century. His son, Thomas, became a trader or mercer and rose in public standing to become mayor of Arundel in 1659. His eldest son, also Thomas, (1655-1690/1), was also a mercer and a tailor. It was Thomas junior's first son, James, (1680-1752) who established the family fortune and settled at Chilham in Kent.

Like his father and grandfather, James also became a mercer but moved to London in the footsteps of an uncle, becoming apprenticed to a goldsmith and later establishing himself as a banker in his own right under the name of James Colebrooke & Co. He apparently declined the offer of a baronetcy but in 1742 was granted what became the family arms with the motto 'Sola bona quae honesta' (those things only are good which are honest). He invested heavily in land, including estates in Middlesex (amongst which was Stebunheath or Stepney), Sussex and Chilham Castle and estate in Kent. He enlarged the estate and improved the village of Chilham and left instructions in his will that a family mausoleum should be built in St Mary's Church, Chilham. When James Colebrooke died in 1752, he had established political and social connections as a gentleman and had considerable landed estates with his wealth estimated at the very considerable sum of £800,000. James and his wife Mary left a daughter and five sons, ensuring '...the continuation of the Colebrooke dynasty...it is in this next generation of

---

[2] Sutherland, M, *Sola Bona Quae Honesta: The Colebrooke Family 1650-1950*, 1998, p2

[3] Following the fortunes of the Colebrooke family becomes confusing because of the common habit of using of the same few Christian names generation after generation.

Colebrookes, in particular, that political power was established and connections forged with the landed gentry.[4]

Sir Edward's grandfather

Sir Edward Colebrooke's grandfather, George Colebrooke (1729-1809) was the youngest son of James Colebrooke and was probably born at Chilham. James's eldest surviving son, Robert, inherited the Chilham estate on his death but his other two surviving sons, George and his elder brother, James (1721-1761), also had a privileged start in life. They were both educated at Leyden University in the Netherlands before taking up positions in their father's bank. Their father died when they were relatively young – James was 31 and George was 23 – and they inherited the banking business, its premises in Threadneedle Street, London and several estates.

In 1751, James junior had bought, together with other land in the Reigate area of Surrey, the manor, mansion house and advowson[5] of Gatton Park. This was to be his country seat and was purchased with an astute eye on the benefits that came with the estate since, from 1451 when Gatton had been created a borough, it was authorised to return two members to parliament, the ownership of Gatton Park giving ' ... uncontested control of one of the parliamentary seats for the borough'[6] (the other being under the control of an adjacent estate). This 'uncontested control' was bought and sold with the estate although the Member of Parliament for Gatton actually represented very few persons (at the time of the Reform Act in 1832, Gatton was described as the third most rotten borough in the country). It was, though, a coveted route into Parliament and political influence.

---

[4] Sutherland, p9
[5] The right to appoint the minister of the parish church.
[6] Sutherland, p20

The creation of the baronetcy

James Colebrooke, in accordance with his purchased right, was duly returned as Member of Parliament for Gatton in 1751, remaining Member until his death in 1761, having been 're-elected' in 1754 and 1761. He and his brother George supported the government loyally, which in turn helped them secure lucrative government contracts. In 1759, the Prime Minister described James as '...among the principal and most responsible men in the City...'[7] and towards the end of the same year, he was rewarded with the greatest prize to which a commoner could aspire, being created a baronet in recognition of his support, '...with special remainder, failing heirs of his body, to his brother George.'[8] In other words, a hereditary aristocratic title was created for him that would be passed on to his sons or, failing sons, to his brother George and his descendants. The title he took was Sir James Colebrooke of Gatton.

Sir James enjoyed his reward for political support for less than two years as he died in May 1761. He had no surviving sons so the baronetcy passed to his brother who bought Gatton Park from James's two daughters and became Sir George Colebrooke of Gatton. He had no interest in becoming MP for Gatton as he was already MP for Arundel. He had secured his election in 1754 by means of a good deal of undisguised corruption,[9] returning to where the Colebrooke family had their roots and where his brother James then had substantial landholdings. He was re-elected MP for Arundel in 1761 and 1768.

Sir George did not have his brother's success in the pursuit of wealth, speculating unwisely and eventually becoming bankrupt. For a good number of years, though, he revelled in the

---

[7] Sutherland, p21
[8] Sutherland, p21
[9] Sutherland, p23

Sir George Colebrooke by Sir Joshua Reynolds, President of the Royal Academy and the most sought-after portrait painter of the time.
From the collection at Wrotham Park

lifestyle made possible by wealth. A token of this lifestyle remains in the portrait he commissioned from Sir Joshua Reynolds, President of the Royal Academy and the most sought-after portrait painter of the time. At the age of only 32, on the death of his brother James, he became the head of the bank that he and James had inherited from their father, changing the bank's name to 'Sir George Colebrooke & Co'. Key involvement of others in the business led to further name changes, including, by 1771, 'Sir George Colebrooke, Lessingham & Binns'.

In Parliament, he took a close interest in the East India Company, participating in most East India debates until 1772. Outside Parliament also, he was deeply involved in the company's affairs, becoming Chairman in 1769, 1770 and 1772.

During his stewardship, when corrupt practices benefitting the Directors were commonplace, the East India Company ran into serious financial difficulties and Sir George, with some justification, was held substantially responsible. Disorder in public financial affairs was exacerbated in 1772 by a general financial crash in the City of London. One result of this was the Regulating Act of 1773 which attempted to reduce the East India Company's influence and appointed the first Governor General to India.

Sir George withdrew from active involvement in the East India Company after the Regulating Act but the retention of a considerable degree of independence by the East India Company was attributed to him – and it was not until almost a century later, after the Indian Mutiny in 1857, that the Crown assumed complete control of India. By the election of 1774, Sir George was seriously affected not only by the affairs of the East India Company but also because of his own financial affairs, which were in such disarray that he did not stand for re-election to Parliament. His bank was one of the first to have been affected by the crash of 1772, finally closing in 1773. Sir George had invested heavily, not only in East India Company stock but also in property and land (including land in Antigua, Grenada, Dominica and America) and various commodity speculations (including hemp, flax, logwood, alum and lead), many of which were unsuccessful.

The purchase of land in Scotland

In 1770, '...he was reported to be anxious to buy land in Scotland...'[10] and, in 1771, he purchased substantial estates in Lanarkshire from the fourth Earl of Selkirk, including the baronies of Crawford and Crawfordjohn and mines at

---

[10] Sutherland, p28

Leadhills and Wanlockhead, where lead was extracted but where, tantalizingly, small amounts of silver and gold had also been extracted since the sixteenth century.[11] His anxiety to buy land in Scotland was almost certainly because, with a different legal system in Scotland, he saw it as a way of protecting at least some of his financial interests as his affairs in England began to unravel. The acquisition of, literally, a gold mine must have seemed a true stroke of luck – but, in fact, the mines only ever yielded small amounts of gold. With the Scottish estates came the patronage of Crawfordjohn Church and Sir George is recorded to have exercised his right to appoint the minister in 1793.[12] With the Scottish estates also came the honorary title of 'Hereditary Keeper of the Castle of Crawford' – a worthless title as Crawford Castle (also known as Lindsay Tower) had been a ruin for several centuries. A local author noted:

> There exists a rumour throughout the Upper Ward that when Sir George Colebrooke took possession of his Lanark-shire property, he sent down marbles to the old castle of Crawford, the ancient abode of the Lindsays, his intention being to make the ruined tower again habitable. But if so, his plans were never carried out. Instead he contented himself with a room or rooms in the old inn of Abington.[13]

He spent lavishly, however, on his own properties in London and Surrey, including a town house in Arlington Street, off Piccadilly, before moving to Soho Square. He also employed Capability Brown to make improvements and additions to Gatton Park, (amongst which was a folly to mark the constituency's place of assembly). In short, he over-extended himself and

---

[11] *Gold, Power and Allure*, exhibition, Goldsmiths Hall, London, July 2012
[12] Reid, Thomas, *A History of the Parish of Crawfordjohn, Upper Ward of Lanarkshire, 1153-1928*, p90
[13] Reid, pp93-94

could not meet his commitments and in January 1777 he was declared bankrupt. According to his grandson (Sir Edward), writing many years later: 'He was reduced to walking when he had been used to living in splendour.'[14]

Gatton Park was sold but without, apparently, the title, which Sir Edward was to inherit in due course. The family went to live in France at Boulogne-sur-mer, depending mainly on Sir George's wife's private income. Evidently, though, his lands in Scotland were to prove as useful as he had anticipated. This land brought an income, so that '...so long as George was abroad and outside the jurisdiction of the British bankruptcy laws, he could appropriate this income to any purpose he wishes, without any interference from his creditors.'[15] Eventually, Sir George reached an agreement with those to whom he owed money, which allowed him to return to live in England in around 1789, and he and his family settled in a house in The Royal Crescent, Bath.

As was common practice, whilst in the employment of the East India Company, Sir George had used his influence to secure positions in the service of the company for two of his sons - James Edward (1761-1838) and Henry Thomas (1765-1837, Sir Edward's father) - both of whom went to work in India.

When Sir George died, his remains and later those of his wife, were interred in the Colebrooke Mausoleum at Chilham. He was survived by his sons, James Edward and Henry Thomas and the baronetcy passed to James Edward, his third and eldest surviving son. The Lanarkshire estates, however, were left to his two infant granddaughters Belinda and Georgiana

---

[14] Colebrooke, TE, *The Life of Henry Thomas Colebrooke*, Trübner, London, 1873, p1
[15] Sutherland, p31

(whose father, Sir George's second son, predeceased their grandfather) to provide them with an income.

Georgiana died unmarried, her interest in the estates passing to her sister, and on Belinda's death her husband made his life interest in the estates over to Henry Thomas,[16] very likely because he had no interest in administering land so far from London but also perhaps in recognition of Henry Thomas's guardianship of the sisters on the death of their father.

Sir Edward's father

Henry Thomas Colebrooke, FRS, the fourth son of Sir George Colebrooke, was educated privately at home, his father not having the resources to provide the kind of education he had received himself. He received no special encouragement to be a scholar[17] but demonstrated a studious nature early in life with a particular aptitude for classical languages, French and mathematics. He told his parents that he hoped to follow a profession that would enable him to continue his studies and the Church seemed a suitable environment in which to do this. His father thought differently, however, and along with his elder brother, James Edward (known as Edward) and in common with many sons of wealthy families, he took up an appointment as a 'writer' (clerk), their positions in India secured through the patronage of their father.

Both Edward and Henry made their careers in the Indian administration. Edward, who had his first appointment in India in 1777 and inherited the baronetcy on his father's death in 1809, resigned and returned to England in 1821. He re-established the family's connection with the county of Kent, buying an estate near Tunbridge Wells on land that still bears the name

---

[16] Reid, p94
[17] Reid, p95

Henry Thomas Colebrooke (Sir Edward Colebrooke's father)
From Sir Edward Colebrooke's biography of his father

'Colebrooke'. After about five years, unhappy with life in England, he returned to India but was found guilty of malpractices in 1829 and suspended from the East India Company. Although he stayed on in Delhi for a while, he returned to Tunbridge Wells, where he lived until his death in1838. His remains were interred in the family mausoleum in Chilham.[18]

Henry began his life in India in 1783 in Calcutta. It took him almost a year to secure his first post – a minor position in the Board of Accounts - but, in 1786, he moved to Tirhut as Assistant Collector of Revenue. He apparently felt quite out of step with the drinking and gambling lifestyle of the majority

---

[18] *The Morning Post*, London, Saturday 17 November 1838, issue 21177

of his ex-patriate colleagues in Calcutta and was pleased to leave. His subsequent positions saw him move location twice more by 1893, during which time he studied and wrote about the state of husbandry in Bengal, criticising British policy and the East India Company's trading monopoly. Despite a heavy work load, Henry managed to further his studies, ranging over several disciplines but focusing particularly on Hindu law and Indian languages, especially Sanskrit.

Henry amply fulfilled his commitments to the East India Company, with his interests in law and languages leading to senior appointments. He also became an eminent and much respected scholar, best known for his knowledge of Sanskrit but also studying Hindu sciences and astronomy, botany and geography. He was a true polymath, studying and writing on several Indian languages and Indian traditions and holding high office in various scientific societies, including President of the Bengal Asiatic Society.[19] He is still recognised as an authority in Sanskrit.

By 1806, he considered that he had accumulated a sufficient fortune to return home to England and devote himself to a life of study. However, his return was delayed by being honoured with election to the Council of Calcutta in 1807 for a period of five years. He was quoted as achieving this 'elevated position' on the Governor-General's Council '...entirely from his abilities, indefatigable attention to business, and superior acquirements in oriental literature'.[20] At the same time, he must have given all appearances of settling in Calcutta rather than planning a return to England since - as was not uncommon amongst the British men in the Indian Administration - he entered into a relationship with an Indian woman, with

---

[19] Colebrooke, p383
[20] Sutherland, p43

whom he had two children: Sophia (born 1809) and John (1810-1827).[21]

In 1810, however, at the age of 45, his domestic circumstances became complicated as he met Elizabeth Wilkinson, recently arrived in India in financially straitened circumstances after the death of her father. They married on 9 July 1810 in Calcutta – in the same year as his illegitimate son John was born. With Elizabeth, he had three sons in quick succession: George Vernon, born 3 June 1811, Henry Herbert, born 17 May 1812 and Thomas Edward, born 19 August 1813. Family life was cut short though. According to Sir Edward (Thomas Edward), who was to become his father's bio-grapher, the early death of his brother Henry Herbert at the age of two, contributed directly to the untimely death of his mother:

> ...the loss of one of them by a prolonged infantine malady undermined the health of their mother, and she was carried off after a short illness at the very time that they were preparing for departure.[22]

Mrs Elizabeth Colebrooke died of a liver condition in October 1814, aged 29, when Thomas Edward was just one year old. Two months later and thirty two years after leaving to work in India, Henry Thomas left India, leaving his illegitimate chil-dren behind, to return to England with his two legitimate sons. His wife was buried in the Lower Circular Road Cemetery, Calcutta, her memorial inscription stating that she was 'pious, benign and exemplary'.[23]

---

[21] Sutherland, p43
[22] Colebrooke, p293
[23] Sutherland, p43

Initially, father and sons went to live in Bath with Lady Mary Colebrooke, Henry Thomas's widowed mother, but the family all later moved to London.[24] Here, Henry Thomas threw himself into his work, concentrating on the study of geology and chemistry and creating a private laboratory in his home.[25] He probably took little part in the upbringing of his children. Indeed, he was absent for the year 1821-22, travelling to South Africa to resolve problems regarding land he had bought on the journey home from India. Whilst in South Africa, he was instrumental in proposing changes to the judicial system, which were later introduced, including the adoption of English law. Surprisingly, in view of his father's experience, he entered into a number of speculative enterprises on his return to England. These included investment in a company involved in the production and public distribution of oil (as opposed to coal) gas. He was also instrumental in the founding of the Royal Asiatic Society.

Henry Thomas Colebrooke is perhaps the best known of the Colebrooke family. His life was distinguished, not only by his humane and empathetic contributions to the administration of India but also by the extraordinary depth and breadth of his academic work and scholarly publications, particularly with respect to studies in Sanskrit, in which he was a pioneer and which led to him being described as the first great Sanskrit scholar of Europe. Surprisingly, he received no British honours for his achievements although he was made a foreign member of the French Institute and of the Imperial Academy of St Petersburg. On his father's behalf, Sir Edward felt this oversight keenly and made it one of his life's objectives to record and celebrate his father's achievements and, so far as he could, to further the causes that were dear to him. In his biography of

---

[24] Sutherland, p43
[25] Sutherland, p43

his father, Sir Edward gives a list of the many and various academic bodies of which he was a member.

Of all the Colebrookes, many of whom led lives of intrigue and corruption, it was perhaps Henry Thomas who most closely upheld the family motto: 'Sola bona quae honesta'. His son, Sir Edward, was to follow his father's moral example, in many ways leading an exemplary life.

Chapter 2

Early life

Until the age of 21, Thomas Edward Colebrooke had no idea of the affluent titled life he was to lead. His elder brother, George Vernon, was expected to inherit the baronetcy from his uncle James, who had no male heir.

Born in Calcutta and baptised there on 25 May 1814, he was just 18 months old when he left India for England with his widowed father. For the first few years of his life, Thomas Edward and his brother George Vernon were brought up by their grandmother but she died when he was only five. By then, the household included their two cousins, Belinda and Georgiana, for whom his father, Henry Thomas, had become guardian on the death of his eldest brother. They were then in their teens and it is likely that, along with nannies, they had a significant role in continuing the upbringing of the two boys. Many years later, though, Sir Edward noted in the biography of his father that his father took time to encourage his sons in the study of science.

Sir Edward hinted in this biography that his elder brother, George Vernon, was academically brighter than he was: 'a young man of brilliant talents, and the object, to his father, of the highest hope and pride'.[1] The brothers both went to

---

[1] Colebrooke, TE, *The Life of Henry Thomas Colebrooke*, Trübner, London, 1873, p379

Eton College. Then, following the well-established family pattern, their father recommended Thomas Edward for an appointment in India with the East India Company, in preparation for which, he attended the East India College at Haileybury, Hertfordshire. George Vernon, meanwhile, was given a Cambridge University education. He graduated with a Bachelor of Arts degree from Trinity College in 1832.[2]

Thomas Edward arrived in India on 19 June 1832, at the age of 18. His first appointment was Assistant to the Commissioner of Revenue and Circuit in Allahabad and in 1834 he became Joint Magistrate and Deputy Collector in the town.[3] In 1835, though, news reached him of Vernon's untimely death on 9 February at his father's home in Argyll Street, London.[4] Knowing that his brother had been for his father 'the companion of his old age and the sharer of his studies, and his attendant during his long illness'[5], he understood that Vernon's death would have been an unbearable blow to his father. Summoned from India and doubtless beginning to see his own reshaping future, he took leave of absence to return to England to comfort his father, leaving India on 9 October 1835.[6]

The opportunity for Thomas Edward Colebrooke to make something of his life and to further his father's memory came as a gift of fortune. He can never have imagined in his youth that the Colebrooke title and lands would be his but when his brother died in 1835 he knew that, in time, he would inherit the Scottish lands owned by his father and, since his uncle had no heir, the Colebrooke title would also be his. He simply had

---

[2] Wrotham Park archive
[3] Sutherland, M, *Sola Bona Quae Honesta: The Colebrooke Family 1650-1950*, Sawd Books,1998, p47
[4] Wrotham Park archive
[5] *Journal of the Royal Asiatic Society*, London, 1890, p499
[6] Sutherland, p47

to wait and there was plenty of time on the long journey home from India to consider what he would do with both.

He arrived home around January 1836, a year after his brother's death, and found his father in poor health. A year later, in January 1837, his father too died, leaving Thomas Edward, aged only 24, the Lanarkshire estates that his grandfather had bought, and which Henry Colebrooke had inherited from his wards Belinda and Georgiana.[7] The London Electoral Register of 1838 shows Thomas Edward living with a Thomas Livermore at 41 York Terrace, Regents Park[8] but the income from the Lanarkshire lands made him immediately wealthy and he soon moved to a new home at 18 Park Lane, London. This was a freehold house designed by Sir John Soane, with about six acres of garden,[9] overlooking the grounds of the Duke of Wellington's house, No 1 London or Apsley House,[10] - a prestigious address indeed – and he began to enjoy the pleasures of the wealthy.

As his father's only surviving son, he felt a heavy responsibility to achieve success and to further his father's work and scholarly standing. His father's knowledge of and affection for India influenced Thomas Edward profoundly and helped to shape

---

[7] According to Thomas Reid on p94 of *A History of the Parish of Crawfordjohn, Upper Ward of Lanarkshire, 1153-1928*, when Sir George died, he left the Lanarkshire lands not to his son James Edward, who inherited the baronetcy, but to the daughters of George, his eldest son, who predeceased him. '...the younger, Georgiana Harriet, died unmarried. Belinda married [and] at her death...her husband, who had a life interest in the property, made this over to Henry Thomas Colebrooke, third son of Sir George Colebrooke, who held it from 1825 to 1837.'

[8] Search.ancestry.co.uk/Browse/Print_d.aspx/21b8e50a918ad6091fff75eb3 6etf754/494204040.jpg, accessed 12.10.12

[9] London Electoral Register, 1841, Search.ancestry.co.uk/Browse/Print_ d.aspx/241572e3e374f14ef63be5e46bc27370/494149684.jpg, accessed 12.10.12

[10] **Daily News**, Classified advertisements, Wednesday 19 March, 1856, Issue 3069

his own lifelong interests. He adopted his father's interest in India and South East Asia and this influenced the causes he supported and acquaintances he made and impelled him later to write a detailed but curiously detached biography of his father based on his father's papers.

Less than two years after his father's death, on 5 November 1838, his uncle, Sir James Edward Colebrooke, the third baronet, also died. Thomas Edward was in Rome when the death was announced in the press[11] but he returned to London with all speed. His return home to London and immediate step up to the aristocracy changed his life for ever. 'Both title and property were reunited after a lapse of twenty nine years...'[12]

Already wealthy, at the age of only 25, Thomas Edward Colebrooke, who had expected to work as a clerk in India, succeeded to the title of 4th Baronet Colebrooke of Gatton, Surrey (the ancestral title created in 1759 by his great uncle), Hereditary Keeper of the Castle of Crawford (the title that came with the land acquired through his grandfather's land speculations and retained through his bankruptcy) and Lord of the Manor of Stepney (associated with land and property bought by his great grandfather).[13]

Gatton brought him a title but no land. Crawford Castle was a ruin so his Scottish title also brought him nothing. However, he now owned land and property in Middlesex, associated with the manor of Stepney (including housing and other interests in Shoreditch, Hackney, Spitalfields, Bethnal Green, Stoke Newington, Bow, Cambridge Heath and Whitechapel – all poor areas of the East End of London). As owner of the

---

[11] *The Morning Post* (London, England), Saturday, November 17, 1838; Issue 21177. *19th Century British Library Newspapers: Part II*.

[12] Reid, Thomas, *A History of the Parish of Crawfordjohn, Upper Ward of Lanarkshire, 1153-1928*, Turnbull & Spears, Edinburgh, 1928, p94

[13] Pine, L G, *The New Extinct Peerage, 1884-1971*, London, 1972, p.81

Crawford Castle – a ruin for many centuries

freehold manor of Stebunheath, otherwise Stepney, he was also owner of the freehold tolls of hay and straw sold in the market of High Street Whitechapel.[14] Sir Edward's chief inheritance, though, was the 29,604 acres of grouse moor and tenant farms in Lanarkshire, that had brought with them the Scottish title. The estate included, near to the small town of Biggar, the ancient parish of Crawfordjohn, the small community of Abington and the greater part of the village of Crawford.[15]

Sir Edward's leave of absence from the Bengal Civil Service lapsed after five years and he never returned to India.

---

[14] From the list of Knights of the Shire for the County of Middlesex, 1853, Search.ancestry.co.uk/Browse/Print_d.aspx/46631ed1af2f3cc1f99ec82330b479e6/493979467.jpg, accessed 12.10.12
[15] Conversation between the author and Mr Brian Lambie of the Biggar Museum Trust, 27.12.2012

Chapter 3

London life for the
new aristocrat 1839–57

On inheriting the Colebrooke baronetcy, Sir Edward set about establishing himself quickly in aristocratic society in London, his residence in Park Lane being perfectly situated to do so. As a new nobleman, he looked for an early opportunity to be introduced to the young Queen Victoria – this being accomplished at St James' Palace in June 1839, a little over six months after he inherited his title.[1]

It seems that his entry to high society came easily and invitations to aristocratic social events followed quickly – perhaps not surprising, given his youth, wealth and eligibility. At the same time, Sir Edward joined learned and society organisations, such as the Royal Society, where he could make the sort of contacts and acquaintances appropriate for a cultured young aristocrat. He also became a member of the Athenaeum Club in London, described as a scholarly gentlemen's club.

On 11 March 1840, less than a year after his presentation to the Queen, Sir Edward was amongst the guests at a grand dinner at the Theatre Royal, Drury Lane, to honour George Byng Esq MP for his public and private services. It was a

---

[1] *The Standard* (London, England), Thursday, June 06, 1839; Issue 4668. *19th Century British Library Newspapers: Part II.*

curious event, where, by boarding over the theatre pit to make it level with the stage, 1200 men from upper echelons of society could dine in public, while spectators, including Mrs Byng and other wives, looked on.[2] None the less, he had 'made it'!

He began to lead a fashionable lifestyle and doubtless held his head high among high-ranking contemporaries on 22 May 1841, when he attended the Eton College Anniversary Festival, at Willis's Rooms, King Street, St James[3] to celebrate the 400th anniversary of the foundation of the school. 'The dinner was served in a style of elegance rarely surpassed and nothing was omitted that could give éclat to the fourth centenary festival of that distinguished seat of learning.'[4]

He bought himself a 142 ton schooner, named Ginevra (after a poem by Shelley), and sailed it around Britain and in the Mediterranean. As a yachtsman, he became a member of the Royal Thames Yacht Club[5] and was elected to the prestigious Royal Yacht Squadron at Cowes on the Isle of Wight.[6] He also had his portrait painted – the painting is attributed to Frederick Richard Say.

By August 1839, Sir Edward had acquainted himself with his Scottish estates but mindful of his father's and his grandfather's energetic examples, plainly felt that he needed to do more than lead the life of a landowner and socialite. However,

---

[2] *The Charter* (London, England), Sunday, March 15, 1840; Issue 60.
[3] Willis's Rooms was a suite of Assembly Rooms which were available for hire.
[4] *The Morning Post* (London, England), Monday, May 24, 1841; Issue 21950. *19th Century British Library Newspapers: Part II*
[5] *The Morning Post* (London, England), Thursday, June 21, 1855; pg. 3; Issue 25419. *19th Century British Library Newspapers: Part II*
[6] *Hampshire Telegraph and Sussex Chronicle etc* (Portsmouth, England), Saturday, July 21, 1855; Issue 2911.

Sir Edward Colebrooke, attributed to Frederick Richard Say, 1843
Private collection/Photo@Christies images/The Bridgeman Art Library

while studious, he lacked his father's academic drive and had none of his grandfather's taste for business. Moreover, he was cautious and considered his actions carefully, perhaps at least partly because of the unexpectedness of finding himself a baronet. However, both his grandfather and his uncle had been Members of Parliament, as had others of his predecessors so Parliament seemed a natural path to investigate.

Taunton

Politically of Liberal inclinations, he looked for a seat where he would appeal to similarly minded voters. He had no association with Honiton in Devon but sought election there in 1841. He was unsuccessful[7] but learned that one of the Liberal members for Taunton, was resigning. Although he had no connection with Taunton either, in February 1842 Sir Edward presented himself to the electors of Taunton as a candidate for the vacant seat.[8] A few days later, he was formally nominated, as was a Conservative party candidate. Both addressed the electors and a show of hands was taken. The Conservative was declared the winner but Sir Edward disputed the result and demanded a poll, which took place the following day when Sir Edward polled a majority of 57.[9]

At the age of 29, he had achieved a seat in Parliament – then an unsalaried honour. The Taunton constituency was a shared seat – a not uncommon situation then. His fellow member was the Right Hon Henry Labouchere, MP, a man of already considerable experience in Parliament. It was an ideal beginning to parliamentary life and he learned much under the tutelage of Labouchere. He was soon working for his

---

[7] *The Morning Post*, letter, June 19, 1841
[8] *Freeman's Journal and Daily Commercial Advertiser* (Dublin, Ireland), Friday, February 4, 1842; Issue N/A.
[9] *The Era* (London, England), Sunday, February 13, 1842; Issue 177

constituents: on Saturday 18 June 1842 Sir Edward, with Labouchere, represented the people of Taunton to Prince Albert at Buckinghan Palace.[10] By March 1843, he was one of the fifteen members of a Select Committee to inquire into the laws affecting aliens.[11]

India

Sir Edward decided early in his career to perpetuate his father's love of India with a determination to speak up for those with little or no voice. In early March 1844, he gave notice of a motion in Parliament: 'That the demands of the Governor General of India upon the Ameers of Scinde, and the manner in which those demands were enforced, and which led to the dethronement and imprisonment of those princes, and the seizure of their country, were inconsistent with the honour and true policy of this country,'[12] – a move scarcely calculated to make friends amongst senior members of the government! In 1848, Sir Edward was nominated to the select committee on the growth of cotton in India,[13] and by 1850, he was calling for 'a select committee to inquire into the rights of succession of the allied and dependent princes of India'.[14]

By 1850, his parliamentary confidence had grown and he spoke in Parliament of the population of India being oppressed.

---

[10] *The Morning Post* (London, England), Monday, June 20, 1842; pg. 5; Issue 22284. *19th Century British Library Newspapers: Part II.*

[11] *The Morning Post* (London, England), Monday, March 20, 1843; Issue 22517. *19th Century British Library Newspapers: Part II.*

[12] *The Morning Chronicle* (London, England), Monday, March 4, 1844; Issue 23197.

[13] *The Morning Chronicle* (London, England), Friday, February 18, 1848; Issue 24438.

[14] *The Morning Chronicle* (London, England), Wednesday, February 13, 1850; Issue 25060.

He felt that, without a more detailed inquiry than any that had hitherto been made, it was impossible to decide upon the means of developing the resources of the country.'[15]

In 1852, he again displayed his natural humanity towards the rule of India – a characteristic that was to be apparent on innumerable subsequent occasions and in many different contexts. A select committee was proposed to enquire into all other matters relating to the administration of Indian affairs under the East India Company including revenue, expenditure, and administrative proceedings. Many considered it too great a task but Sir Edward was supportive[16] and went further in suggesting several further areas of enquiry.[17] Unsurprisingly, he duly became a member of the Select Committee on the Indian Territories[18] – one of the very few members who had seen service in India.[19]

Railways

The 1840s and 1850s were the period of rapid and widespread railway development and Sir Edward showed an early interest in their development in Britain and continued to involve himself throughout his political career. In May 1844, he reported on discussions on the Leeds and Bradford Railways Bill, giving considerable detail relating to capital, number of subscribers, dimensions, length, anticipated traffic and so

---

[15] The Morning Chronicle (London, England), Wednesday, June 19, 1850; Issue 26068.
[16] The Morning Post (London, England), Tuesday, April 20, 1852; pg. 4; Issue 24449. 19th Century British Library Newspapers: Part II.
[17] Freeman's Journal and Daily Commercial Advertiser (Dublin, Ireland), Wednesday, April 21, 1852
[18] Liverpool Mercury etc (Liverpool, England), Tuesday, April 27, 1852; Issue 2392.
[19] The Examiner (London, England), Saturday, May 14, 1853; Issue 2363.

on.[20] In 1852, with Labouchere, he was one of a deputation representing West Country constituencies, discussing charges on the Great Western Railway.[21]

Ireland

The first record of his interest in Ireland was noted in April 1847 over the poor relief (Ireland) bill, where his concern was evident in a discussion on the neglect of the peasantry by landlords.[22]

Scotland

Significantly also though, at an early stage of his political career, he began to involve himself in issues relating to Scotland. His interventions on Scottish policy related in particular to education and social reform and even as a new MP, he was not afraid to argue according to his conscience. On 24 May 1844 he demonstrated a conviction that bigotry had no place in education when he argued in Parliament for '... a return of the parochial schoolmasters who have retired, or have been removed from situations, in consequence of their secession from the Established Church,[23] subsequent to the month of May 1843...[24]

---

[20] *The Bradford Observer; and Halifax, Huddersfield, and Keighley Reporter* (Bradford, England), Thursday, May 02, 1844; pg. 6; Issue 530. *19th Century British Library Newspapers: Part II.*

[21] *The Morning Chronicle* (London, England), Saturday, May 22, 1852; Issue 26648.

[22] *The Examiner* (London, England), Saturday, April 17, 1847; Issue 2046.

[23] Education in Scotland was run by the established Church of Scotland. In May 1843, around a third of the clergy seceded from the established church, with members of the laity following, forming themselves into the evangelical Free Protesting Church of Scotland. It marked the formal breach between the church and state which had been developing for several years and rendered the Church of Scotland less able than ever to deliver an acceptable level of education.

[24] *Caledonian Mercury* (Edinburgh, Scotland), Monday, May 27, 1844; Issue N/A.

In matters relating to social reform, he again showed his belief in fairness, that men should work if they were able and not receive something for nothing. In 1845, on the Poor Law Amendment (Scotland) Bill, he drew on his growing experience of an Englishman in Scotland in giving his opinion. After some discussion on the over-generosity of the current provision,

... Sir Thomas Edward Colebrooke proposed from his experience of English law for the past 10 years and from his practical knowledge of the poor law system in Scotland he was decidedly of the opinion that able-bodied men should have no right to relief.[25]

His views on reform led within a few years to him being described 'as a leading reformer in England along with the likes of Cobden and Bright'.[26]

In 1847, he was on his first Scottish-context parliamentary select committee investigating sites for churches in Scotland.[27] His interest in Scotland, stemming from increasing involvement in his inherited lands in Lanarkshire was already beginning to suggest to him that representing a constituency in the south west of England did not fit comfortably with his Scottish interests and in 1851, the press reported that he was to be a candidate for the Falkirk burghs.[28]

London versus Taunton

Despite representing Taunton, Sir Edward never went to live there. His home remained in London and his life and affairs

---

[25] *The Morning Chronicle* (London, England), Tuesday, July 15, 1845; Issue 23624.

[26] *Caledonian Mercury* (Edinburgh, Scotland), Thursday, April 24, 1851; Issue 20087.

[27] *Daily News* (London, England), Wednesday, March 10, 1847; Issue 243.

[28] *Daily News* (London, England), Thursday, January 16, 1851; Issue 1450.

were focused on London and it seems there were times when the attractions of the West Country were secondary to London life. At the annual meeting of the Taunton Agricultural Association in December 1845, an occasion for classes and political groupings to mix and when the local Members of Parliament would reasonably have been expected to attend, Labouchere thanked the assembled company for drinking the health of himself and Sir Edward Colebrooke, who intended to have been there 'but for being detained in town by business that prevented him leaving.'[29]

He began to immerse himself in political life in London. He supported nominees for parliamentary seats, taking a particular interest in Middlesex, stemming from his inheritance of the manor of Stebunheath (Stepney). When Mr George Byng, the Member for Middlesex, died, Sir Edward was one of a large committee formed to organise a by-election, attending a meeting on 19 January 1847 of Liberal electors from Middlesex, in the Central Committee Rooms at The British Coffee House in Cockspur Street, London.[30] The committee sat daily as they endeavoured to secure their candidate's return.[31]

By February 1852, it seems that the voters of Taunton had become dissatisfied with Sir Edward. They may well have disliked the fact that Sir Edward was not local and spent little time in Taunton; they may have disliked the fact that he spent time in Scotland and had already put himself forward for the constituency of Falkirk; they may have felt he should have been more active in Parliament - Hansard shows that his

---

[29] *The Morning Chronicle* (London, England), Tuesday, December 2, 1845; Issue 23744.
[30] *The Morning Post* (London, England), Wednesday, January 20, 1847; pg. 6; Issue 22817. *19th Century British Library Newspapers: Part II.*
[31] *The Morning Post* (London, England), Monday, July 26, 1847; pg. [1]; Issue 22975. *19th Century British Library Newspapers: Part II.*

contributions to parliamentary proceedings were relatively few; they almost certainly found some of his views too radical. (He voted against the abolition of the Corn Laws as their new MP in 1842 but in 1846 supported their repeal – legislation that angered many landowners[32] and 'lost him the friendship of a large section of his constituents.')[33] For whatever reason, a local man, more of a traditionalist than Sir Edward, announced himself as a candidate for Taunton in opposition to Sir Edward.[34] When the candidates addressed the electors, Sir Edward was not present and in the election, he came third,[35] losing his seat.

As was not uncommon, there were charges of bribery and, after an investigation, it was declared a void election.[36] Despite not having been proved guilty of any offence himself, Sir Edward decided not to stand in the subsequent by-election,[37] suggesting (together with his failure to address electors at the time of nomination) that his interests and intentions were moving away from Taunton. His absence from the new Parliament was met with much regret.[38]

When the Report of the Select Committee on the Indian Territories was published later in 1852, Sir Edward was no

---

[32] *The Morning Post* (London, England), Tuesday, January 14, 1890; pg. 5; Issue 36686. *19th Century British Library Newspapers: Part II.*

[33] Scrapbook, Lanark Local History Library, 1906, Ref:1906, p65

[34] *The Standard* (London, England), Tuesday, March 02, 1852; Issue 8599.

[35] *Manchester Times* (Manchester, England), Saturday, July 10, 1852; Issue 385.

[36] *Daily News* (London, England), Monday, April 18, 1853; Issue 2155.

[37] *The Huddersfield Chronicle and West Yorkshire Advertiser* (West Yorkshire, England), Thursday, April 30, 1853; pg. 5; Issue 161. *19th Century British Library Newspapers: Part II.*

[38] *The Sheffield & Rotherham Independent* (Sheffield, England), Saturday, July 24, 1852; pg. 8; Issue 1712. *19th Century British Library Newspapers: Part II.*

longer in Parliament but reference to his work was included.[39] He considered the issue inadequately dealt with in the report and of such importance that, without the public platform of parliamentary debate to express his views, he took the unusual step of publishing his views privately. He announced the publication in an advertisement among the classified advertisements in *The Morning Chronicle*:

> This day is published, sewed, price 1s, a letter to Thomas Baring, M.P., on the Indian Civil Service, by Sir Edward Colebrooke, Bart., London, Uphan & Beet, 46 New Bond Street'.[40]

The Press responded to his 'letter' supportively, referring to his six years' experience in the Indian Civil Service. Quoting Sir Edward's letter, the article was extremely critical of the rottenness of the Indian Civil Service, staffed by young men of often dubious ability from England and it was of the opinion that the select committee had failed to address this in their report.[41]

Social life

Sir Edward's rapidly improving social life in London was reason enough to keep him in the capital. He was a very eligible bachelor and was invited to an ever increasing number of social engagements. In May 1845, he was just 32 when he was among what the press described as '...a select circle of about one hundred and fifty of the leading members of the

---

[39] *The Morning Post* (London, England), Thursday, October 21, 1852; pg. 4; Issue 24596. *19th Century British Library Newspapers: Part II.*
[40] *The Morning Chronicle* (London, England), Wednesday, December 22, 1852; Issue 26831, Classified ads
[41] *The Examiner* (London, England), Saturday, March 12, 1853; Issue 2354.

aristocracy...'[42] invited to a 'Matinee Musicale' hosted by the Duke and Duchess of Somerset at the family mansion in Park Lane in honour of a foreign royal guest. Over the following months, he was to become a regular guest of the Duke and Duchess of Somerset at dinner parties at Wimbledon Park, their 're-embellished' and improved out-of-town property.[43] And within a few years, he was described as one of their select circle of friends at the elegant (and, it appears, frequent) entertainments at their Park Lane mansion.[44] It is apparent that considerable stamina was needed to keep up with the social calendar of high society and survive the lateness of many events: in July 1847, for example, Sir Edward attended a Soirée Dansante in Knightsbridge, at which the press reported that dancing began shortly before 11 and 'was kept up to a late hour'.[45]

As a Member of Parliament, Sir Edward began to attend the many regular social events for those in the London political world, including parliamentary dinners. In February 1846, he was 'received' at the Levée[46] of Speaker of the House of Commons.[47] Large numbers of MPs attended these events, which followed dinner for a select few. Sir Edward would have to wait only a year to be one of the exclusive group who gathered beforehand for dinner, attending the Speaker's

---

[42] *The Morning Post* (London, England), Saturday, May 24, 1845; Issue 23201. *19th Century British Library Newspapers: Part II.*

[43] *The Morning Post* (London, England), Friday, November 28, 1845; pg. 5; Issue 22461.

[44] *The Morning Post* (London, England), Monday, June 09, 1851; pg. 5; Issue 24179. *19th Century British Library Newspapers: Part II.*

[45] *The Morning Post* (London, England), Wednesday, July 14, 1847; pg. 6; Issue 22965. *19th Century British Library Newspapers: Part II*

[46] A levée was originally a reception held by a monarch or other high ranking person on rising from bed. The term came to be applied to a formal reception at court or given by someone of high rank.

[47] *Daily News* (London, England), Monday, February 23, 1846; Issue 29.

Parliamentary dinner on 13 February 1847,[48] and continuing to attend these functions each year.

Sir Edward was soon also attending events in the highest political society and forging political liaisons. In June 1848, he was one of the 'leading members of the aristocracy' mentioned in the press attending a soirée given by Lady John Russell (the Prime Minister's wife) at Downing Street.[49] In March 1851, he attended a soirée hosted by Lady Russell at the premier's private residence in Chesham Place[50] and in March was at a party given by Lord and Lady Palmerston on Saturday 8 March at their mansion in Carlton Gardens.[51] In early 1852, having been sacked by the Prime Minister, Palmerston's own actions contributed to the fall of the Russell government. Very likely in an attempt to forge allies, Sir Edward was invited to the Russell London home twice in quick succession in the early part of 1852, for a reunion on 27 February[52] and to a dinner for 'leading members of the aristocracy' on 13 March 1852.[53]

Attending the theatre was a social event, where one went to be seen at least as much as to see the production. On 2 July 1845, Sir Edward was among the 'royal and distinguished personages present' at a production of French plays at Haymarket

---

[48] *The Standard* (London, England), Monday, February 15, 1847; Issue 7026. *19th Century British Library Newspapers: Part II*

[49] *The Morning Post* (London, England), Thursday, June 15, 1848; pg. 6; Issue 23252. *19th Century British Library Newspapers: Part II.*

[50] *The Morning Post* (London, England), Tuesday, March 04, 1851; pg. 5; Issue 24096. *19th Century British Library Newspapers: Part II.*

[51] *The Morning Post* (London, England), Monday, March 10, 1851; pg. 5; Issue 24101. *19th Century British Library Newspapers: Part II.*

[52] *The Morning Chronicle* (London, England), Monday, March 1, 1852; Issue 26577.

[53] *The Morning Chronicle* (London, England), Monday, March 15, 1852; Issue 26589.

Theatre attended by Queen and Prince Albert.[54] Clearly, he was rubbing shoulders with those at the very top of society.

Whilst entering these new and fashionable worlds of the aristocracy and of Parliament, Sir Edward's interest in India led him to join the Royal Asiatic Society, an organisation founded by his father. By 1843, when he was only 30, he was a Vice President and chairing meetings,[55] and he continued to support the society all his life. He was also involved in other organisations connected with India as well as with people who came from or had connections with India. On 12 January 1846, he was at a meeting at the Oriental Club to mark the retirement of an eminent lord who had served in India.[56]

He also joined numerous other learned societies and attended the social events given by these societies. As a member of the Royal Society, he began to attend their 'conversaziones'[57] regularly. In February 1846,[58] and again in 1848,[59] he was present at Royal Society soirées also attended by Prince Albert. There were several 'conversazione' meetings at the Royal Society each year and Sir Edward became a regular attender,[60] and in later years became President for some time.[61] He was

---

[54] *The Morning Post* (London, England), Thursday, July 03, 1845; pg. 5; Issue 22334. *19th Century British Library Newspapers: Part II.*

[55] *The Era* (London, England), Sunday, November 19, 1843; Issue 269.

[56] *The Morning Post* (London, England), Tuesday, January 13, 1846; pg. 6; Issue 22499. *19th Century British Library Newspapers: Part II.*

[57] A conversazione was a meeting for conversation or discussion, especially of the arts.

[58] *The Standard* (London, England), Monday, February 23, 1846; Issue 6720. *19th Century British Library Newspapers: Part II.*

[59] *The Morning Post* (London, England), Monday, April 03, 1848; pg. 6; Issue 23189. *19th Century British Library Newspapers: Part II.*

[60] *The Morning Post* (London, England), Monday, March 01, 1847; pg. 6; Issue 22850. *19th Century British Library Newspapers: Part II.*

[61] Reid, Thomas, *A History of the Parish of Crawfordjohn, Upper Ward of Lanarkshire, 1153-1928*, Turnbull & Spears, Edinburgh, 1928, p97

a member of the Statistical Society, and attended their meetings at their rooms in St James Square.[62] In 1846, he was one of a small group from the Oriental Club entertaining a senior Ottoman statesman[63] and in 1847, he was presented to Louis Philippe, the King of France, at a reception.[64]

From 1852, he may have been out of parliament but as an eligible aristocrat, he was certainly not out of fashionable society. His attendance at a society wedding at St Martin-in-the-Fields in October 1852 was considered worth reporting,[65] as was his arrival among fashionable society in Brighton in January 1853.[66] In September 1856, he was reported to be at fashionable Cowes on the Isle of Wight with his yacht, *The Ginevra.*[67]

Sir Edward used some of his time out of Parliament to make two visits – in 1854 and 1855 - to the Crimean War. He wrote detailed letters home to friends, one of which, in small, neat handwriting, is known to have been forwarded to the Prime Minister. In it, he describes himself as an amateur. He comments on the poor performance of the English army but says '...on the whole I am very cheery with regard to the position of our army'. The letter was sent to the Prime Minister with a cover letter describing Sir Edward's comments as '...the judgement

---

[62] *Daily News* (London, England), Tuesday, February 20, 1855; Issue 2732.

[63] *The Morning Post* (London, England), Monday, July 06, 1846; pg. [1]; Issue 22648. *19th Century British Library Newspapers: Part II.*

[64] *The Morning Chronicle* (London, England), Thursday, January 14, 1847; Issue 24095.

[65] *The Morning Post* (London, England), Wednesday, October 27, 1852; pg. 5; Issue 24601. *19th Century British Library Newspapers: Part II.*

[66] *The Standard* (London, England), Friday, January 07, 1853; Issue 8866. *19th Century British Library Newspapers: Part II.*

[67] *Hampshire Advertiser & Salisbury Guardian* (Southampton, England), Saturday, September 27, 1856; pg. 8; Issue 1726. *19th Century British Library Newspapers: Part II.*

of a sensible man on the prospects of our Army there'.[68] Sir Edward also published a journal of the visits in 1856. There is no clear reason why he chose to visit a war zone and to make a return visit. The government fell in 1855 over the appalling conditions in the Crimea[69] and Sir Edward's correspondence and journals contributed, with the reports of other civilians and journalists, to the understanding of the war and to the military reform that followed. He must have been moved by what he witnessed as he contributed £21 (a fairly generous donation when compared to others) to a fund in recognition of the work of Florence Nightingale. The fund was to establish an institution for the 'training, sustenance and protection of nurses and hospital attendants'.[70]

---

[68] National Archive, Kew, PRO/30/22/11F, among Lord John Russell papers, letter to Sir Denis Le Marchant, dated 22 October 1854, from Balaclava.
[69] Heald, Henrietta (ed) Chronicle of Britain and Ireland, Chronicle Communications Ltd, Farnborough, 1992, p908
[70] *The Morning Post* (London, England), Monday, December 10, 1855; pg. [1]; Issue 25564.

Chapter 4

Lanarkshire life 1839–1857

The first visit of the new Colebrooke baronet to South Lanarkshire was on 8 August 1839. Sir Edward arrived by stage coach, the only means of transport then available (– the railway from London came to the area about ten years later[1]). The Day Book of the Abington Inn records that Sir Edward was met at Beattock by J Johnston, one of the regular boys employed by Mrs Hunter who ran the thriving coaching inn in the village of Abington, within the ancient parish of Crawfordjohn. The record of this first visit is noticeable for the highly unusual absence of a coaching charge attached to it: a customer would normally pay a charge as well as a coaching tax.[2] Waiving the charges for the new landlord would have been judged to be starting on a good footing from the outset!

There would have been considerable excitement at the prospect of meeting the new young landlord, particularly as the previous landowner, his father, had neglected his lands on the Clyde. An

---

[1] The Caledonian Railway was formed in the 1830s to link the local railways around Glasgow and Edinburgh to the railway network of England and reached Beattock in 1847, opening to Edinburgh in 1848 and Glasgow in 1849. Prior to the formation of the Caledonian Railway, there was no rail link between the Scottish and English railway systems. From 1841, the quickest route from London to Glasgow was by train from London to Liverpool and then by sea from Liverpool to Glasgow.
[2] Day Book of the Abington Inn, 1839

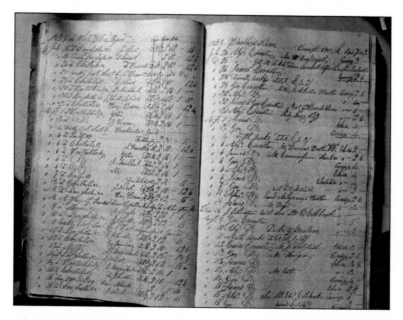

The Day Book of the Abington Inn, open to the page recording
Sir Edward's first visit
Courtesy of the Biggar Museum Trust

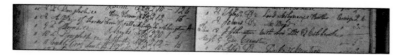

Detail from the Day Book of the Abington Inn, recording Sir
Edward's first visit
Courtesy of the Biggar Museum Trust

article in the Glasgow Herald some twenty years later reflected
on this first meeting between Sir Edward and those who lived
on his Scottish lands and the hopes and expectations that
his tenantry held, hopes that he more than lived up to in the
ensuing years:

> At that time he was a young man, as yet untried and
> unknown, and the speeches delivered on the occasion were
> necessarily limited to general expressions of goodwill,

coupled with hopes that in him those long neglected estates would find an enlightened and improving proprietor, and his tenants a kind friend and a liberal landlord.[3]

Apart from property owned in East London, his Lanarkshire lands and honorary Scottish title (Keeper of Crawford Castle) were almost all Sir Edward had to cling to in the world. With his parents and siblings dead, his title of Baronet of Gatton totally worthless (the lands had been sold) and no connection with the Colebrooke seat created by his great grandfather at Chilham in Kent, he had decided to investigate his Scottish inheritance.

The wild and hilly lands he found were grazed by cheviot sheep and some cattle. There was also arable land and extensive grouse moors. Abington was a meeting place for coursing clubs (indicating a very popular local sport) and most of the residents of the village were tenants on the Colebrooke estate.[4] Sir Edward must have liked what he saw as he held a ball shortly after his arrival,[5] and, according to the classified advertisements carried in the *Caledonian Mercury* on 31 August 1839, he paid £3-13s-6d (about £3.70 then or about £300 in 2014[6]) for a game certificate for the year 1839 up to 24 August in order to exploit his valuable grouse moors. A servant to Sir Edward Colebrooke, William Temple, is listed as a 'gamekeeper being assessed' with a 'certificate B' costing £1-5s.[7]

---

[3] *Glasgow Herald* (Glasgow, Scotland), Thursday, September 20, 1860; Issue 6456

[4] Reid, Thomas, *A History of the Parish of Crawfordjohn, Upper Ward of Lanarkshire, 1153-1928*, Turnbull & Spears, Edinburgh, 1928, pp142-3

[5] Conversation between the author and Mr Brian Lambie of the Biggar Museum Trust, 29.12.2012

[6] www.measuringworth.com (retail price index)

[7] *Caledonian Mercury* (Edinburgh, Scotland), Saturday, August 31, 1839; Issue 18667.

The wild and hilly countryside around Abington

Establishing a foothold in Scottish society

Sir Edward moved quickly to establish himself as a public personality, being put forward for public office as early as 5 November 1839. Reported in *The Morning Chronicle*, the *London Gazette* announced commissions signed by the Lord Lieutenant of the County of Lanark for three men to be Deputy Lieutenants of the county, including Sir Thomas Edward Colebrooke, Bart.[8] By 1841, he was sufficiently established to be a guest of honour among three hundred guests, at the dinner of the Highland Society's Agricultural Show at Berwick on 29 September.[9]

---

[8] *The Morning Chronicle* (London, England), Wednesday, November 6, 1839; Issue 21825.

[9] *The York Herald, and General Advertiser* (York, England), Saturday, October 09, 1841; Issue 3602. *19th Century British Library Newspapers: Part II.*

A champion of local affairs

Sir Edward was to become 'much more than a mere Scottish laird'[10] soon becoming active as a Scottish landowner, taking an interest in local farming and involving himself in local affairs, even though, in 1842, he won a parliamentary constituency that was hundreds of miles away in the south west of England. He started contributing to the planning of important events in the Lanarkshire agricultural calendar. On 7 August 1844, he was one of the 'noblemen and gentleman' present at The Great Meeting of the Highland and Agricultural Society of Scotland in Glasgow, the purpose of which was to discuss the annual great cattle show.[11]

Sir Edward was happy to continue to host several coursing meetings each year on his land. The sporting press reported the Abington Spring Meeting in April 1856, recognising that Sir Edward's hospitality was well known;[12] by the following year, Sir Edward seems to have improved the courses on his Crawfordjohn land as the press reported the 'ground more adapted for good trials' and the 'hares plentiful and stronger'.[13] For the Biggar Club autumn coursing meeting in 1858, the hares were good and Sir Edward's hospitality was again acknowledged.[14] By 1862, Sir Edward felt that these meets were causing excessive damage to his lands and he withdrew the permission – which had so long been enjoyed - to course

---

[10] Reid, p97

[11] *The Standard* (London, England), Saturday, August 10, 1844; Issue 6260. *19th Century British Library Newspapers: Part II.*

[12] *Bell's Life in London and Sporting Chronicle* (London, England), Sunday, April 06, 1856; pg. 6

[13] *Bell's Life in London and Sporting Chronicle* (London, England), Sunday, October 04, 1857; pg. 5

[14] *Bell's Life in London and Sporting Chronicle* (London, England), Sunday, October 10, 1858; pg. 8

over his lands.[15] The disappointment of local hare coursers will have been considerable.

He began to take an interest in the welfare of his tenant farmers, preparing the way for an involvement at a practical level that was to earn him genuine respect and popularity among those whose lives depended on his management of the Colebrooke estates.

Politics

He gradually became involved in local politics also. In January 1846, he was at an Anti-Corn Law meeting in Glasgow. It had been called by the Lord Lieutenant, the Duke of Hamilton, who was absent due to ill-health so, as Deputy Lieutenant, Sir Edward's role in the meeting was important. The Lord Lieutenant sent a letter reaffirming belief in free trade and the issue of universal suffrage was also raised,[16] and it would have been understood that Sir Edward espoused the same views.

Over a few years, he developed a natural affinity with Lanarkshire and its people and realised that Taunton and its people were never going to have the same emotional hold. He began looking for a suitable Scottish constituency and in 1851 a report in the *Falkirk Herald* and elsewhere stated that Sir Edward was to become a candidate to represent the Falkirk District of Burghs.[17] No subsequent record has been found of what happened to this candidature but he did not become MP for Falkirk. None the less, he had clearly indicated his interest in representing a Scottish rather than an English

---

[15] *The Sporting Gazette* (London, England), Saturday, November 01, 1862; pg. 11; Issue 1

[16] *The Morning Post* (London, England), Thursday, January 22, 1846; pg. 6; Issue 22507. *19th Century British Library Newspapers: Part II.*

[17] *Daily News* (London, England), Thursday, January 16, 1851; Issue 1450.

constituency - and this was very likely one of the factors that led to him losing his seat in Taunton the following year.

Finding himself out of parliament in 1852 made the sharing of his views very difficult and he resorted to taking private advertisements in the press on more than one occasion to alert the public to issues which would have been the subject of parliamentary press reports, had he been in Parliament. He was out of Parliament for almost five years, when '... he spent most of his time at Abington, where he applied himself to the improvement of his estate. His enterprise attracted widespread attention, and very soon he had established for himself a place in the life of the county.[18]

A home in Scotland

Initially, Sir Edward's 'home' remained London as there was no ancestral home in Lanarkshire waiting for him to take possession. On his visits to the area, therefore, he gave his patronage to the Abington Inn or stayed with other members of the aristocracy in the area. At the time of the general election in 1857, it was reported that he '...issues forth... from Wishaw House every day', suggesting that, in the absence of a home of his own, this, the home of the Lord Provost, Lord Belhaven, was where he stayed.[19] In August 1861, he was again reported to be a guest at Wishaw House.[20]

Business at the coaching inn declined from 15 February 1848, when the Caledonian Railway opened the line from Beattock to Glasgow. Abington Station, paid for by Sir Edward, was opened on the same day.[21] Doubtless finding alternative

---

[18] Scrapbook, Lanark Local History Library, 1906, Ref:1906, p65
[19] *Glasgow Herald* (Glasgow, Scotland), Monday, March 23, 1857; Issue 5740.
[20] *Glasgow Herald* (Glasgow, Scotland), Saturday, August 10, 1861; Issue 6733.
[21] Information from John Lindsay to author, 24.10.2012

employment for Mrs Hunter and her family, he took the Abington Inn for himself having it extended and developed by John Stewart, the county architect,[22] into a striking baronial gothic house, which was to become his Scottish seat and 'one of the finest mansions in the county'.[23] He was then often referred to as 'Sir Edward Colebrooke of Abington'.[24]

He had the course of the Carlisle to Glasgow road altered in Abington to gain privacy in his new Scottish home. However,

Abington House, early 1860s
From *The Upper Ward of Lanarkshire*, Volume 1, by G V Irving and A Murray, 1864

---

[22] Scrapbook, Lanark Local History Library, Newspaper cutting, unidentified newspaper, February 1939, p012
[23] Haddow, George, *Pictorial Guide to Upper Clydesdale*, Norman Hunter, Port Glasgow, 1907, p35
[24] *Glasgow Herald* (Glasgow, Scotland), Monday, May 28, 1860; Issue 6357

he allowed access to the upper waters of the Clyde on his lands for the purpose of fishing - so long as it was single line fishing. He would not permit double line fishing - or netting, which he described as '...an abomination to the true sportsman'.[25] The only restriction was '...with regard to a small part about half a mile in extent, opposite his house and pleasure-grounds, which are close to the river.'[26] It was helpfully pointed out that '...anglers may find their way past this part of the river by the roads which run parallel and on either side.'[27]

Accident

On Saturday 10 September 1853, Sir Edward had a serious accident which, in a man less determined, might well have ended a career before it had really begun – indeed, it could have ended his life. The report in the *Glasgow Herald* stated that '...when shooting on his estate at Abington, Sir Edward Colebrooke... unfortunately shattered his right hand. [The doctor] ... performed an amputation the same evening...[28] Other newspapers gave more detail: '...met with a serious accident on Saturday, his gun having gone off while he was in the act of loading it...'[29] The fact that this accident is never referred to again (except that later photographs clearly show that he had no right hand) is testimony to Sir Edward's determination not to let such a misfortune deter him from the path he had by now, at the age of 40, determined for himself.

---

[25] *The Caledonian Mercury* (Edinburgh, Scotland), Friday, September 5, 1862; Issue 22828.

[26] *The Caledonian Mercury* (Edinburgh, Scotland), Friday, September 5, 1862; Issue 22828.

[27] *The Caledonian Mercury* (Edinburgh, Scotland), Friday, September 5, 1862; Issue 22828.)

[28] *Glasgow Herald* (Glasgow, Scotland), Friday, September 16, 1853; Issue 5283.

[29] *The Examiner* (London, England), Saturday, September 17, 1853; Issue 2381.

The opportunity to return to national politics

Sir Edward looked to restart his career in national politics with the general election in April 1857, when it was announced that he would oppose the standing Tory member for Lanarkshire, Mr Alexander Baillie Cochrane, who, as recently as January in the same year, '...had been allowed to walk the course unchallenged'[30] in a by-election following the death of the previous Member of Parliament.[31] The *Caledonian Mercury* reported favourably on Sir Edward's candidature:

> LANARKSHIRE. – No incident has yet occurred respecting the coming elections of more importance than the opposition to be offered to the return of Mr A. B. Baillie

Photograph of Sir T Edward Colebrooke, 1866-69
Parliamentary Archives, PHO/2/2/118
This photograph, taken about fifteen years after the gun accident, clearly shows that Sir Edward had no right hand.

---

[30] Scrapbook, Lanark Local History Library, 1906, Ref:1906, p65
[31] *The Morning Post* (London, England), Monday, March 16, 1857; pg. 2; Issue 25961. *19th Century British Library Newspapers: Part II.*

Cochrane for Lanarkshire. We have pleasure in directing attention to the address of Sir Edward Colebrooke who announces himself a candidate on Liberal principles. Sir Edward appeals with justifiable satisfaction to his votes when sitting for an English constituency between 1842 and 1852, in favour of commercial reform, repeal of the corn and the navigation laws, of colonial reform, and the other liberal measures which were enacted during that time. On such legislation, Glasgow flourishes. Mr Cochrane at that time did his best and worst, all he could, to obstruct such commercial reforms, as he now opposes the enlargement of the county franchise, a measure which Sir Edward promises to support.[32]

As a near neighbour (Baillie Cochrane's estates and seat were in nearby Lamington), the men would have been well acquainted and Baillie Cochrane's animosity and anger must have run high against the English interloper. Excitement in the press also ran high. The *Caledonian Mercury* kept up its support:

Sir Edward Colebrooke, the gentleman in the county who was marked out by Liberal principles, by Parliamentary experience, extensive property, and universal popularity is now before the electors as a candidate for their suffrages.[33]

while the *Glasgow Herald* supported the sitting MP, although admitting certain weaknesses:

County of Lanark. – We hinted in our last that opposition was threatened to Mr Baillie Cochrane in the County. This has assumed the form of an address from Sir Edward Colebrooke of Abington, who sat in Parliament for some

---

[32] *Caledonian Mercury* (Edinburgh, Scotland), Thursday, March 19, 1857; Issue 21053.
[33] *Caledonian Mercury* (Edinburgh, Scotland), Friday, March 20, 1857; Issue 21054

years for the burgh of Taunton. We do not think Mr Cochrane is in the slightest danger; but the very fact of opposition shows that with his admitted ability, he has certain weak points, of which advantage is now taken...[34]

Sir Edward was well received at a meeting of electors in Hamilton at which he supported the extension of the franchise.[35] There were further meetings in Airdrie, Coatbridge, Trongate in Glasgow and Lanark and Sir Edward wrote at length in the press where his views on education were also aired for the first time.[36] Considerable verbal battles took place between the candidates: '...the speeches of the two candidates in that election are still worth reading, and the inhabitants of the county must have derived great enjoyment from that oratorical duel which was carried into every part of the district'.[37]

With considerable apprehension, therefore, Sir Edward put himself forward as Liberal candidate for the constituency of Lanarkshire – a constituency that had been represented by a Conservative for the previous two decades and where his landowning near-neighbour Conservative opponent was well-known, a Scot, and supported by the principal local newspaper.

> No contest had taken place in the county for twenty years. Four elections had passed without a breath of opposition, and the Liberals had paid not the slightest attention to registration, while the Conservatives had retained all their machinery.[38]

---

[34] *Glasgow Herald* (Glasgow, Scotland), Friday, March 20, 1857; Issue 5739.

[35] *Glasgow Herald* (Glasgow, Scotland), Monday, March 23, 1857; Issue 5740.

[36] *Glasgow Herald* (Glasgow, Scotland), Monday, March 23, 1857; Issue 5740.

[37] Scrapbook, Lanark Local History Library, 1906, Ref:1906, p65

[38] Scrapbook, Lanark Local History Library, 1906, Ref:1906, p65

Despite these apparent disadvantages, on 27 March 1857, Sir Edward was elected Member of Parliament for Lanarkshire, the county in which he owned his inherited estates and to which he had grown increasingly attached – and which was the largest constituency represented by a single Member of Parliament.[39] He had not expected to win. The margin was 36 votes representing the districts of Glasgow, Lanark, Airdrie, Hamilton, Strathaven, and Biggar. Cochrane was not at the result while Sir Edward's appearance was received with enthusiastic cheering.

In his acceptance speech, Sir Edward spoke of his connections with Lanarkshire:

> I cannot boast of ancestral connection like my hon. Opponent; but, when I say that my family has been connected for more than 80 years with this county, I think I have some right to take an interest in its affairs. And...I do not stand forward for the purpose of fighting a personal contest with my hon. Opponent, but on account of the principles which I uphold and which I desire to advance....[40]
> ...Throughout my life, the object of my ambition has been to represent in Parliament a county with which I am so nearly connected; and it shall be my endeavour, far more by actions than by words, to do justice to the confidence you have placed in me...[41]

Voting had been on a show of hands and Cochrane demanded a poll. The Conservative-supporting *Glasgow Herald* felt Cochrane had been cheated and there was predictably a bitter aftermath to the election. A letter appeared in the press,

---

[39] Hansard, speech by Sir Edward Colebrooke, 1.3.1860
[40] *The Morning Post* (London, England), Monday, April 06, 1857; pg. 2; Issue 25979. *19th Century British Library Newspapers: Part II.*
[41] *The Morning Post* (London, England), Wednesday, April 08, 1857; pg. 2; Issue 25981. *19th Century British Library Newspapers: Part II.*

from George Vere Irving (Cochrane's secretary) claiming Sir Edward's corrupt practices during the election and that election should be void.[42] Cochrane did everything he could to unseat Sir Edward and was seen by the more Liberal *Caledonian Mercury* (which wrote of '....a county long oppressed by aristocratic influence'[43]) as malicious. When the election expenses, ('much for hire of horses and carriages') were published in April, Cochrane's (£4974 – or about £390,000[44]) exceeded Sir Edward's (£3374 – or about £270,000[45]), prompting the comment that the amount spent was often not related to success.[46] Mention of a petition to parliament against Sir Edward by Cochrane was also recorded,[47] although, remarkably, it was also noted that some well-known Lanarkshire members of the Conservative party had contributed towards the costs of defending Sir Edward. The general opinion was that there could be '... little doubt that Mr Cochrane will display that discretion which is the better part of valour, in withdrawing his petition.'[48]

The new Liberal Member of Parliament for Lanarkshire

The furore eventually blew itself out (indeed, in 1860 Baillie Cochrane was to become MP for Honiton in Devon, although he retained his ancestral connections with Lamington.[49]) With

---

[42] *Caledonian Mercury* (Edinburgh, Scotland), Friday, May 22, 1857; Issue 21108.

[43] *Caledonian Mercury* (Edinburgh, Scotland), Tuesday, May 26, 1857; Issue 21111.

[44] www.measuringworth.com (retail price index) 2014 equivalent

[45] www.measuringworth.com (retail price index) 2014 equivalent

[46] *Glasgow Herald* (Glasgow, Scotland), Friday, April 30, 1858; Issue 5913.

[47] *Glasgow Herald* (Glasgow, Scotland), Monday, May 25, 1857; Issue 5767.

[48] *Caledonian Mercury* (Edinburgh, Scotland), Friday, June 26, 1857; Issue 21138.

[49] *Glasgow Herald* (Glasgow, Scotland), Thursday, September 20, 1860; Issue 6456.

the election outcome settled, Sir Thomas Edward Colebrooke, Bart., the new Member of Parliament for Lanarkshire, quickly settled into combining the role of Deputy Lord Lieutenant with that of parliamentary representative and the heightened public profile that this entailed. He

>...became immediately an active member of the House of Commons, and in those matters which affected Scotland he was ever watchful. County business never had a more jealous champion, and on several occasions the stand he took for the county, as opposed to the city, interests brought upon him the displeasure of the citizens of Glasgow.'[50]

He began to work on the matters of social, political and educational reform that he considered so important, beginning with issues of policing, university reform, asylum protection and electoral reform. So in October 1857, he was one of the Commissioners of Supply[51] whose responsibility was to establish a police force for Lanarkshire.[52] He also began to take a prominent social role: on 16 September 1857, he was one of the 'prestigious company', led by the Lord Provost, with Dr David Livingstone (the Scottish missionary and explorer in Africa) when Livingstone was presented with the freedom of the City of Glasgow at City Hall.[53]

---

[50] Scrapbook, Lanark Local History Library, 1906, Ref:1906, p65

[51] Commissioners of Supply dealt with local administration in Scotland. Their original purpose was to collect taxes but they later assumed responsibility for much of local government. They lost most of their responsibilities to the County Councils that were created in 1889 and were abolished in 1930.

[52] *Caledonian Mercury* (Edinburgh, Scotland), Wednesday, October 14, 1857; Issue 21232.

[53] *Caledonian Mercury* (Edinburgh, Scotland), Thursday, September 17, 1857; Issue 21209.

He began to find himself under public scrutiny with regard to charitable patronage: he contributed £10-10s (approximately £800[54]) to an Indian relief fund in addition to a subscription he had already made to the same fund in London and related to this, supported a move to raise subscriptions to help needy people with no entitlement to claim from any public fund.[55] In 1859, he was a 'generous subscriber' on the retirement of the editor of The Scotsman, a man known to hold enlightened political principles and liberal opinions.[56] He was also listed as a patron (with many other notable persons, beginning with the Queen) of the First Glasgow Music Festival in aid of the Glasgow Royal Infirmary and the Asylum for the Blind.[57]

Education

Sir Edward's interest in education became apparent very early: in November 1857, he was at a meeting in Edinburgh to discuss the improvement of Scottish universities, where his proposals included opening up the universities to what were referred to as the lower classes.[58] Sir Edward's knowledge of practices and reforms in England proved to be invaluable - as it was on many subsequent occasions in suggesting reforms in Scotland. He recognised the heritage of the Scottish universities, especially St Andrews, Aberdeen and Glasgow – 'of popish foundation' and Protestant Edinburgh of later foundation and that they all had high reputations in Europe. He insisted, though, that reform was necessary in same way

---

[54] www.measuring worth.com (retail price index) 2014 equivalent

[55] *Glasgow Herald* (Glasgow, Scotland), Friday, September 25, 1857; Issue 5820, Classified ads

[56] *Caledonian Mercury* (Edinburgh, Scotland), Saturday, June 25, 1859; Issue 21762, Classified ads

[57] *Glasgow Herald* (Glasgow, Scotland), Monday, June 27, 1859; Issue 6169, Classified ads

[58] *Caledonian Mercury* (Edinburgh, Scotland), Monday, November 9, 1857; Issue 21254.

as it had been necessary at the universities of Oxford and Cambridge.[59] He became one of the Acting Committee of the Association for the Improvement and Extension of the Scottish Universities. This acting committee sought several improvements: the encouragement of excellence in literature and philosophy; an increase in the efficiency of professorial instruction, while safeguarding its distinctive Scottish character; an increase of professorial endowments with provision for retirements; the extension to graduates of a share in university government; and an improved system of examinations.[60] Such proposals were radical and attracted hostility in the same way as similar proposals for reform met with opposition at Oxford and Cambridge. A decade later, he spoke of the paramount importance of education in fitting those who had acquired the franchise for its duties and responsibilities.[61]

Other issues

Sir Edward became involved in much besides education: in January 1859, he was one of those who attempted to prevent the Glasgow Lunatic Asylum from being used as a site for a barracks, a move, he felt, that would have destroyed the institution. He saw the asylum as a valuable facility and he actually visited it, '...so that [he] might more satisfactorily urge the claims of the Asylum for protection...' [62]

He made it widely known that he supported a widening of the franchise and an improvement in the electoral system and he

---

[59] *Caledonian Mercury* (Edinburgh, Scotland), Thursday, December 31, 1857; Issue 21299.

[60] *The Bradford Observer* (Bradford, England), Thursday, January 07, 1858; pg. 3; Issue 1151. *19th Century British Library Newspapers: Part II.*

[61] *Glasgow Herald* (Glasgow, Scotland), Wednesday, October 14, 1868; Issue 8980.

[62] *Glasgow Herald* (Glasgow, Scotland), Friday, January 14, 1859; Issue 6029.

voted in Parliament in support of the Reform Bill. He defended his vote at a meeting in Glasgow in April 1859, where his stance on electoral reform was greeted by a unanimous vote of confidence.[63]

Banking crisis

While Sir Edward was starting to devote himself to issues of improvement, protection and reform that he considered so important, there was, in 1857, a crisis in the Scottish banking system when two Scottish banks – the Western Bank and the City of Glasgow Bank – suspended payments. Sir Edward willingly helped in attempts to resolve the situation (as did Alexander Baillie Cochrane indicating that within months of the animosity of the general election, they had arrived at a working relationship). He was one of a meeting in Glasgow of noblemen, merchants and manufacturers – '... the most influential meeting to have assembled in many years...to consider the present financial crisis, to express their confidence in the Scotch banks and to determine how the difficulties might be best met and public confidence restored.'[64]

The crisis led to discussion, particularly in England, of whether a distinct Scottish banking system with separate bank notes was sustainable while many shareholders supported the troubled banks from their private resources and expressed confidence in the Scottish system. Sir Edward proposed a committee to monitor events and to take whatever steps were necessary. 'Confidence depended' he said, 'less on legislation than on the character of the people who carried

---

[63] *Caledonian Mercury* (Edinburgh, Scotland), Thursday, April 14, 1859; Issue 21701.

[64] *The Morning Post* (London, England), Thursday, November 19, 1857; pg. 5; Issue 26174.

it out.'[65] Many people of means undertook to support Scottish credit and agreed to accept transactions of the two banks. 'Altogether an extraordinary spirit of unanimity and hopefulness prevailed in this gathering of merchants, manufacturers and landed proprietors.'[66] Nevertheless, despite determined efforts over a frenetic few weeks, on 31 December 1857, the Western Bank was wound up[67] amid accusations of malpractice among the directors and the City of Glasgow Bank followed suit not long afterwards. Nothing Sir Edward or anyone else could do could salvage the banks from the scandal that surrounded their demise.

In the mid-1850s, Sir Edward is likely to have met Elizabeth Margaret Richardson, his future wife, although it is possible that he had known her some years. She was Scottish, the daughter of John Richardson of The Kirklands, Roxburghshire, a lawyer in Edinburgh who was also a parliamentary solicitor in London[68] - and a friend of Sir Walter Scott. They probably met socially when Sir Edward was in Scotland although their meeting could have been through her father when he was working in London.

[65] *Caledonian Mercury* (Edinburgh, Scotland), Wednesday, November 18, 1857; Issue 21262.
[66] *The Bradford Observer* (Bradford, England), Thursday, November 26, 1857; pg. 6; Issue 1145. *19th Century British Library Newspapers: Part II.*
[67] *The Bradford Observer* (Bradford, England), Thursday, January 07, 1858; pg. 3; Issue 1151. *19th Century British Library Newspapers: Part II.*
[68] http://thepeerage.com/p4824.htm, accessed 15.9.12

Chapter 5

Family life

In January 1857, a few months before Sir Edward re-entered Parliament, notice of his marriage appeared in the press:

On the 15th inst., at St Pauls' Knightsbridge, Sir Edward Colebrooke, Bart., to Elizabeth Margaret, second daughter of John Richardson, Esq., of the Kirklands, Roxburghshire, by Hon and Rev R Liddell and the Rev Sir John Seymour Bart.[1]

St Paul's was a recently built church where society weddings were beginning to take place: two ministers officiated and both were members of the aristocracy, leaving no doubt that it was very much a society occasion. Both Sir Edward, at 43, and his bride of 33 were of advanced years to be embarking on marriage for the first time. Their first home was almost certainly Sir Edward's bachelor residence on Park Lane but they moved to 37 South Street, off Park Lane, Mayfair, early in 1859. This was a substantial property rented from the Duke of Westminster's Grosvenor Estate and was to be the Colebrookes' London home until Sir Edward's death. It was

---

[1] *The Morning Post* (London, England), Saturday, January 17, 1857; pg. 8; Issue 25912, Births, Deaths, Marriages and Obituaries, *19th Century British Library Newspapers: Part II.*

Photograph of Lady Elizabeth Margaret Colebrooke, probably about 1860
From the collection at Wrotham Park

renumbered in 1872[2], becoming 14 South Street and was demolished in 1978.[3]

A private life had never been of great importance for Sir Edward: as a single man and an eligible bachelor, he had probably been happy to live in the public eye, enjoying seeing his name in the many newspaper reports of the social comings and goings of high society. Marriage changed that and time away from the public gaze became increasingly important. Such time was difficult to find in Abington and London where, as a member of the aristocracy, Lord Lieutenant and a Member of Parliament, he was a 'celebrity' and his movements were of great public interest, especially among his constituents and others in Scotland.

---

[2] *The Survey of London*, Vols 39 and 40, 'The Grosvenor Estate in Mayfair', 1977, Part II, p266
[3] *The Survey of London*, Part II, p340

The Colebrooke children

The Colebrookes' first child, Margaret Ginevra, was born on 19 November 1857. She was named Margaret, after her mother but was known as Ginevra (the name of Sir Edward's yacht!) or Ginny. She is recorded as being born at Crawfordjohn[4] in Lanarkshire but this is improbable. Crawfordjohn was one of the communities on Sir Edward's Scottish estate but it was very small with no special medical provision. It is more likely that Ginevra was born in Edinburgh, where medical facilities would have been the best that money could buy and appropriate to the social standing of the Colebrookes. If she was born in Edinburgh, her birth would have been registered there as well as in Crawfordjohn – dual registration being permitted at the time.[5]

Sir Edward and Lady Colebrooke's second child, named Henry after his illustrious grandfather, was born a year later on 3 November 1858. The birth of a son and heir to the Colebrooke estates was the cause of very great celebration on Sir Edward's estate. There was 'great rejoicing and festivity' in Abington on 12 November[6] and on 24 November:

> ...the tenantry and a few friends, to the number of 34, sat down to dinner to celebrate and express their joyful feelings at the auspicious event....The Chairman, in proposing the toast of the evening, said – We are met here this evening to unite our congratulations to Sir Edward and Lady Colebrooke, and of rejoicing together on account of a son and heir being born to their estates. He [the Chairman] felt

[4] http://freepages.family.rootsweb.ancestry.com/~londonaye/colebrooke_family.htm
[5] Conversation between the author and Mr Brian Lambie, founder of the Biggar Museum Trust, 29 March 2012
[6] Scrapbook, Lanark Local History Library, 1906, Ref:1906, p65

convinced that he expressed the sincere wishes of everyone present when he said that we fervently hope and trust that this auspicious and joyful event may prove a source of enduring comfort and happiness to the honoured parents, and that the young heir to those extensive estates, brought up, as he will be, under the happy influences of wise parental instructions and an excellent example, may, with God's blessing, be long spared, and endowed with those talents and virtues that will enable him to be an ornament in the elevated sphere which, in the natural course of events, he will be called upon to occupy.[7]

The Colebrookes' joy was to be sadly short-lived, however, as Henry died on 1 May the following year. Sir Edward was in Lanarkshire campaigning for re-election in the general election to the constituency he had served since 1857, while Lady Colebrooke and her son were in London. Sir Edward was hurriedly called to London to experience personal tragedy coincide with political triumph. In stark contrast to the euphoria in the Scottish press the previous year, a simple announcement was made among the deaths announcements in London and local newspapers: 'At 37 South Street, London, on the 1st inst., Henry, infant son of Sir Edward Colebrooke, Bart.'[8] The stark juxtaposition of triumph and tragedy was recorded in the *Upper Ward Almanac and Handbook* with singular brevity: 'Election of Sir E Colebrooke MP. His Son died.'[9]

The agony of Henry's death caused the Sir Edward and Lady Colebrooke to reflect on what constituted an appropriate

[7] *Glasgow Herald* (Glasgow, Scotland), Friday, December 3, 1858; Issue 6006.

[8] *Caledonian Mercury* (Edinburgh, Scotland), Wednesday, May 4, 1859; Issue 21717, Births, Deaths, Marriages and Obituaries *and*

The Morning Post (London, England), Thursday, May 05, 1859; pg. 8; Issue 26639. *19th Century British Library Newspapers: Part II.*

[9] *Upper Ward Almanac and Handbook*, 1860, R Wood, Lanark

environment in which to bring up their family. The metropolis at the time was dirty and disease (particularly cholera) was rife. It was not the best place in which to bring up healthy children. The Colebrookes lived a substantial part of each year in Lanarkshire where Sir Edward attended to Scottish and constituency business. However, when Parliament was sitting, home had to be near to Westminster, and 37 South Street was convenient for Parliament and the political and society dinners and parties that were an essential part of the life of an aristocrat and Member of Parliament. It seems likely, though, that Henry's death prompted the Colebrookes to seek an alternative home outside London, where their children could live more freely and healthily than in London. As late as 1875, when their youngest child was ten and when the construction of sewers had made London much cleaner and when, indeed, the Colebrooke family spent a lot of time there, Lady Colebrooke wrote in a letter:

> I am sure London was never intended as an abode for Children, in fact I wonder how the most robust live, always swallowing soot, and often the very dirtiest of dust. Instead of wondering at the amount of deaths here I wonder as many people survive as do in this great, yellow, choky dirty Babylon.[10]

Ottershaw Park near Chertsey in Surrey was purchased in August 1859, only three months after Henry's death, and although only a little more than twenty miles from London and easily accessible by train, the air and environment was clean and altogether healthier than in London.

There are several possible reasons why they chose Ottershaw. Woking Station was attractively close - London being only

---

[10] *The Colebrooke Letters*, 20.4.1875

forty five minutes away by train. Sir Edward may have visited the area previously with his aristocratic acquaintance, Sir Denis Le Marchant, who lived at Chobham Place, Bagshot. It is also likely that Sir Edward knew of the area from contacts. A nurseryman by the name of Gavin Cree from the town of Biggar – close to Sir Edward's Scottish estates and almost certainly well known to Sir Edward as he worked for all the local landowners[11] - had a relation who had run a plant nursery in Addlestone, only a mile or so from Ottershaw, and probably talked of the area.

Helen Emma (known as Nelly) was born in 1860, in London. By Autumn 1861, it seems that the Colebrookes trusted a Chobham doctor sufficiently for Lady Colebrooke to have their fourth child, Edward Arthur, at home at Ottershaw Park on 12 October 1861.[12] Newspapers had learned caution as the celebrations of his birth were not reported in the same way as Henry's. But, after two daughters and at the age of 48, Sir Edward had an heir. Caring for his health and educating his heir was to take time, effort and anguish for Sir Edward and Lady Colebrooke but in due course Edward Arthur was to inherit the baronetcy from his father.

Mary Elizabeth (known as Molly) was born in London on 21 May 1863 and the Colebrooke's last child, Roland (named after Lady Colebrooke's brother) John, sometimes known as Rolly, was born on 22 July 1864.

The household

The Colebrooke lifestyle meant that a large household was necessary. At the time of the 1861 census, Sir Edward, Ginevra

---

[11] Yeates, Patricia, *The Cree Nurserymen of Lanarkshire and Surrey*, Cree Family History Society, 1992, p17
[12] *The Caledonian Mercury* (Edinburgh, Scotland), Wednesday, October 16, 1861; Issue 22480, Births, Deaths, Marriages and Obituaries.

and Helen were at 37 South Street and the rest of their household included a butler, an under butler, a groom, a housekeeper, a cook, two housemaids and two nurses. Had Lady Colebrooke been at home, it would also have included a lady's maid. For the 1871 census, the family were all in London and with the number of children now five, the number of staff had increased. The household now included a butler, a housekeeper, two housemaids, two kitchen maids, a nurse, two nursemaids, a lady's maid, two footmen, a groom, an instructress (Mary Stubbs), and a tutor. This tutor was Mr W F Rawnsley, a young man who was to go on to have a significant role in the lives of the Colebrookes. After he left their employment, he became a regular correspondent giving them advice and seeking advice from them. Much of the information about the Colebrookes' private life is drawn from the letters they sent to him (*The Colebrooke Letters*).

It seems that at one point one of their staff was black as Lady Colebrooke wrote of 'our beloved Negress',[13] and the household was often supplemented – wherever the family were – by Lady Colebrooke's sisters Joanna and Helen and her brother Roland. Lady Colebrooke managed the household – something that, at a time when all communications were handwritten, kept her endlessly busy.

When the family travelled, some of the servants went with the family and some travelled ahead to make preparations. Going to Abington on 7 August 1873, their servants were in a train accident although, to the Colebrooke's relief, none were injured:

> We followed ... that fearful accident. I trust none may forget the awful Lessons of that awful night... Mrs Matheson was

---

[13] *The Colebrooke Letters*, 16.3.1873

so nervous at starting,...<u>Their</u> carriage – the last but one of the front part of the train leapt three times over and shook and swayed – but righted itself - Her description of the whole thing, the 2 hours dead silence <u>after</u> the accident ... is very striking....[14]

The Colebrookes' fashionable lifestyle

The Colebrookes led a fashionable lifestyle, which included having their portraits painted by prominent artists. These family portraits were all exhibited at the Royal Academy.[15] Sir Edward had his image painted more than once by the society portraitist George Richmond; Lady Colebrooke was painted on the occasion of their marriage in 1857 by Sir Francis Grant (1803-1878);[16] a group picture of Ginevra, Helen and Edward Arthur was painted in 1862 by Robert Thorburn (1818–1885)[17] and individual portraits of Ginevra, Helen and Mary were painted by E Taylor in 1868 and of Edward Arthur in 1869.[18] As was fashionable at the time, Sir Edward and Lady Colebrooke also had 'cartes de visite' (visiting cards) produced with their photographs on them.[19]

---

[14] *The Colebrooke Letters*, 7.8.1873

[15] There are references to these portraits in the National Portrait Gallery but the whereabouts of most of the pictures, if indeed they still exist, is unknown. A lithograph by Richard James Lane dated 1860 after a painting by George Richmond is probably the best known image of Sir Edward Colebrooke and the NPG holds copies (Ref NPG D34021 and NPG D22364).

[16] Sir Francis Grant was a Scottish portrait painter. He painted Queen Victoria and many distinguished people and served as President of the Royal Academy. National Picture Gallery, RA Cat 73

[17] National Portrait Gallery, RA Cat 806

[18] National Portrait Gallery, RA Cat Nos 576 (Master Edward), 784 (Nelly), 787 (Mary), 804 (Ginevra)

[19] The 'cartes de visite' (albumen prints dated 6 March 1861) of both Sir Edward and Lady Colebrooke are in the National Portrait Gallery collection, Ref NPG Ax51744 (Lady Colebrooke) and NPG Ax51745 (Sir Edward)

They went to the studio of Camille Silvy,[20] '...one of the most in-demand portrait photographers of mid-19th century London...even Prince Albert sat for Silvy'.[21]

Sir Edward, perhaps surprisingly in view of the fact that he had no right hand, enjoyed horse riding and was often to be seen on Rotten Row in Hyde Park. In February 1873, he was injured in a fall. Lady Colebrooke complained how busy she was '...and attending on my poor Husband, whose horse fell a week ago with him in that <u>most</u> Rotten Row, and so sprained his <u>useful</u> shoulder, I have had a busier Life than usual......'[22]

The family growing up

Edward Arthur

Ned was not as academically bright as his parents would have liked. Reference is made to this on numerous occasions in Lady Colebrooke's letters to Rawnsley. He also suffered generally poor health. He was a weak and sickly child, something which frequently dictated the actions and activities of the rest of the family. The Colebrooke's energies were focused on ensuring Ned would fulfil his position as fifth baronet when his time came and in this Rawnsley's role was important. Lady Colebrooke commented gratefully to Rawnsley on '...the care you have taken of Edward's unfortunate little body, as well as his mind....' and added: 'I trust to live to see him a broad

---

[20] Arriving in London in 1859, Camille Silvy introduced London to the 'cartes de visite' craze that had swept Paris. These were small photographs of eminent people that were collected in albums as a means of demonstrating taste or connections.

[21] Murray-Fennell, Michael, 'Focus on a 19th century innovator', *Country Life*, 23 June 2010, p141

[22] *The Colebrooke Letters*, 22.2.1873

chested man, and as much of an athlete as an English country gentleman need be.'[23]

By the end of April 1872, Ned was at Summerfield Preparatory School, Oxford, and the education of the other children continued at home. There would have never been any question of the girls going away to school and Roland's turn to go away to school was a year or two away. By 1874, new tutor, Mr A Gibson, taught them – and Ned, when he was home. Gibson wrote to Rawnsley, summing up the Colebrooke boys:

Neither of the boys is extra quick; and Roland will soon be overtaken by Mary in Latin, though the latter has only ½ an hour a day with me. I hope I shall make something of Edward and that he will obtain a fair place at Eton. But he labours under one great disadvantage viz that he has not been "pulled up" for inaccuracy at school. I make a very great point of accuracy; and consequently my temper is tried very severely at times. But I hope that in the course of a few weeks I shall have brought him round to my way of thinking. He is very fairly studious and seems anxious to get on – which is half the battle.[24]

Ned began well at prep school, although his academic ability and his health continued to concern his parents:

...... Edward writes as if he were <u>quite</u> happy there. I do not mean that he says so, but from the tone of his letters we judge him to be so. Furthermore we have heard from [an acquaintance] that when he took his boy down there, he found Ned racing and tearing about, and screaming and shouting with a quantity of boys and as <u>happy as possible.</u> Let us hope that his learning will flourish, as well as his

---

[23] *The Colebrooke Letters*, 9.10.1871
[24] *The Colebrooke Letters*, 2.10.1874

body. I felt <u>so</u> thankful to feel he was safe there, for I always think people are so weak in thinking that they, and they alone, can look after their delicate sons.[25]

At their first meeting, the matron at the school, Mrs Maclaren, had evidently been shocked by Ned's appearance but the school's regime seemed to improve Ned's health quickly:

> ...I saw when we took Ned to Summerfield <u>how</u> shocked Mrs Maclaren was at his appearance. But I did my best to re-assure her. Certainly her treatment has answered <u>admirably</u>. He looks a different boy, brown, upright, and <u>far</u> less diffident than he was. We were delighted with the change in him.[26]

Lady Colebrooke believed that Ned's difficulties as a scholar were the result of his health problems and that his positive response to the regime at his preparatory school were proof of this:

> The accounts of Ned are capital and Mrs Maclaren thinks he <u>looks</u> a shade less delicate and certainly <u>is</u> stronger. I do not wonder she thinks of him as "<u>so</u>" good. I always felt it a <u>privilege</u> to have to guide anyone as "pure in spirit" as he is. All his miserable, sad, peevish ways when he was ailing, were I knew, but the body dragging down as gentle and patient and pure a soul as God ever put into a child. I am so glad she understands him.[27]

Edward Arthur was never in robust health – indeed all the children seemed to suffer a lot of illnesses, except, perhaps, Mary. Coughs, colds, bronchitis, measles and mumps all put in

---

[25] *The Colebrooke Letters*, 28.4.1872
[26] *The Colebrooke Letters*, 15.6.1872
[27] *The Colebrooke Letters*, 28.5.1872

an appearance in the Colebrooke household. When Ginevra had mumps in early 1874, she was kept away from the other children for three weeks. In July 1872, Ned had scarlatina but mildly so he remained at Summerfield.[28] In early 1873 he had whooping cough.[29] In spring 1873,

> ...<u>both</u> boys had Bronchitis ... and all colds, and ...as the Doctor <u>would</u> keep the boys apart (for fear of whooping cough returning) I had my hands full. Poor Ned was <u>in</u> <u>agonies</u> at going back to school. I think it was the whooping cough's depressing effects that made him thus.[30]

Ned had great difficulties with his studies, so that any success was celebrated and mentioned in letters. In August 1873, he was third in his class at Summerfield and in 1874 he received a prize for his holiday project. Writing in December 1874, Lady Colebrooke seemed pleased with her son's attitude:

> I must say Ned picks up an amount of information that is curious for a boy of thirteen and once he has read a thing carefully it is there for ever, at least as long as his memory lasts. But then when he gets a book he likes as much as French History or anything of that sort he is dead to the World! And lies like a deaf Log on the Floor. Mr G says he is getting on pretty well with his Lessons.[31]

His time at Summerfield began well but after a while the conditions seemed to deteriorate: 'People are complaining how <u>much less well</u> their children are taught than before, and

---

[28] *The Colebrooke Letters*, 6.7.1872
[29] *The Colebrooke Letters*, 26.5.1873
[30] *The Colebrooke Letters*, 16.3.1873
[31] *The Colebrooke Letters*, 30.12.1874

I think how <u>horribly</u> full Summerfield is for <u>such</u> a small House.'[32] She was also shocked by:

> ...how <u>very</u> much corporal punishment is now used at Summerfield...I do not pay very much attention to the very horrid accounts of baths &c. &c. which all boys report, but I am shocked about the punishments! They have evidently got more boys than they can manage... Still I must say <u>Ned does get on</u>. I do <u>not</u> think they have a nice set of boys there, ...[33]

Ned remained at the school but never quite made the grade with his 'verses' (knowledge of Classics) and his chances of getting a place at Eton were uncertain. An Eton education, in Sir Edward's mind, was absolutely essential so the Colebrookes came to some arrangement that Ned would start early at Eton and prepare for the beginning of term. This turned out to be a disastrous false start. Lady Colebrooke told Rawnsley all about it:

> You know Browning was to arrange – as agreed last Easter, for him to wait in some safe House until he was ready for him in Sept. My husband had written twice lately to Browning about it. When he took Edward down, Mr Browning was not come back from Rome, and had made no provision for Edward whatever. A bed was found next door! a boy not having come back.... Edward took a bad place failing <u>in verses</u> – Sir Edward had so begged Mr Gibson to work him hard at them. Edw'd got a cold and I went down to see him and found what really was the matter – was his horror and worry at the swearing, gambling &c. of the <u>very</u> bad set of boys into which he had got. To make a long story short, after his father and others had

---

[32] *The Colebrooke Letters*, 7.8.1873
[33] *The Colebrooke Letters*, 19.2.1874

consulted what to do, and Sir E. had made sundry expeditions to Eton, Mr Browning relented! and said he <u>would</u> take E. in Sept. (He had told us he did not know <u>when</u> he could take E. and we might make some other arrangement!) and he ...and others my husband consulted agreed it was best to take Edward away on sick leave. My husband <u>could</u> <u>not</u> let him stay with <u>such</u> a set of boys! And we mercifully found a Vacancy at an excellent <u>school.</u> – Mr Lockwood at Sevenoaks, (you may have heard of it ...) Edward seems in bliss there. His headaches quite gone. The boys seem to work and play hard, and they are a most gentlemanlike set of boys.[34]

Sir Edward remained very concerned about Ned and his grasp of the Classics and arranged that Rawnsley (then no longer employed by the Colebrookes) should provide some extra work for his son. Writing himself from Ottershaw Park to Rawnsley in August 1875:

I have been distressed to find how slow Edward is with his verses. The exercise you set him has cost him much labour and I had to help him once or twice. He is not at all well today and this may account for it; but I am clear that he ought not to attempt anything more difficult at present. This you will judge of as you receive his copy. Unless you send him something express I will give him the examination paper which Mr Lockwood [headmaster at Sevenoaks School] sent me as a specimen of his school work and he shall send you something more by the end of next week. He gets on well with Virgil but I have no doubt Mr Lockwood is right that he is behind what might be expected of a boy of his age and I have thought a good deal of your kind offer of giving him help in his Christmas holidays. There is nothing

---

[34] *The Colebrooke Letters*, 7.6.1875

I should like better for a month of the time. But we could not think of asking you to undertake such a charge except as a professional engagement...I hope you will be able to make out your visit to Abington...

Yours truly

Edw'd Colebrooke[35]

A good standard of Classics was essential for entry to Eton College. Sir Edward himself was an able classicist and believed utterly in the value of the classics as a sound educational base. In considerable dismay over his heir's apparently low ability, he wrote from Abington to Rawnsley again at the beginning of September.

My son is rather slow at his work and I was obliged to give him some help which I told him to include in his verses when finished. Two of them were unnecessary, it seems, but even with these helps he has boggled very much at easy bits and only overcame one the 9th verse by finding the original in his dictionary. I must add that they were to me unnecessarily difficult. I was fairly floored by the first and hunted out the original in Ovid. I should not have thought of "applicat" for drives nor "hospes" in verse 3 for driver. I never heard of "Apolline" in the former copy and do not think it good Latin. My version was "Nullus adest Phoebi qui levet arte milum". That I think is better than Ovid's. You see I am quite interested in my son's exams. but I am sorry for his sake that so much importance is attached to them.[36]

Edward Arthur was confirmed in Bournemouth (why there is unknown) in May 1876, in time for his second start at Eton College. Lady Colebrooke was reassured: 'It is such a comfort

---

[35] *The Colebrooke Letters*, 5.8.1875

[36] *The Colebrooke Letters*, 6.9.1875

to me to think of Edward receiving, as I trust he will receive, at Easter, the Holy Communion before going to Eton'.[37] Sir Edward wrote to Rawnsley about Ned's start at Eton – blighted, it seems, by ill-health again: 'Edward made a good start at Eton and seemed very happy but he came home last week suffering from the effect of a bilious attack which has thrown him back.'[38] He was giving cause for concern again the following year:

Ned has been back at Eton this month past and I am sorry to say had a very bad cold at the beginning of the term. Entre nous we often wonder if we can keep him there. We hope he will go into the Diplomatic service; so by and bye I shall think of sending him abroad. It is so provoking how the climate of Eton affects him.[39]

Somehow Ned survived Eton and the next stage of his education was discussed. Lady Colebrooke wrote to Rawnsley:

I think Ned told you we think of Cambridge for him. His father could not send him to Christ Church. And we were not disposed for Baliol, besides he would not have been equal to Baliol Honours I think, so his name is down at Trinity College Cambridge and I trust he will be up to the mark in his Euclid next April, when he must go up ... Ned is ten times as strong since he left Eton, works much better, has had no bronchitis. (He used to have it there perpetually) and is I am happy to say, a capital shot! Who would have thought it? [40]

In the event, his parents changed their minds as Ned actually went on to Christ Church, Oxford.

---

[37] *The Colebrooke Letters*, 25.3.1876
[38] *The Colebrooke Letters*, 4.7.1876
[39] *The Colebrooke Letters*, 23.10.1877
[40] *The Colebrooke Letters*, 10.11.1878

The girls

The three Colebrooke girls were academically brighter than both boys. In October 1874, Mr A Gibson, then the Colebrooke tutor, wrote to Rawnsley from Abington House:

> ... My work with the girls is most interesting. I decidedly think that they have most of the talent which belongs to the family – undoubtedly the lion's share.[41]

The curriculum at home was largely determined by Lady Colebrooke. There was a tutor in the household from Rawnsley's appointment onwards, whose role was apparently primarily to teach mathematics and classics. Masters or instructresses with relevant skills were engaged as necessary. So, at different times, there was a French and German national in the household and others were engaged to teach Italian, music and art and, when they were in London, they went out for dancing lessons. Ginevra and Nelly worked well at algebra and Mary had a gift for Latin. Ginevra helped in instructing the younger children and they seem to have derived real pleasure from serious study. Lady Colebrooke wrote:

> Ginevra and Nelly are in great delight, having found some old Latin books of yours and theirs which they thought were lost![42]
>
> and
>
> The girls have been busy with German and Macauley[43] this half, and both have been reading <u>much</u> to themselves.

---

[41] *The Colebrooke Letters*, 2.10.1874
[42] *The Colebrooke Letters*, 26.5.1873
[43] The reference is to *The History of England* by Lord Macaulay (1800-1859)

As for Nelly, I think I will make a list of the books she has <u>devoured</u> since this time last year...no Trash![44]

Ginevra

Ginevra, being the eldest, enjoyed certain privileges – such as a trip with her parents to Rome from their stay in Cannes in 1872. She was certainly excited at the prospect: 'I am going to Rome next week with Papa and Mama. Won't it be nice to see it? We are going by sea to Genoa I think and from Genoa by rail - I should rather see Rome almost than any other place.'[45] The trip to Rome seems to have been a real tonic and gave Lady Colebrooke time to reflect on her children:

> ...the Children have been most flourishing at Cannes... Edward is <u>not</u> "rosy" yet but is of a darker yellow than formerly with an orange tawny shade in his cheeks! Roland is as happy and cheery as ever and mercifully he has had no colds...Nelly is as clever and contemptuous and stormy as ever. Molly as practical, and matter of fact. She is growing very handsome and is very like one of Andrea del Sarto's children who do <u>not</u> look holy in his "Holy Families". How I laughed when...asked...if Ginevra "was ever naughty"? I told him what a tyrant and sinner she used to be, and how old age has calmed her down.[46]

With her family and family friends, Ginevra spent her fifteenth birthday in Ottershaw in 1872.

> In the morning we had a paperchase and in the evening we acted charades, we acted the word Incapable, it was great

---

[44] *The Colebrooke Letters*, 15.11.1873
[45] *The Colebrooke Letters*, 12.1.1872
[46] *The Colebrooke Letters*, 17.3.1872

fun. [A guest] brought us a lot of crackers with caps inside, and one great big cracker with a cloak inside.'[47]

At seventeen, her mother described Ginevra as a great martinet[48] in dealing with her younger brothers. She also began to enjoy adult socialising. 'Ginevra has been to one or two parties. Her first party at home delighted her. Her first party out was at Lambeth...' She added that Ginevra's health would prevent her joining the world of debutante balls and parties: 'I am glad she is not going to have "a season" she is not strong enough.'[49] In September though, in Abington with her father and siblings, she assumed her mother's position for the shooting season, while her mother was detained in the south, arranging Roland's recuperation following illness.

> Ginevra is Hostess at Abington and they expect a Houseful tomorrow. I hear she performs her duties in a most exemplary way, and writes Nelly tells me "heaps of letters daily"! Nelly has been called in to late dinner, [ie with the adults] much to her indignation! It is so dull she says.[50]

In 1884, Ginevra (then twenty seven) had a break in Devon, during which time she went to a Reform demonstration in Exeter. Ever maternally concerned, Lady Colebrooke was relieved that the meeting was '...mercifully unaccompanied with Chair or head breaking.'[51]

Helen

Helen (Nelly) sometimes wrote to Rawnsley to tell him what the children were doing. 'You asked me what we have been

---

[47] *The Colebrooke Letters*, 20.11.1872
[48] *The Colebrooke Letters*, 20.4.1875
[49] *The Colebrooke Letters*, 20.4.1875
[50] *The Colebrooke Letters*, 4.9.1875
[51] *The Colebrooke Letters*, 16.10.1884

doing lately? we have been chiefly playing playing chess I should say', she wrote in 1874.[52] In March 1875, the family were returning from the south of France and she wrote for her mother from an hotel in Paris: 'Mama is so very busy that she asked me to write for her... We went to the play last night it was one of Offenbach's the music was very pretty. We hope to be in London by tomorrow evening.'[53]

Lady Colebrooke delighted to see her studious daughters. Of Nelly she wrote: 'I wish you saw her over Boswell's Johnson! I meet her creeping up and down stairs in the wildest state.' but she worried about how best to plan their education.

> I am pondering much in my mind over the education of the whole family...I wish I knew at what occupation to work each child the hardest. Ginevra and Nelly are busy with their father at Todhunter.[54] I think Ginevra explains herself better than Nelly in a difficulty, and tho' she is not nearly as quick, takes in her Algebra quite as quickly as Nelly. The master thought so too last year...'[55]

Mary

Mary seems to have been strong, sensible, practical and good-looking. From the family visit to France in 1871, at the age of eight, she wrote to Rawnsley, with her mother's help, giving a good impression of what they saw and did. Lady Colebrooke saw Mary (as well as Roland) as '...true Britons, [who] very much prefer their own Country in many ways, tho' they both

---

[52] *The Colebrooke Letters*, 2.4.1874
[53] *The Colebrooke Letters*, 11.3.1875
[54] The reference is to Isaac Todhunter, a nineteenth century mathematician.
[55] *The Colebrooke letters*, 13.1.1874

of them thoroughly enjoy the pleasures of the table! And eat steadily on at all the foreign dishes!!'[56]

Mary seems to have become something of a support to her mother: – 'Mary your excellent Mary (you remember your prophecy?) is the comfort of my Life. Always strong, always sensible, always useful.'[57] In September 1875, Mary, then twelve, was a genuine help to her mother in Ottershaw, while the rest of the family were in Abington. Lady Colebrooke wrote to Rawnsley: 'I never needed a secretary more, but Molly – indefatigable Molly, has helped me both to add up my accounts and entertain Roland.[58] When she was fifteen, her mother described her as '...a monster but such a nice monster, so practical and pleasant... and with less of a temper than earlier.' She also loved dogs.[59]

Roland

> ... I like all the family very much, especially Mary and Roland. The latter is an exceedingly nice cheerful boy, and, apart from lessons, nobody could be more interesting and charming. He has a great deal more spirit than Edward, who at times seems somewhat moody and irritable: but I think he is a well-disposed boy on the whole....[60]

So wrote Gibson, their tutor. Roland, the Colebrookes' youngest child, was not of a strong constitution and missed a lot of schooling due to ill health. When Lady Colebrooke wrote to Rawnsley in November 1872 (Roland was then eight), she was so pleased with the way Summerfield School

---

[56] *The Colebrooke letters*, 24.11.1871
[57] *The Colebrooke Letters*, 7.6.1875
[58] *The Colebrooke Letters*, 4.9.1875
[59] *The Colebrooke letters*, 10.11.1878
[60] *The Colebrooke Letters*, 2.10.1874

was working out for Ned, she really wanted to send Roland there as well: 'I am longing to be able to send Roland, but I don't think Mrs Maclaren would thank us for doing so at present. He is <u>such</u> a scrap and has grown smaller than ever of late owing to his teething. ...'[61] 'Scrap' though he was, Roland had began to learn to ride.[62]

Lady Colebrooke's sister, Joanna Richardson, seems to have involved herself in the details of Roland's schooling. She wrote to Rawnsley from Abington in August the following year:

'No, [it] is not the kind of book I want for Roland, and so I am troubling you again as perhaps you may be able to invent another...I should fear there is not the faintest chance of his passing his examination but if I could contribute to one question being answered correctly, I should be glad, and for this reason write, for any kind assistance to you.'[63]

By February 1874, preoccupied with a fire that had damaged Abington House, they were looking for a suitable preparatory school for Roland, not too far from Ottershaw,[64] and in April the following year, they seemed satisfied:

The poor little scrap Roland goes on Saturday – if all be well – to that repository of precious, delicate and backward children at Farnborough. I have such faith in school discipline and school Life, and above all fresh Country air working wonders for delicate boys, that I send Roland with a quieter heart than mothers would imagine.[65]

---

[61] *The Colebrooke Letters*, 12.11.1872
[62] *The Colebrooke Letters*, 12.6.1872
[63] *The Colebrooke Letters*, 29.8.1873
[64] *The Colebrooke Letters*, 19.2.1874
[65] *The Colebrooke Letters*, 20.4.1875

Lady Colebrooke's heart was not to remain quiet for long. At the same time as Sir Edward and Lady Colebrooke were coping with Ned's false start at Eton, as well as the wedding of Lady Colebrooke's sister in Ottershaw, everything seemed to go wrong for Roland.

> Our last sorrow has been our worst; the dangerous illness of dear little Roland. ... his father saw him ten days after he went, and reported "all well". I did not go for fear of "upsetting" him. But after 3 weeks and more I went and <u>was</u> horrified. He looked poor dear little fellow, as if he were fast going into an atrophy. We had him up to consult the Doctor. He put him to bed <u>at once</u> and there he has been ever since, and there he will be for many a day I fear ... As soon as we can arrange about a Doctor... we hope to take him off bodily to O. He pines for quiet poor little man. He was so brave he struggled on at Farnborough without a murmur they told me, and was so steady at his Lessons. I fancy it must have been Whitsunday he got a chill. Everything <u>except lungs</u> was congested, and there was internal inflammation as well...[66]

Roland had contracted scarlet fever, which was complicated by bronchitis. In 1875, Lady Colebrooke spent much time at Ottershaw Park, caring for him. Winter in Abington, with its damp and cold weather, was not the best place for him to recover and once he was a little stronger, it was decided that he needed time to recuperate where the climate was mild so Lady Colebrooke began looking for a property in the Bournemouth area, where her sister Joanna was to take care of Roland, with Nelly for company. She wrote to Rawnsley from Ottershaw:

> He is <u>really</u> better, can walk, coughs much less, has a <u>capital</u> appetite, and looks much better also. Of course we have our ups and downs, but get on very much like that snail you

---

[66] *The Colebrooke Letters*, 7.6.1875

remember that went up the 20 feet Pole falling down 4 of the 5 feet it climbed daily. Still we hope to get up to the top at last, and I trust much to Bournemouth for taking away the remains of Cough, and I trust also for adding some flesh to the poor skeleton. We hope to get there on the 18th and kind Joanna descends from the remote parts of Northumberland, to chaperone Roland and Nelly aided by our good French governess who we are re-engaging. We hope she may get Roland on in French, History &c. in an _easy_ way... Any way a little French will be better than nothing. The Doctor thinks it will be long ere he can do real work again.[67]

At the same time, Rawnsley received a letter from Sir Edward in Abington:

We have good accounts of Roland. He has really begun to walk again and some of the most unpleasant symptoms which interfered with it have subsided. Lady Colebrooke settles him at Bournemouth on the 20th and then joins me here.[68]

In March the following year, Sir Edward wrote again, reporting on a visit to see Roland in Bournemouth:

The accounts of Roland are excellent. We thought him much improved when we were at Bournemouth, and the reports of him since from Doctor and friends were most cheering. We are to have him up I trust at Easter...'[69]

He wrote again in July:

... Roland has quite got the use of his legs again and I think will be quite the better of Scotch air. We think of starting for

---

[67] *The Colebrooke Letters*, 4.9.1875
[68] *The Colebrooke Letters*, 6.9.1875
[69] *The Colebrooke Letters*, 25.3.1876

the North at the end of this month. Is there any chance of you coming our way?[70]

Roland had clearly been very ill indeed and it seems likely that he was permanently weakened but Lady Colebrooke reported the following year: 'Roland fed on Porridge and Cream, is better than he has been since his scarlet fever and Bronchitis.'[71] But as Roland improved, so Lady Colebrooke had cause to worry about Sir Edward himself. Writing from Abington:

> Sir Edward had a sad accident in July which thank God left no bad results. His horse excited at Woking Station, by the constant noise while it was waiting, bolted just as he was mounting, knocked the groom down and flung him against a paling, mercifully not a wall. He had slight concussion of the Brain and was much bruised and shaken, but we kept him entirely quiet for ten days ...and at the end of that time he was alright again, only weak. He followed us here when we all came at the beginning of August.[72]

It seems Roland was still spending time in Bournemouth in early 1879 as Lady Colebrooke wrote to Rawnsley: 'I am here with Roland for a little change, but hope to be home [London] tomorrow. We do not expect to be away from London at Easter.[73]

By 1884, Rawnsley was running his own school, Winton House, and he probably considered offering Roland (then twenty) a position, despite the many gaps in his education. Writing from Abington, Lady Colebrooke responded:

> You are very kind about Roland but I am afraid it would be almost impossible to manage a visit to Winton House. We

[70] *The Colebrooke Letters*, 4.7.1876
[71] *The Colebrooke Letters*, 23.10.1877
[72] *The Colebrooke Letters*, 23.10.1877
[73] *The Colebrooke Letters*, 28.3.1879

are going to be guided ... as to our Winter – or I trust <u>early Spring</u> movements and in the meantime I <u>trust</u> he will be able to stay at Home and work at his German.'[74]

In 1885, Lady Colebrooke reported: 'Roland on the whole has kept wonderfully well, but having got a chill out driving last week, he has been laid up for ten days and more, but is better.'[75]

The next account of Roland is in 1888, when, thirteen years after his serious illness, Lady Colebrooke still commented first on his health, implying his constitution had been much weakened. None the less, at the age of twenty four, he was well enough to travel:

'Roland has been much better this autumn, and went off "on his own Hook" to Moravia this Autumn, with a delightful Italian Cousin who has nursed him through more than one Illness. He went to pay a visit to three Countesses, who adore him, German, Austrian and Italian. Mother and two married daughters![76]

Autumn in Abington

When Sir Edward was a Member of Parliament, there was generally no autumn session of Parliament and then the whole family moved to Abington for a few months, arriving in time for the beginning of the grouse shooting season on 12 August. They normally held a party to mark the opening of the season when the sport was to shoot black grouse and partridges and to go trout fishing in the Clyde.[77] The annual stay in Abington

[74] *The Colebrooke Letters*, 16.10.1884
[75] *The Colebrooke Letters*, 31.10.1885
[76] *The Colebrooke Letters*, 7.1.1888
[77] *The Colebrooke Letters*, 6.7 1872

was also the occasion for the family to visit their dentist in Edinburgh. 'It considerably lessens the terrors of the dentist's chair, to the unfortunate children, taking them in to shop in Edinburgh, so I think I shall always keep this delightful entertainment for the Autumn in Scotland.'[78] Lady Colebrooke wrote.

Sir Edward's public positions meant that the Colebrooke social life in Scotland was public knowledge and their departure for Abington House from London was newsworthy. For instance, a news items in the *Morning Post* at the beginning of August 1885 included: "Sir Edward Colebrooke M.P., Lady Colebrooke and family have left for Abington House, their seat in Lanarkshire.'[79] They entertained extensively in Abington and visited acquaintances. Even a small social gathering was reported in the press.

The month of August, just after their arrival from the south and while the weather was still mild, was particularly hectic socially. In 1874, Ginevra wrote of preparations for large-scale entertaining:

> Papa is going to give a garden party at Abington this year and he is going to get a wooden house for the people to dance in. I think it will be great fun. It is going to be on the 25th or 26th. Papa is going to get some fireworks for it.'[80]

Ned wrote later, confirming details: 'They are building a wooden house for dancing in. It is as big as the dining room and library together.'[81] Meanwhile, Lady Colebrooke wrote of

---

[78] *The Colebrooke Letters*, 12.11.1872
[79] *The Morning Post* (London, England), Tuesday, August 04, 1885; Issue 35294. *19th Century British Library Newspapers: Part II.*
[80] *The Colebrooke Letters*, 25.7.1874
[81] *The Colebrooke Letters*, 12.8.1874

having a 'garden or rather <u>field</u> party to most of the County, a tenants' dinner, a school feast, all in one week'.[82]

In 1875, Sir Edward wrote to Rawnsley, telling of their new playroom at Abington and of a new game they had invented: 'My play room is an immense success. A neighbour is going to build one at once and I expect to give a name to the new game ...'[83] The neighbour may well have been Alexander Baillie-Cochrane, since, despite their political differences, the two men became the best of friends.[84] On the occasion of a visit of Prince Leopold to Baillie-Cochrane's home, Lamington House, in 1876 Sir Edward was one of the guests after dinner at a private theatre performance.[85]

The autumn of 1877 was no less busy:

> We have had many friends with us this Autumn, but not so many as last year, tho' at one time the House was <u>quite</u> full for a little dance we had. Lamington and Abington together made up about 15 Couples. The great event of the Autumn was the making and opening of a little wooden railway of Neds and Rolands. The first day a most distinguished Company whirled down it. It is about 130 yards long, and there are stations and seats at the Stations. We had a nice little escapade to Aberdeenshire Sir E. having business in Aberdeen, ... and [came] home by lovely Dee side <u>most</u> delicious Braemar, (where I always think the air <u>perfect</u>), and up Clunie and down the Spittal of Glenshee to beautiful Dunkeld. Then G and I went off to a <u>beautiful</u> ball given by the Caledonian Hunt on its Centenary. I never saw so many

[82] *The Colebrooke Letters*, 6.8.1874
[83] *The Colebrooke Letters*, 6.9.1875
[84] Information in correspondence from Brian Lambie, 5.6.2011
[85] *The Englishwoman's Domestic Magazine* (London, England), December 01, 1876, pg 321; Issue 144.

beauties together for long! And they all looked so much better than in London.[86]

In 1878 Lady Colebrooke wrote:

We had some very pleasant relays of guests when we first came down, and great were the deeds done at Lawn Tennis[87]; and many and many were the guests who whirled down Ned's railway. After that we had many engagements, and I have been to Fife, and Carstairs, Midlothian, Dalziel, Coltness and Northumberland.[88]

In 1884, the family stayed at Newton House in Abington[89], while work was carried out at Abington House, with the result that the family returned south earlier than usual, around the end of October. The work was barely completed when the family returned the following year. Lady Colebrooke wrote:

We only got in here at the end of July, and had we <u>not</u> come then, I believe we should <u>never</u> have got in. There were about 50 workmen still in the House when we came! – of all descriptions – We only lost the last about three weeks ago! and the House still remains unpapered and unfurnished in many Places. The two schoolrooms have made a charming Dining Room. The Wood work of the new part of the House is so nicely done and a charming 1½d paper we have put up on the Staircase makes that and the Corridor look <u>so</u> well. Those papers are well worth knowing about. The Paper is made in Norway, from the pulp of the fir tree and it is printed in Scotland...it is only lately people have

---

[86] *The Colebrooke Letters*, 23.10.1877
[87] The modern game of Lawn Tennis dates from the early 1860s with the first clubs founded in the early 1870s. The Colebrookes were therefore very much in tune with what was then the new fashion for the game.
[88] *The Colebrooke Letters*, 10.11.1878
[89] *The Colebrooke Letters*, 16.10.1884

noticed it – tho' it has been out several years. It wears I am told quite admirably.[90]

By 1887, they were entertaining at Abington House again in grand style with a garden party to celebrate Queen Victoria's Golden Jublilee.

Winter comes early in Lanarkshire, so a good autumn was always particularly enjoyed. Even in late summer, weather was often poor, prompting Ned to write to Rawnsley in August 1871: 'Mama is quite miserable because there are hardly any flowers out,'[91] and again in 1874: 'We have had

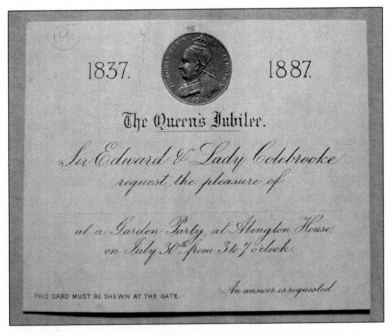

The Colebrookes' Golden Jubilee garden party invitation
Courtesy of the Biggar Museum Trust

---

[90] *The Colebrooke Letters*, 31.10.1885
[91] *The Colebrooke Letters*, 2.8.1871

hardly any fine weather here.'[92] But in 1878, Lady Colebrooke wrote:

> What a beautiful Autumn it has been! At least what a beautiful late Summer and early Autumn it was! Suddenly in the middle of September we had the most extraordinary storm of Wind and rain, and since then the weather has been much broken, until lately when we seem to be settling steadily down into an Arctic Winter. [93]

In 1885, the autumn was cruel. Lady Colebrooke wrote: 'We have had a terrible Autumn. The worst here since I was married! Frost, and whirlwind and Deluge having been our portion all through September and greater part of October.'

Most years, the mild autumns of the south were unknown because of commitments in Scotland. But in 1875, Lady Colebrooke was kept in the south, caring for Roland: 'I had no notion how beautiful Surrey is in Sept.!! The commons perfect! Our Garden is quite a blaze of Colour also, and oh! what glorious weather.'[94] The following year, they were in Ottershaw in January, thoroughly enjoying the milder weather: 'What a delightful change of weather! We are all roaming right and left after our long captivity in the frost.'[95]

Christmas

The Colebrookes generally remained in Abington until around Christmas, when, at least when the children were young, they moved to Ottershaw and at that time (1860s and early 1870s) Christmas was usually celebrated at Ottershaw Park where the

---

[92] *The Colebrooke Letters*, 12.8.1874
[93] *The Colebrooke Letters*, 10.11.1878
[94] *The Colebrooke Letters*, 4.9.1875
[95] *The Colebrooke Letters*, 2.1.1876

family entertained privately, relaxed and had a lot of family fun. Their social gatherings there were relatively small scale, with friends from neighbouring estates, including Mr William Gibb of Sheerwater Court, who was later to pay for the tower and the bells at Christ Church, Ottershaw and Sir Denis Le Marchant, Sir Edward's friend of long standing who lived in Bagshot.

Ottershaw Park had been bought as a healthy place in which to raise the young Colebrookes but it also allowed the family to live a more anonymous life than in Abington or London. Although the mansion was grand by any standards, Sir Edward had little or no public role or public obligations in Ottershaw so was able to lead a private life. His skills and position were sometimes called upon but he was never in the public eye in the same way as in Scotland and London.

Spending Christmas in Ottershaw caused tension for Sir Edward, though, as his constituents in Lanarkshire expected him to attend Christmas-time events around his constituency. On Boxing Day 1862 (by which time he was father to four very young children), the *Caledonian Mercury* published a letter from Ottershaw Park, in which Sir Edward apologised for his absence from a dinner on 23 December at the Elphinstone Arms, Biggar, given for the author of a book 'Biggar and the House of Fleming'. He wrote: 'I am sorry that my absence from Scotland will prevent my being present...It [the book] is a valuable contribution to the history and antiquities of our neighbourhood...' The item made it clear that Sir Edward's absence was seen as the absence of a local dignitary, describing him as '... of Crawford, M.P. for the county of Lanark', and Sir Edward's mention of 'our neighbourhood' indicated that he felt his duty was to Lanarkshire.[96]

---

[96] *The Caledonian Mercury* (Edinburgh, Scotland), Friday, December 26, 1862; Issue 22924.

Absence from Scotland was never easy for Sir Edward as all his working interests were there. However, Ottershaw Park was increasingly seen as 'home'. In April 1867, when he knew he should have been in Lanark he was held 'at home' in Ottershaw by family illness. The *Glasgow Herald* published a letter from Sir Edward, written from Ottershaw Park (which he described as 'home') but written as Member of Parliament for Lanark, regarding his absence from an important meeting in Glasgow on the Reform Bill. He wrote '...in consequence of serious illness in my family, I am unable to leave home at present.'[97] The press, though, provided him with the means of overcoming the difficulty of being a father in Surrey and a Member of Parliament for a constituency several hundred miles away as he was able to include in the letter an explanation of his own views, which were duly published.

Ottershaw Park

When their family was young, the Colebrookes spent substantial amounts of time in spring and early summer in Ottershaw. Sir Edward was sometimes absent, attending to parliamentary business in London and staying at 37 South Street. It is likely that Lady Colebrooke and the growing Colebrooke family spent much more time in Ottershaw than did Sir Edward himself. In Ottershaw, the children's health and well-being was safeguarded - but a train to Woking Station and a fly[98] from there to Ottershaw meant he could join his family fairly easily.

Sometimes Lady Colebrooke joined Sir Edward in London or stayed with him in Abington while the children were cared for by servants. In June 1872, Helen made this clear in a letter from Ottershaw: 'Mama has gone up to London today for the

---

[97] *Glasgow Herald* (Glasgow, Scotland), Saturday, April 27, 1867; Issue 8521.

[98] A fly was a one horse carriage that was hired out – in effect, a taxi.

rest of the week [and] of course Papa has gone too.'[99] In November of the same year, Sir Edward and Lady Colebrooke remained in Abington while the governess took the children to the South.[100]

In May 1873, when the Colebrookes were all in the south, there was a fire at Abington House. It meant that Sir Edward had to rush to Abington and missed the Ascension Day service in Ottershaw, something that seems to have been important for the family – possibly, even, a day of remembrance for Henry, their dead son. Lady Colebrooke wrote in a letter from London: 'We go to Ottershaw D.V. on Saty. Sir E. to Scotland on Weds, to see poor shattered Abington House, where it is a wonder we were not all burnt long ago.'[101] The fire plainly caused substantial damage as the following February, Lady Colebrooke wrote: 'The awful fire took our thoughts from everything else.'[102]

Mr W F Rawnsley

The Colebrooke children were probably educated by governesses until 1870 when Sir Edward and Lady Colebrooke advertised for a tutor – primarily for Edward Arthur, who, at the age of eight and a half and heir to a title and estates, had to be prepared for entry to preparatory school with a view to following in his father's footsteps to Eton College at the age of 13. The young man by the name of W F Rawnsley first visited the Colebrookes at Ottershaw Park in May 1870. He already had some experience as a tutor and this impressed Sir Edward and Lady Colebrooke:

> I have not time...to tell you how safe we feel we are in trusting little Edward into your hands, and I am sure you will

---

[99] *The Colebrooke Letters*, 12.6.1872
[100] *The Colebrooke Letters*, 12.11.1872
[101] *The Colebrooke Letters*, 26.5.1873
[102] *The Colebrooke Letters*, 19.2.1874

help to keep him as "unspotted from the world" as he is at present. Tho' he may learn slowly, I always feel growth is slow where roots are deep.[103]

Rawnsley was to play an important part in the lives of Sir Edward and Lady Colebrooke and all the children. Ginevra was already twelve years old when he came to tutor her younger brother, while Mary was ten, Helen nine and Roland was six. He quickly gained the trust of the whole family providing lessons for all the children, though mainly for Ned.

The Colebrooke Letters suggest a stable period from mid-1870 to autumn 1871 with Rawnsley at the educational helm in Ottershaw. He took a firm hand with their education, but also organised fun for the children. Early in the new year of 1871, when the family had spent Christmas at Ottershaw, he organised the children to perform a drama at the impromptu 'Theatre Royal, Ottershaw', supported by the governess, Miss Reeve and a Mr A Lillie. From the surviving programme, it is evident that there was a degree of cross-gender characterisation, (which must have provided much hilarity) so that all the children could be involved, including Roland who was then only seven.

The tutor and governess joined in the fun too, with the adults performing a piece on their own. Later in the year, Rawnsley moved with the family to Abington to continue lessons there. Other teachers were engaged to fulfil particular needs, sometimes on a short-term basis.

The position of tutor was frequently a young man's first position after university and was often seen as a stepping stone to a position as junior master in a public school. Rawnsley

---

103 *The Colebrooke Letters*, 13.6.1870

stayed only about a year with the Colebrookes, leaving them for a position at Uppingham School in late 1871. The year he spent with them, however, seems to have been beneficial for the whole family, out of all proportion to the brevity of his stay:

> Sir Edward and I feel very much indebted to you for what you have done for our children, and I do not doubt of your success with others, seeing <u>how</u> much Edward is improved during the year. I ought to add seeing also, how you have helped Nelly to dry that fountain of tears, which used to flow so constantly last Autumn.[104]

Lady Colebrooke goes on to thank Rawnsley for improving their own relationship with the children:

> Sir Edward desires me to say that he feels grateful to you, not only for what <u>you</u> have done for the Children, but for putting <u>us</u> in the way of managing them better ourselves...[105]

When, a year after Rawnsley's departure, they had concerns about leaving their dog, Norah, at Ottershaw Park when they were absent, they made a gift of her to Rawnsley, when he stayed a few days with the family in Ottershaw after Christmas.[106] He remained in contact with the family, while other tutors came and went, for the rest of Sir Edward and Lady Colebrooke's lives, corresponding in particular with Lady Colebrooke and providing advice that was respected on the children's education. Even after their deaths, he maintained an interest in their children, as is clear from newspaper cuttings and obituary letters pasted into the back of *The Colebrooke Letters.*

---

[104] *The Colebrooke Letters*, 9.10.1871
[105] *The Colebrooke Letters*, 9.10.1871
[106] *The Colebrooke Letters*, 4.12.1872

THEATRE ROYAL, OTTERSHAW.

ON FRIDAY, JANUARY 6, 1871.

WILL BE PERFORMED

DOMESTIC ECONOMY.

John Grumley swore by the light of the moon,
And the green leaves on the tree,
That he would do more work in a day
Than his wife could do in three.
Old Ballad.

CHARACTERS :

John Grumley.................................Mr. W. F. Rawnsley.
Joey..Miss Nelly Colebrooke.
Mrs. Grumley.................................Miss Reeve.
Mrs. Shackles................................Mr. A. Lillie.
Mrs. Knagley.................................Miss Colebrooke.
Peggy Brown..................................Master Colebrooke.
Polly..Miss M. Colebrooke.
Sally..Master R. Colebrooke.

TO BE FOLLOWED BY

BOX AND COX.

Box, (a *Journeyman Printer*) ....Mr. Arthur Lillie.
Cox, (a *Journeyman Hatter*) ....Mr. W. F. Rawnsley.
Mrs. Bouncer, (a *Lodging House Keeper*) ....Miss Reeve.

VIVAT REGINA!

LARKIN, TYP., CHERTSEY.

Programme from the Theatre Royal, Ottershaw
Reproduced by permission of Surrey History Centre

London

The Colebrookes spent periods of time in their London house, even in the early days when the children were very young. As early as 1861, the census (in April) recorded the family as being at 37 South Street. They were also living at their London home at the time of the 1871 census (by which time Florence Nightingale was their next-door neighbour). It seems likely that their main home was the South Street house as the children grew older and in particular when Ned and Roland were away at their preparatory schools and the girls found London shopping and society more interesting than rural Ottershaw. In 1874, Lady Colebrooke wrote – from a visit to Ottershaw: "We all went shopping in London yesterday - Ginevra and Nelly of course spent a considerable time at a newly discovered Pawnbrokers where there were many Coins to be had!"[107] They continued to visit Ottershaw and there are several mentions of day visits in *The Colebrooke Letters*. As the children grew older, however, it was left empty for long periods or was let out. In 1874, for example, it was rented by a Viscount and Viscountess for the autumn[108] and in an undated letter (probably from the late 1870s), Sir Edward offered Ottershaw Park to Sir Erskine May[109] for a period of recuperation:

My dear May

If you want rest and quiet and escape from London, why should you not go and grab a few weeks at Ottershaw? Lady Colebrooke has been disturbed at the thought of nobody being there during the winter months...it would give us both great pleasure if we thought that you were

---

[107] *The Colebrooke Letters*, 13.1.1874
[108] *The Morning Post* (London, England), Tuesday, August 25, 1874; pg. 5; Issue 31872. *19th Century British Library Newspapers: Part II.*
[109] Sir Thomas Erskine May was Clerk of the House of Commons and is still recognised as an authority on parliamentary practice and procedure.

settled there and recovering your strength in the Surrey air...Lady Colebrooke jumped at the idea of offering it to you. It has been occupied during the summer and our tenants have only just left...
Yours very truly
Edw Colebrooke[110]

It is not known whether Sir Erskine May took up the offer, but it is clear that Ottershaw Park was rented out not infrequently, the last tenants of Sir Edward being Lord and Lady Brabazon[111] in 1882-3.

Time away from home

The Colebrookes took holidays and other breaks and some of these generated press comment.

In 1862, with three very small children, a holiday in Scotland saw them at the Wemyss Bay Hotel, at Wemyss Bay - a village on the coast of the Firth of Clyde. From there, 'Sir Edward Colebrooke, M.P. for Lanarkshire, his lady and family' were reported to have left for the West Highlands.[112]

The mild climate of fashionable resorts on the south coast of England tempted them. In 1866, they were on the 'Southsea Visitors' List' - a list of notable persons staying in this Hampshire town, together with their holiday addresses. 'Sir Edward Colebrooke, Bart., M.P., Lady Colebrooke, family, and suite, [from] Abington, Scotland' were reported

---

[110] Parliamentary Archive, document ref: ERM/10B/54
[111] Lady Brabazon (the Countess of Meath from 1887) founded several charitable institutions including the Ministering Children's League, which built the Meath Home, an orphanage, in Ottershaw. It is now the Meath School.
[112] *Glasgow Herald* (Glasgow, Scotland), Tuesday, September 16, 1862; Issue 7077

to be staying at Southsea Mansion. The town was a newly fashionable resort and, with both Portsmouth and Southsea station and various hotels, (including the Southsea [Beach] Mansion) opening that same year, Sir Edward and his family were very much trend setters among the fashionable elite.[113]

In September 1870, they took a holiday from Abington to the Highlands[114] and in September two years later, Lady Colebrooke's sister, Joanna Richardson, reported to Rawnsley:

> It pours steadily all and every day which is not cheering for the prospect of a week's expedition to the West which the Colebrooke family hope to make. Sir E and my sister and Ginevra are going to Loch Gare to Mr Reeve, and Nelly and Ned chaperoned by their Uncle Roland are to go with them as far as Ardrishaig and then come home somehow, sleeping somewhere on the way![115]

In November, Lady Colebrooke referred to the holiday saying that she and Sir Edward had been 'wandering about a good deal' and that they had enjoyed the visit to Loch Gare, where Ginevra had enjoyed crabbing.[116]

In 1873, the children left Abington ahead of their parents to avoid the risk of illness. Lady Colebrooke wrote:

> They are all gone south, and are at Hastings. The Measles were rife here, and the Doctor did not wish Roland to get it before his long journey, and in this most inclement climate;

---

[113] *Hampshire Telegraph and Sussex Chronicle etc* (Portsmouth, England), Saturday, November 17, 1866; Issue 3574 *and Hampshire Telegraph and Sussex Chronicle etc* (Portsmouth, England), Saturday, November 24, 1866; Issue 3576.

[114] *The Colebrooke Letters*, 19.9.1870

[115] *The Colebrooke Letters*, 9.9.1872

[116] *The Colebrooke Letters*, 12.11.1872

so they settled there on Wedy last, and are supremely happy there with "Aunt Helen" [her sister], delightful shops including two with Coins, and plenty sea anemones. .....[117]

In 1878, they chose the fashionable Isle of Wight - the family were reported on 16 January being new arrivals at the Bonchurch Hotel in Ventnor.[118]

The family also enjoyed days out, both in Scotland and in the south. In 1871, Ned wrote to Rawnsley that they had visited '...the National Gallery [of Scotland] on Saturday and there were such pretty pictures. I liked those of Fra Angelico and Francia the best. The journey was very dusty and the train an hour late.'[119] In a letter written in July 1872, Lady Colebrooke mentions that they visited Shap Fell[120] and Ginevra wrote that they had been out on a good many picnics and that they had been great fun.[121] In 1873, Nelly wrote to Rawnsley: 'Been to see boat race, driving down to Barnes in a carriage and having lunch there,'[122] adding that they had also visited the Temple Church in London. A letter of February 1873 suggests a visit to the House of Commons to hear the debates and in 1874, Nelly wrote of going to see 'Semiramide' by Rossini at the Opera.

Going abroad

Their most significant breaks, though, were abroad and were not so much holidays as escapes in search of a health-promoting

---

[117] *The Colebrooke Letters*, 15.11.1873

[118] *The Hampshire Advertiser* (Southampton, England), Wednesday, January 16, 1878; pg. 4; Issue 3296. *19th Century British Library Newspapers: Part II.*

[119] *The Colebrooke Letters*, 2.8.1871

[120] *The Colebrooke Letters*, 6.8.1872

[121] *The Colebrooke Letters*, 26.8.1872

[122] *The Colebrooke Letters*, 31.3.1873

climate. Following Queen Victoria's example in taking her haemophiliac son, Leopold, to the French Riviera in the colder months for health reasons, the Colebrookes too, for several years from at least the early 1870s, spent the worst of the winter months in the south of France, primarily, it seems, so that Ned could benefit from the warmer climate. 'It is a <u>most</u> healthy place Everyone says for children as the air is full of salt. One must inhale iodine I should think.[123] Lady Colebrooke commented.

They were horizon-broadening experiences for all the family. The winter of 1874-75 was spent in Biarritz. The family visited places as tourists, spending some days in Italy, and tried foreign food. Lady Colebrooke wrote to Rawnsley in January 1875 from Hotel Gardens, Biarritz, of the food they had sampled on a day in the French Basque Country: "Our first dish at Hendaye at Luncheon nearly killed the Colebrooke family but it was carried off. It was a dish like macaroni but it <u>was</u> hundreds and hundreds of little white sand eels!!!![124]

Lady Colebrooke suggested that spending weeks away from home was not what she would have chosen to do in other circumstances:

> I don't at all enjoy spending my Xmas in exile and pine for my people... [and] my friends sadly. It will seem sadly unlike Christmas day here I fear, but I shall try and make the Children as cheery as possible and have ordered a cake to make up for Plum Pudding...The Children have told you what a pleasant little expedition we made along the coast the other day...The Riviera is really <u>perfect,</u> and the peeps up some of the valleys quite beautiful. If I had time I could make some such nice sketches...No! give me a nice clear

---

[123] *The Colebrooke Letters*, 12.12.1873
[124] *The Colebrooke Letters*, 13.1.1875

frosty English day. It is far more healthy than this I am sure. Nevertheless I am bound to say in spite of colds, constant colds, the children are flourishing, and Roland's face is <u>almost</u> round! He spends all his spare time picking up the minutest shells on the sea shore, which are carefully stowed away in pill boxes.[125]

Even away from Britain, they were kept abreast of events in Britain and especially in Sir Edward's constituency by frequent letters and newspapers. 'We shall soon be thinking of packing up again. Sir E and I hoped to get to Rome, but I fear Sir E will have to go home about some horrid Glasgow business and Scotch Education...'[126]

Tutors were engaged while the family were in the south of France, emphasising that the stay was not simply a long holiday. The children were allowed a short break from their studies or, as Helen put it in 1871, 'We are going to have a week of whole holidays this year instead of a fortnight of half.'[127] In 1875, Lady Colebrooke wrote: 'The Colebrooke family are fearfully busy, with <u>two</u> french Teachers and a drawing Master. A professor from Bayonne on the "Logic of Grammar" is excellent....'[128] However, there was also time to relax and Sir Edward bought the equipment for the fashionable new game of lawn tennis, which the family played a good deal.[129]

Family man

Sir Edward had a surprisingly modern view of a father's role in the family. He plainly accepted cross-gender drama by his

---

[125] *The Colebrooke Letters*, 22.12.1871
[126] *The Colebrooke Letters*, 22.12.1871
[127] *The Colebrooke Letters*, December 1871
[128] *The Colebrooke Letters*, 13.1.1875
[129] *The Colebrooke Letters*, Feb1875

children under Rawnsley's direction; he also helped with his own children's schooling – the girls as well as the boys, and particularly in Latin and Greek. As many Victorians, Sir Edward was a very good classicist – indeed was reported to have been 'a classical scholar of great repute'[130] and believed the classics were essential to a good education. When the governess, Miss Stubbs, took a holiday in the Lake District, Lady Colebrooke wrote: 'Sir Edward is beginning Latin today with Ginevra and Nelly and I am going to read all sorts of things with them. Sir Edward too and I are busy reading French with Mad'lle to improve our Conversation.'[131] In 1876, Lady Colebrooke told Rawnsley that the children were working hard with Sir Edward in the Ottershaw schoolroom.[132] He also personally took the children on outings, reporting from Abington in 1872, for instance, that: '...I took all the young folk to our Gymnasium in the town yesterday and Edward's performances along the horizontal ladder were the admiration of the whole party and he evidently enjoyed it which I do not think he did last year....'[133]

With a large family, Lady Colebrooke was kept fully occupied managing the household, the children's schooling and the family's health. She frequently acted independently of Sir Edward in these matters, while he was occupied with his various public duties – as with her search for a suitable recuperation home for Roland in Bournemouth. She planned and took decisions on her own regarding schooling. She also managed the family's complex public and private social calendar and sometimes had to manage Sir Edward's business as well as her own.[134]

---

[130] Scrapbook, Lanark Local History Library, 1906, Ref:1906, p65
[131] *The Colebrooke Letters*, 6.7.1872
[132] *The Colebrooke Letters*, 2.1.1876
[133] *The Colebrooke Letters*, 27.8.1872
[134] *The Colebrooke Letters*, 19.2.1874

Church

The family were religious and there are numerous references in Lady Colebrooke's letters that make this clear. Of Ned at Summerfield, she wrote to Rawnsley:

> If we have <u>any</u> faith at all surely we can trust God to take care of those we have committed to His keeping. I can only say, I <u>know</u> who I have believed and <u>am</u> convinced that He can and will help others to do for one's child far better than one ever could have done oneself.[135]

'The old chapel', Abington – possibly originally the Colebrookes' private chapel.
Courtesy of the Biggar Museum Trust

This picture was taken in the 1970s by Brian Lambie of the Biggar Museum Trust when the building was used as a garage and firewood store. The structure has a round-headed window, unusual for a working building and the interior was apparently lined with tongue and groove wood and painted green with some stencilling. The presence of a ventilator on the roof certainly suggests that it was a place for people to meet.

---

[135] *The Colebrooke Letters*, 28.4 1872

In Abington, they did not have a church built as they did in Ottershaw. Sir Edward may have felt that the provision of a building for the Church of Scotland would cause antagonism within the community and towards himself since the Free Church[136] was strong in the area. The United Free Church building dates from 1861 although services had been taking place from about 1844.[137] Providing the building for the Established Church was left to Sir Edward's son, although services were held by the parish minister in the schoolroom and later in the village hall.[138] It is possible that a wooden structure on the site of Abington House was used by the Colebrookes as a private chapel. It was known as 'the old chapel' up to recent times.[139] Furthermore, Sir Edward had inherited the patronage of Crawfordjohn Church and the family attended services there.

It was to Ottershaw, where the Colebrookes had their own church that they came for important religious family occasions. On 4 June 1872, Ginevra and 32 other young people were confirmed there by the Bishop of Winchester and the whole family gathered in Ottershaw for the occasion. She received several gifts. To Rawnsley, she wrote: 'Thank you very very much for the book you sent me I like it so much and I shall always read out of it... Mr Gibb gave me a book called "The book of Praise" it has all the hymns I like best in it.'[140] Sir Edward had to squeeze attendance into his busy parliamentary schedule: Ginevra wrote in the same letter to Rawnsley: 'Papa came down just for the service but he had to go up again immediately after it.' Ginevra's first Communion also took

---

[136] The Free Church was the result of a schism in the established Church of Scotland in 1843
[137] Haddow, George, *Pictorial Guide to Upper Clydesdale*, Norman Hunter, Port Glasgow, 1907, p40
[138] Haddow, p40
[139] Information from Brian Lambie, the founder of Biggar Museum Trust
[140] *The Colebrooke Letters*, 5.6.1872,

place in Ottershaw about a fortnight later. In June 1875, Lady Colebrooke's sister Helen – a lady of mature years by then – was married in Ottershaw.

The family also gathered at the church for Ascension Day services. These services had special significance for the Colebrookes as Ascension Day almost always falls in May, the month in which their son Henry died. Lady Colebrooke wrote to Rawnsley: 'Yes! <u>how</u> I love Ascension day for its own Sake, and for the blessing that followed it, and follows it still.'[141] The Colebrookes provided a reference to the Ascension in the (then) only chancel window and they probably saw Christ Church as dedicated to the Ascension and to Henry.

Ottershaw was clearly important to the Colebrookes. Ottershaw Park was bought as a healthy alternative to the

Christn Church Ottershaw

[141] *The Colebrooke Letters*, 26.5.1873

The Ascension window, Christ Church, Ottershaw: probably an integral part of the memorial to Henry Colebrooke

noise and dirt of London. It was a retreat for the Colebrookes and, for a while, somewhere to which to escape from the pressures of Parliament and London social life and where Sir Edward and his family could assume relative anonymity and relax. However, he took a personal interest in running the estate adopting new techniques and improving methods in Ottershaw as well as in Abington. It is unlikely that Ottershaw was ever seen by Sir Edward as his first home as his sense of duty meant Abington House was where he belonged. In the aristocratic listings of the time, Ottershaw Park is always mentioned as his second seat. The family's attachment to Ottershaw is clear, though, from the fact that Sir Edward remained churchwarden for several years after selling the estate, taking the time to travel down from London to attend to parish business.[142]

---

[142] Brush, Pamela, *Christ Church Ottershaw: History and Guide*, Ottershaw, 2004, p8

Social conscience

Sir Edward and Lady Colebrooke both contributed generously to charitable causes, in Abington and Ottershaw and also in the parts of Stepney where Sir Edward owned property. He supported the London Hospital in Whitechapel on many occasions. Lady Colebrooke supported four 'ragged children' paying for their clothing and arranging for their lessons.[143] Lady Colebrooke plainly also supported people with physical disabilities as in a letter of June 1872, she referred to giving a party in Ottershaw for her 'Cripples'[144] (a word then with no pejorative connotations). In July she wrote of the new museum in a deprived area of East London where Sir Edward owned inherited property:

> We had a <u>very</u> interesting afternoon...at the Bethnal Green Museum, so saw much of the people, and I talked with many and was so pleased to find how much they appreciate it, and one very sensible workman with whom I conversed evidently thinks it will do much good in keeping people from the Public Houses at night...[145]

When in Abington, Lady Colebrooke made shawls for elderly women in the locality[146] and in Crawfordjohn, endeavoured '...to get up a friendly Society for Young Women which I trust may do some good in this wicked valley....'[147]

Author

Sir Edward wrote several books, most notably a biography of his father (published in 1873) – a dedicated attempt to pull

---

[143] *The Colebrooke Letters*, 22.2.1873
[144] *The Colebrooke Letters*, 15.6.1872
[145] *The Colebrooke Letters*, 6.7.1872
[146] *The Colebrooke Letters*, 6.8.1872
[147] *The Colebrooke Letters*, 12.11.1872

Frontispiece of Sir Edward's biography of his father, Henry Thomas Colebrooke

together the body of his father's work with a strangely detached account of family life.

In 1856, he published a journal of his visits to the Crimean War in 1854 and 1855. He also wrote a biography of and edited the papers of a now largely forgotten statesman and governor of India, who gloried in the name of the Honourable Mountstuart Elphinstone – a huge task, for which he received considerable praise. He wrote several other works, several of which had been digitised by 2012 and made available online (see Appendix).

Lady Colebrooke and politics

Lady Colebrooke supported her husband and shared his political beliefs. These often crept into her letters to Rawnsley

but seldom as angrily as when Queen Victoria was created
Empress of India:

> My dear Mr Rawnsley, how shall I begin on Politics?
> D'Israeli makes my blood boil; and his last speech is quite
> sickening. First insulting the House by talking that twaddle
> about Whitaker &c. &c. and then insulting his co Ministers
> and Russia with that Act of defiance about sustaining the
> "empire"! I hope you heard L'd Justice Jenner's speech,
> that on the new Coinage for England it would still be Dei
> Gratia – for India "D'Izzy Gratia". It is a miserable piece of
> business altogether, and I fear ... that it will be "the begin-
> ning of the end" of our Monarchy. The Q. is so sensible that
> had D'Israeli had the Courage to speak the truth all this
> mischief would not have occurred. I am thankful I am not
> to pray for the "Prince Imperial", but how will it sound in
> India "God save the Empress"? D'Israeli is making a mess
> of everything and I cannot repine! I must stop tho' I have
> many things to say...[148]

For someone in Sir Edward's position who juggled several
public roles at the same time, a private life was difficult. It
is clear, though, that his family was very precious to him. He
enjoyed leisure time with his family and spent as much time as
he could with them.

By 1887, Sir Edward's health was failing and Christmas had
been spent quietly at the South Street house:

> Nelly and I had a quiet Xmas for Ned [then 26], Ginevra
> [30] and Roland [23] are in the South, and Molly [24]

---

[148] *The Colebrooke Letters*, 25.3.1876,

was away ...... and we too did <u>not</u> see much of each other, as we were like buckets in a well, reading alternately to my husband! for his eyes were so bad he could not read himself. What a jumble we read to be sure! Politics, Travels, Biographies, Novels, Children's Stories &c. &c.[149]

Sir Edward had married and had his family late but his life with Lady Colebrooke and the children, away from the public gaze, was very important to him. Despite heavy demands on his time, he always did his best for his family, in particular for his heir, whose physical and intellectual weaknesses proved such a challenge on so many occasions.

[149] *The Colebrooke Letters*, 7.1.1888

Chapter 6

London life from 1857: among the elite of society

Marriage in January and election to the parliamentary seat of Lanarkshire in March made 1857 a milestone year in Sir Edward's life, the complexity of which increased considerably from then on. As Member of Parliament he now had political responsibility for the people of Lanarkshire in addition to his responsibilities as a major landowner. To his by now well established personal social life in London was added the parliamentary and social obligations of a politician, all of which, within a short while, were to be complicated by family responsibilities. His lease on 18 Park Lane expired, the property was put up for sale[1] and, in 1859, he and Lady Colebrooke moved to 37 South Street, Mayfair, a property near to Hyde Park that he rented from the Grosvenor Estate and which was to be his London home for the rest of his life.[2] Designed by the architect J P Gandy-Deering and built around 1835, the house was described in the *Morning Post* as being:

> ...a spacious and elegant mansion...furnished in the best taste, having a stone-floored hall, two stone staircases and

---

[1] *Daily News*, Wednesday 19 March, 1856, Issue 3069, Classified advertisements

[2] The Survey of London, Vol 29, *The Grosvenor Estate in Mayfair*, The Athlone Press, University of London for the GLC Part I, p340

**14 (37) South Street front: the Colebrookes' town house in Mayfair,
(Numbers 14-24, even, right to left, c1931, demolished 1978)**
Reproduced courtesy of *The Survey of London*

on the principal floor, a drawing room nearly thirty five
feet long with a fine prospect commanding the entire
Park view.'[3]

South Street was renumbered in 1872, when the number
of their house became 14,[4] although in her letters, Lady
Colebrooke continued to use 37 for several years.

The Colebrookes entertained in London but on a smaller scale
than in Abington as their town house, though large by modern
standards, was on a more modest scale. Sir Edward was a
guest, though, at the grandest houses in London, sometimes
alone and sometimes with Lady Colebrooke and later with his
children.

---

[3] *The Morning Post*, 28 July 1835, cited in 'The Survey of London',
Vol 29, The Grosvenor Estate in Mayfair
[4] Survey of London, Vol 29, *The Grosvenor Estate in Mayfair*, 1977,
Part II, p266

14 (37) South Street back (Numbers 6-14, even, left to right, 1929, demolished 1978)
Reproduced courtesy of *The Survey of London*

Attending high profile social events, serious and learned societies, clubs, theatrical performances, the opening of new museums and other buildings and so on were all part of the life of an aristocrat in London. To this was added the political social round, generally on his own, at least while his children were very young.

Social gatherings of Scots in London were an important way of keeping in touch on matters that affected people hundreds of miles away and made sure Scottish issues were kept distinct from those of England. When a Glaswegian, Sir James Campbell, entertained a group of foreigners and other gentlemen Sir Edward was there in support of Scottish interests[5] and a dinner given by

---

[5] *Glasgow Herald* (Glasgow, Scotland), Wednesday, July 16, 1862; Issue 7024.

Scottish MPs for the Lord Advocate of Scotland[6] at the St James's Hotel, Piccadilly[7] was an opportunity for temporary exiles to catch up on issues of concern to them all.

Aristocratic social life

Many society events remained the preserve of men but an important Society of Arts event in May 1862, was patronised by about three thousand dignitaries, including many women attending in their own right. The event was the Society's first reception of the season at the South Kensington Museum[8], when the new Italian courts were opened for the first time but with three children under four, including the Colebrooke heir of seven months, Lady Colebrooke was needed at home and was unable to accompany her husband.[9]

Sir Edward continued the round of meetings of learned societies and associations, including the fashionable conversaziones of Royal Geographical Society[10] and the Dilettanti Society.[11]

His personal interest in developing his Lanarkshire estates and his commitment to agriculture saw him as one of the

---

[6] The Lord Advocate was the chief legal adviser of the UK government and the Crown for Scottish legal matters, both civil and criminal. The Scotland Act 1998 made changes to the role.

[7] *The Standard* (London, England), Tuesday, July 07, 1863; pg. 6; Issue 12138. *19th Century British Library Newspapers: Part I*

[8] Now the Victoria and Albert Museum

[9] *The Morning Post* (London, England), Friday, May 09, 1862; pg. 7; Issue 27579. *19th Century British Library Newspapers: Part II.*

[10] *The Morning Post* (London, England), Friday, May 16, 1862; pg. 5; Issue 27585. *19th Century British Library Newspapers: Part II.*

[11] The Dilettanti Society was the oldest of the London societies. It was founded in 1732 by a group of young British aristocrats who had all taken the 'Grand Tour' of Italy. They met to dine and discuss painting and the names of many distinguished taste-makers were to be found amongst the society's membership. The society still meets.

distinguished attendees at the Smithfield Club Cattle Show in London – an annual show of fatstock, agricultural implements, seeds, roots and other farm produce.[12]

Once the Colebrooke children were old enough to easily leave with nannies, Lady Colebrooke often accompanied Sir Edward to fashionable royal and aristocratic occasions. They were no strangers at court occasions – for example as guests at Buckingham Palace on the afternoon of 15 March 1866 when the Queen 'held a Court' and where a number of people were presented to her.[13] In December 1871, Sir Edward himself presented a new Member of Parliament, Mr Graham, at the Queen's levée (reception) at St James's Palace, where he was received by Prince Alfred, Duke of Edinburgh on behalf of the Queen.[14]

The Colebrookes also attended events hosted by the most senior members of the nobility. One such gathering was an Assembly[15] in June 1866, hosted by the Duke and Duchess of Devonshire, at Devonshire House in Piccadilly, one of the largest and grandest of the ducal houses in London. Such events were for large numbers of the aristocracy and members of both Houses of Parliament (over seven hundred in this case) and they began late in the evening, after the evening's

---

[12] *The Standard* (London, England), Tuesday, December 09, 1862; pg. 2; Issue 11958. *19th Century British Library Newspapers: Part II.*

[13] *The Dundee Courier & Argus* (Dundee, Scotland), Saturday, March 17, 1866; Issue 3935.

[14] *Glasgow Herald* (Glasgow, Scotland), Tuesday, December 12, 1871; Issue 9968.

[15] An 'Assembly' was a gathering of members of the higher social classes of both sexes. Public 'Assembly Rooms' were built for this purpose but much high class entertaining was still at the homes of the aristocracy, for which they needed large homes. There were few public places of entertainment open to both sexes besides theatres and there were few of those outside London. Upper class men had more options, including coffee houses and gentlemen's clubs.

entertainment at Covent Garden and other theatres had ended. This particular event began around 10.00 pm, with the last guests arriving after midnight.[16] Society hosts and hostesses (events were usually hosted by the lady of the house) maintained an exhausting schedule of social events. So, in March 1869, Sir Edward and Lady Colebrooke attended an evening party which was described as 'the sixth and last reception before Easter', held by a certain Countess de Gret at the family residence in Carlton Gardens.[17] As the Colebrooke daughters became adults, they began to accompany their parents to society functions. On some occasions Ginevra and later Helen stood in for their mother, such as at a society wedding in 1883 at All Saints, Ennismore Gardens which Sir Edward attended with the 'Misses Colebrooke'.[18]

Parliamentary social life

There were many social events which, as a Member of Parliament, Sir Edward was expected to attend. They were an important way of keeping abreast of news and gossip and it was unacceptable to decline invitations without good reason. They were formal occasions with a strict formal dress code and manner of behaviour. They were often also very late in the evening and would have presented Sir Edward with no choice but to stay in London and not return to his family in Ottershaw. Details of a few of these events give the flavour of the social round throughout Sir Edward's political life.

As early as 26 May 1857, he had clearly been received back into political society as he was one of a 'select group of guests'

---

[16] *The Morning Post* (London, England), Wednesday, June 20, 1866; pg. 5; Issue 28868. *19th Century British Library Newspapers: Part II.*
[17] *The Morning Post* (London, England), Monday, March 22, 1869; pg. 5; Issue 29729. *19th Century British Library Newspapers: Part II.*
[18] *The Morning Post* (London, England), Friday, December 07, 1883; pg. 5; Issue 34775.

of the President of the Board of Commissioners for the Affairs of India, at a dinner to celebrate the Queen's birthday.[19]

The Speaker of the House of Commons held a series of full dress[20] Parliamentary dinners every year and most years between 1858 and 1883, Sir Edward attended one of these. The venue for the event was the London home of the Speaker and was for a select group of parliamentarians, which routinely included Sir Edward. These occasions were usually followed by a levée for many more guests.

Dinners given by other senior politicians, including the Prime Minister and Secretaries of State, ensured a hectic social round. In February 1861, Sir Edward attended a grand political banquet for members of the House of Commons given by the Prime Minister, Lord Palmerston, at Cambridge House, his prestigious London residence at 94 Piccadilly.[21]

In 1865, with Lady Colebrooke, he was among a large company at a musical party given by Mrs Gladstone, wife of William Ewart Gladstone, who was then Chancellor of the Exchequer, at their private residence on Carlton House Terrace.[22] In April 1870, again with Lady Colebrooke, he was at an evening Assembly, given by Mrs Childers, wife of Hugh Childers, then First Lord of the Admiralty, at his official residence, Admiralty House, Whitehall.[23] A month later, they

---

[19] *Caledonian Mercury* (Edinburgh, Scotland), Tuesday, May 26, 1857; Issue 21111.

[20] A 'full dress' occasion required the wearing formal attire. For a man at an evening function, this was a dark tail coat and trousers and a dark waistcoat, a shirt with a winged collar and a white bow tie.

[21] *The Morning Post* (London, England), Tuesday, February 05, 1861; Issue 27188. *19th Century British Library Newspapers: Part II.*

[22] *The Morning Post* (London, England), Wednesday, March 01, 1865; pg. 5; Issue 28458. *19th Century British Library Newspapers: Part II.*

[23] *The Morning Post* (London, England), Thursday, April 07, 1870; pg. 5; Issue 30056.

were at another large evening party given by Mrs Gladstone, whose husband was, by then, Prime Minister[24] and in March the following year at a reception, again hosted by Mrs Gladstone at Carlton House Terrace.[25] In June 1870, they were both among 'a numerous and brilliant company' at the Foreign Office, the guests of the Countess Granville, wife of the Earl Granville, who was Leader of the Liberal Party for over thirty years and at that time Secretary of State for Foreign Affairs.[26]

In April 1875, a year after the Liberal defeat in the General Election and the same year as the Marquis of Hartington succeeded Gladstone as Leader of the Liberal opposition in the House of Commons, Sir Edward was one of a small number of guests at a parliamentary dinner given by the Marquis at Devonshire House.[27]

In May 1876, Sir Edward and Lady Colebrooke were among the guests at a reception given by Lady Salisbury, wife of Disraeli's Secretary of State for India. It was held at the family mansion in Arlington Street, off Piccadilly. The event began late - around 11.00 pm – and on this occasion, they were accompanied by Ginevra, who, now eighteen, was attending one of her first society occasions.[28] She also accompanied her parents to the reception given by the Hon Mrs Brand, wife of

---

[24] *The Morning Post* (London, England), Monday, May 09, 1870; pg. 5; Issue 30083. *19th Century British Library Newspapers: Part II.*

[25] *The Morning Post* (London, England), Thursday, March 23, 1871; pg. 5; Issue 30354. *19th Century British Library Newspapers: Part II.*

[26] *The Morning Post* (London, England), Thursday, June 20, 1872; pg. 5; Issue 30743. *19th Century British Library Newspapers: Part II.*

[27] *The Morning Post* (London, England), Thursday, April 22, 1875; pg. 5; Issue 32078

[28] *The Morning Post* (London, England), Thursday, May 11, 1876; pg. 5; Issue 32407. *19th Century British Library Newspapers: Part II.*

Henry Brand, then Speaker of the House of Commons, after the Speaker's dinner in February 1877.[29]

By May 1878, Helen (Nelly) was eighteen and also joining her parents at functions. She was with them for a reception given by Lady Salisbury at her family's London mansion. It was a huge affair where 'nearly 2000 guests honoured Lady Salisbury with their presence' and 'the grand staircase in the principal corridor was artistically decorated with beautiful flowers and exotics' and 'the full band of the Royal Artillery, upwards of 150 strong...played a selection of music' including Gounod, Mendelssohn, Rossini, and others. Following, as it did, a full dress banquet in celebration of the Queen's birthday, given by Lord Salisbury, the Conservative Secretary of State for Foreign Affairs, guests did not begin to arrive until around 10 o'clock. The company included various members of the British and German royal families: the Crown Prince and Princess of Germany - particularly illustrious guests - arrived at twenty to eleven and left about an hour later, in the Queen's carriage. Sir Edward and Lady Colebrooke and the Misses Colebrooke were described as 'general guests' - indicating that they were not royal, diplomatic or foreigners of rank. None the less, it was a glittering occasion at which to introduce Nelly to high society.[30]

In 1883, Sir Edward attended the party given by the Speaker's wife (the Hon Lady Brand), following a parliamentary dinner, accompanied by his daughters but without Lady Colebrooke[31] but three weeks later, they attended together Lady Salisbury's

---

[29] *The Morning Post* (London, England), Thursday, February 22, 1877; pg. 5; Issue 32653.
[30] *The Morning Post* (London, England), Monday, May 27, 1878; pg. 6; Issue 33045. *19th Century British Library Newspapers: Part II.*
[31] *The Morning Post* (London, England), Thursday, April 19, 1883; pg. 3; Issue 34576. *19th Century British Library Newspapers: Part II.*

first reception of the season at the Salisbury's home in Arlington Street[32] and two years later, in April 1885, as Sir Edward stood down from Parliament, they attended Lady Salisbury's reception for members of Diplomatic Corps and both Houses of Parliament.[33]

It is clear that the Colebrookes were guests at many functions hosted by aristocrats of considerably higher status than themselves but such occasions were of great importance in making contacts and alliances and not least in giving the Colebrooke girls opportunities to meet eligible potential husbands. Sir Edward and Lady Colebrooke also hosted smaller scale events themselves. Lady Colebrooke wrote of one such event:. '...I have been fearfully busy – not in the London acceptation of the word! Tho' to be sure I have been inviting nearly 200 "Asiatics" for my husband besides many non Asiatics...'[34]

Sir Edward in Parliament

Sir Edward made his mark early on the floor of the House of Commons when he spoke forcefully for George Gilbert Scott and his Gothic design of the Government Offices in Parliament on 4 August 1859.[35] At the time, Scott was preoccupied with the 'Battle of the Styles',[36] on which he perceived

---

[32] *The Morning Post* (London, England), Monday, May 07, 1883; pg. 6; Issue 34591. *19th Century British Library Newspapers: Part II.*
[33] *The Morning Post* (London, England), Thursday, April 30, 1885; pg. 3; Issue 35212. *19th Century British Library Newspapers: Part II.*
[34] *The Colebrooke Letters*, 25.3.76
[35] http://hansard.millbanksystems.com/commons/1859/aug/04/supply-civil-service-estimates#S3V0155P0_18590804_HOC_42
[36] There was a fierce debate, taken extremely seriously in the highest circles, as to whether the new offices to be built in Whitehall should be in Classical or Gothic style.

his considerable reputation to depend and he was indebted to Sir Edward for supporting his own preferred Gothic style.[37]

In Parliament, Sir Edward became a well-known figure. Reporting on the proceedings in Parliament in 1860, about a year after he had been returned in the General Election of 1859, the *Caledonian Mercury* reported on Sir Edward speaking on an Annuity Tax Bill: "Him all men know for he has lost an arm." He was "liberal and enlightened"[38] and respected as serious and thoughtful but, in all the dogged determination that he was to show throughout his representation of people in Scotland, he could never be a firebrand: the same article in the *Caledonian Mercury* continued: "Sir Edward is a good speaker but lacks fire to make his speeches tell."[39]

In 1861, Sir Edward and Lanarkshire were honoured by the selection of Sir Edward to 'move the address' in the House of Commons in answer to the speech from the Throne at the opening of Parliament on Tuesday 5 February. The choice of Sir Edward seems to have been something of a surprise: the *Caledonian Mercury* (a newspaper normally well disposed towards Sir Edward) wrote:

> Scotland is to be honoured by the selection of a Scotch member to move the Address. Sir Edward Colebrooke is not a young man nor a young member; he was member for Taunton, in Somerset, from 1842-52 and he was elected for Lanarkshire in 1857. The honourable baronet is not one of the stars of the House, but his speeches are far above mediocrity; and if he had a better voice he would

---

[37] Scott, Sir George Gilbert, *Personal and Professional Recollections*, originally published 1879, new edition, ed. Stamp, G, 1995, p184

[38] *The Caledonian Mercury* (Edinburgh, Scotland), Wednesday, February 26, 1862; Issue 22594

[39] *The Caledonian Mercury* (Edinburgh, Scotland), Monday, May 21, 1860; Issue 22043

gain the ear of the members. As Sir Edward is a deputy-lieutenant of Lanarkshire, I suppose he will appear in scarlet uniform, ...[40]

On 5 February, after the Speaker had read the Queen's Speech from the chair (the Queen had read it previously in the House of Lords,) Sir Edward, in the uniform of the Deputy Lieutenant, gave the Address in reply,[41] but was overcome by anxiety. He trembled and stammered and had to call for a glass of water to 'loosen the flow of his words' and even then he was barely audible.[42] The *Caledonian Mercury* wrote that Sir Edward '...was so distressingly nervous that he could hardly get on, and in one part it was to be feared that he would break down altogether'[43]. However, the sympathetic correspondent added that he felt few could do better in such situation. It was not Sir Edward's greatest moment.

In 1868, Sir Edward was returned for the new constituency of North Lanarkshire, after the division of Lanarkshire, which had been the largest constituency in Scotland. This was Sir Edward's fourth parliament and he took the oath for the new parliament on 11 December 1868.[44] Again the respect that Sir Edward had earned was commented upon in the press. Reporting that the Lord Advocate had responded to a toast to five Scottish MPs and himself at a dinner, he made a point of commenting on Sir Edward and one other of the five: '...There

---

[40] *The Caledonian Mercury* (Edinburgh, Scotland), Monday, January 28, 1861; Issue 22258.
[41] *Glasgow Herald* (Glasgow, Scotland), Wednesday, February 6, 1861; Issue 6575.
[42] *Plymouth and Cornish Advertiser*, Wednesday February 13, 1861, Issue 4948
[43] *The Caledonian Mercury* (Edinburgh, Scotland), Monday, February 11, 1861; Issue 22270.
[44] *Daily News* (London, England), Saturday, December 12, 1868; Issue 7056.

are no members sent from any part of the United Kingdom who command more respect in the House than they do.'[45] None the less, Sir Edward never achieved ministerial office (although this was not unusual among Scottish members). In 1870, the *Glasgow Herald* emphasised that he was an 'ordinary' Member in an item dealing with the re-assembling of the House after the Easter recess, when Scottish interests were represented by just three members, including Sir Edward, described as 'rank and file' members.[46]

Sir Edward became known as one of the more serious members of the House of Commons so when, on 22 May 1883, there was a debate in the House of Commons – involving much hilarity in the House - on the subject that the House should adjourn to go to Epsom on Derby Day, Sir Edward was one of the few MPs who tried to discuss the question seriously and who were ridiculed when they tried to prolong the discussion.[47] The motion was overwhelmingly carried, with the expectation that it would set a pattern for years to come.[48]

Scottish issues

Scotland was always the main focus of Sir Edward's contributions in Parliament and he worked tirelessly for the people of the area of Scotland he represented. Chief among his concerns was a broadening of the franchise. He supported the harmonisation of the franchises of England and Scotland, arguing that in Scotland the franchise was too limited with members effectively returned by landed aristocracy since tenants were always

---

[45] *Glasgow Herald* (Glasgow, Scotland), Saturday, December 19, 1868; Issue 9037

[46] *Glasgow Herald* (Glasgow, Scotland), Tuesday, April 26, 1870; Issue 9458.

[47] *Glasgow Herald* (Glasgow, Scotland), Wednesday, May 23, 1883; Issue 123.

[48] *The Graphic* (London, England), Saturday, May 26, 1883; Issue 704

expected to vote with their landlords, and artisans were not enfranchised.[49]

Just a month after his election, together with another Scottish MP, Sir Edward was already preparing to broaden the franchise by bringing in a Bill for the amendment of the law for the Registration of County Voters in Scotland.[50] But Parliament can move slowly: nearly two years later, Sir Edward was taking initiatives on the same topic, endeavouring to have his bill on the Registration of County Voters read a second time. He felt Parliament was treating Scotland as second best and he was particularly annoyed that his bill had been postponed for three weeks while similar legislation for England was considered. He made his view clear that if the franchise in England was being considered, Scotland should be considered at same time,[51] and, Liberal though he was, he supported the Conservative Prime Minister, Lord Derby, in the Reform Bill of 1859.[52]

In March 1867, there was a meeting of opposition Liberals to discuss the Reform Bill at Gladstone's residence in Carlton House Terrace. The meeting was so numerous that it was held in the inner hall with people spilling up the staircase. Gladstone spoke from the first landing: in general, he was opposed because he felt that there were too many conditions to make for fair reform.[53] As in 1859, Sir Edward acted

---

[49] *The Bradford Observer* (Bradford, England), Thursday, May 13, 1858; pg. 3; Issue 1269. *19th Century British Library Newspapers: Part II.*
[50] *Caledonian Mercury* (Edinburgh, Scotland), Monday, April 26, 1858; Issue 21398.
[51] *The Morning Chronicle* (London, England), Thursday, March 17, 1859; Issue 28762.
[52] *The Morning Post* (London, England), Tuesday, January 14, 1890; pg. 5; Issue 36686. *19th Century British Library Newspapers: Part II.*
[53] *The Standard* (London, England), Friday, March 22, 1867; pg. 5; Issue 13299. *19th Century British Library Newspapers: Part II.*

according to his own conscience rather than towing the Liberal Party line. He was in a minority in believing that the reforms proposed were not sufficiently comprehensive and he dissented from the Liberal view that was presented.[54] The Party line was that occupation of land of the requisite value was sufficient to make the occupant a voter but Sir Edward wanted the requirement that a house was on the land – his amendment was not carried.[55] A year later, Sir Edward made two other amendments to the Scottish Reform Bill: firstly to put an end to faggot-voting[56] and secondly to have a 12 month residency requirement to gain the right to vote.[57]

Parallel with reform of the franchise was concern at the level of representation for Scotland in the House of Commons – in other words that the number of Members was too small compared to England. The Scotch Reform Bill sought to address this and, as Member for the largest constituency in Scotland, Sir Edward was much involved. In June 1867, Sir Edward was at a meeting at the Westminster Palace Hotel, with representatives from both political parties where they initiated an attempt to get Scotland proper representation in the House of Commons.[58] At the general election in 1868, this

---

[54] *The Examiner* (London, England), Saturday, April 13, 1867; Issue 3089.

[55] *The Newcastle Courant etc* (Newcastle-upon-Tyne, England), Friday, May 31, 1867; Issue 10040.

[56] Faggot-voting was a common electoral abuse in the United Kingdom until the electoral reforms of the late nineteenth century. Typically, faggot voters satisfied a property qualification by holding the title to subdivisions of a large property with a single beneficial owner. The lack of secret ballot ensured the faggot complied with the landowner's wishes so "faggot voters" would vote according to the wishes of the original landowner. Prohibition of vote buying was difficult to enforce if the faggot was an employee of the landowner. There was no requirement for a voter to be resident; the landowner and faggot voter might both reside outside the constituency.

[57] *The Dundee Courier & Argus* (Dundee, Scotland), Wednesday, May 27, 1868; Issue 4622. *19th Century British Library Newspapers: Part II.*

[58] *Glasgow Herald* (Glasgow, Scotland), Saturday, June 22, 1867; Issue 8569

initiative came to fruition with Lanarkshire divided into two divisions as well as changes to other Scottish constituencies.

As he was preparing to step down from Parliament, Sir Edward was in the House on Saturday 6 December 1884 to hear the Third Reform Bill (giving the vote to around two million agricultural labourers) had been given royal assent and he added his voice to the loud cheers,[59] before going on to preside at a private meeting of Scottish Members at the House to discuss the Redistribution Bill,[60] which led to a further division of Lanarkshire as well as other changes.

Education

Scottish education – of all types and at all levels – received much of Sir Edward's parliamentary energy and he developed an interest and expertise that was widely recognised and respected.

In 1864, there was a widespread view among Scottish MPs that there were many problems to be addressed in Scottish education and that there should be two Royal Commissions to enquire into it.[61] The Scotch Education Bill, debated in London, had as its purpose to set up boards to run schools, after the pattern instituted in England in 1870. A commission had been set up to 'look after the parishes, and to see what schools ought to be planted in them; to overlook the proposed unions of small parishes, and of small burghs with parishes; to draw up rules for the School Board elections; and to settle the number of the members of such Boards in each separate

---

[59] *Glasgow Herald* (Glasgow, Scotland), Monday, December 8, 1884; Issue 293.
[60] *Aberdeen Weekly Journal* (Aberdeen, Scotland), Monday, December 8, 1884; Issue 9306.
[61] *The Dundee Courier & Argus* (Dundee, Scotland), Tuesday, May 10, 1864; Issue 3355. *19th Century British Library Newspapers: Part II.*

locality'.[62] Sir Edward argued that members of school boards should be drawn from the landowning classes; others thought there were too many variable factors to make this practicable and Sir Edward's proposal was not adopted. The outcomes of the commission's enquiries were enshrined in the Scottish Education Act of 1872.[63]

Of more immediate and practical concern to Sir Edward was the second commission, the Scotch Endowed Schools Commission, of which Sir Edward became Chairman. The *Daily News* and other newspapers reported the announcement of this in the London Gazette of Tuesday 17 September 1872:

THE SCOTCH ENDOWED SCHOOLS COMMISSION. – WHITEHALL, SEPT 14.- The Queen has been pleased to appoint Sir Thomas Edward Colebrooke, Bart.; [and six others] to be Her Majesty's Commissioners to enquire into the nature and amount of all endowments in Scotland, the funds of which are wholly or in part devoted, or have been applied, or which can rightly be made applicable to educational purposes, and which have not been reported on by the Commissioners under the Universities (Scotland) Act, 1858; also to inquire into the administration and management of any hospitals or schools supported by such endowments, and into the system and course of study respectively pursued therein, and to report whether any and what changes in the administration and use of such endowments are expedient, by which their usefulness and efficiency may be increased. – *Gazette* [64]

When the commission reported in 1875, it sought to make the provision of Endowed Schools less exclusive: '...to open

---

[62] *Glasgow Herald* (Glasgow, Scotland), Saturday, June 8, 1872; Issue 10122.

[63] *Glasgow Herald* (Glasgow, Scotland), Friday, June 7, 1872; Issue 10121.

[64] *Daily News* (London, England), Wednesday, September 18, 1872; Issue 8235.

access of education in schools, to prevent exclusion on the basis of religious denomination, to largely transfer control from foundations to school boards'.[65]

By 1877, there was a view in the House of Commons that the boards that oversaw individual Board Schools in Scotland were functioning well and that the Board of Education that in turn oversaw the school boards could be abolished, although it was Sir Edward's view that the umbrella board should be retained.[66]

Indian affairs

Sir Edward's other main interest was in matters relating to India. This stemmed from India being the country of his birth, from it being where his father had spent most of his working life and built up extraordinarily rich legacy of scholarly work and from his own few years working there. He knew Hindi – learned at the East India College and in India and his standard was high enough to be able to translate a paper on the constitution of an Indian court, which was published in the *Transactions of the Royal Asiatic Society.*[67] He often involved himself in legislation to do with India, gave advice regarding India to other people, contributed to organisations connected with India and entertained Indian people and others with an interest there. He was known in India for his compassionate interest in the country so that, when he was re-elected to Parliament in 1868, *The Times of India* (reported in the *Glasgow Herald*) was pleased to report the return of 'old

---

[65] *The Aberdeen Journal* (Aberdeen, Scotland), Wednesday, March 17, 1875; Issue 6636.

[66] *Aberdeen Weekly Journal* (Aberdeen, Scotland), Friday, August 3, 1877; Issue 7006.

[67] *The Morning Post* (London, England), Wednesday, January 20, 1858; pg. 4; Issue 26227. *19th Century British Library Newspapers: Part II.*

acquaintances' including Sir Edward, with an interest in 'the prosperity of India'.[68]

His reputation in India had developed over the preceding decade, as well as during his time as Member for Taunton. In March 1858, soon after being elected back to Parliament, he was involved in work on the bill to transfer the government of India from the East India Company to the Crown. The plan was to set up a Council of India, with 18 members, half nominated by the Crown and half elected.[69] Sir Edward contributed to the debate in Parliament, suggesting that the Council should operate '...as nearly as possible in the position of the old Directors.'[70] By May of the same year, the rule of India had been transferred to the Crown. Sir Edward had also got himself on to a select committee concerned with the transport of troops to India.[71]

In 1860, Sir Edward offered, at a meeting of distinguished people at Willis's Rooms in St James, to become the honorary secretary of the elected committee to determine a suitable memorial 'testifying respect for the memory of the late distinguished Indian statesman, the Hon Mountstuart Elphinstone.'[72]

At state functions with an Indian connection, Sir Edward was a natural guest. It was the custom for the various Secretaries of State to host state dinners in celebration of the Queen's birthday and on 25 May 1867, Sir Edward was a guest at the dinner given by the Secretary of State for India. A month later,

---

[68] *Glasgow Herald* (Glasgow, Scotland), Friday, February 19, 1869; Issue 9090.

[69] *The Morning Post* (London, England), Saturday, March 27, 1858; pg. 4; Issue 26284. *19th Century British Library Newspapers: Part II.*

[70] *Glasgow Herald* (Glasgow, Scotland), Wednesday, May 5, 1858; Issue 5915.

[71] *The Morning Chronicle* (London, England), Tuesday, February 9, 1858; Issue 28435.

[72] *The Morning Post* (London, England), Friday, February 17, 1860; pg. 6; Issue 26885. *19th Century British Library Newspapers: Part II.*

the Sultan of Turkey visited London and received various deputations at Buckingham Palace, including one from the Royal Asiatic Society, among whom, as would have been expected, was Sir Edward.[73] Outside Parliament and from a young age, Sir Edward had involved himself in the Royal Asiatic Society, an organisation set up by his father. Attendance at meetings was often sparse, because, according to a press article, the papers given often have 'no vitality and elicit no discussion'.[74] Nevertheless, Sir Edward's support was loyal and he became president more than once. Membership was broad, including nationals of Asian countries.

In 1879, at a summer sitting of the House of Commons, it was proposed to break up the Indian Museum, dispersing its contents to the British Museum, the South Kensington Museum and elsewhere.[75] Sir Edward opposed this break-up, presumably because he felt India was of such importance to Britain as to warrant its own museum. He acknowledged, though, that it was tired and its popularity waning but his solution was to support a proposal for funding of £2000 a year to improve it.[76] In the event, though, the museum was closed.

Sir Edward's knowledge and experience was welcomed on the committee set up to realise the 'so long advocated proposal'

---

[73] *The Morning Post* (London, England), Monday, July 22, 1867; pg. 5; Issue 29208. *19th Century British Library Newspapers: Part II*

[74] *The Morning Post* (London, England), Tuesday, November 21, 1865; pg. 5; Issue 28687. *19th Century British Library Newspapers: Part II*.

[75] The India Museum opened in 1801. It contained artefacts from India and was originally housed in East India House, Leadenhall Street. By 1850s, it was no longer popular and after a couple of temporary homes, it was dispersed in 1879, mostly to the South Kensington Museum (now the Victorian and Albert Museum) where it forms the basis of the museum's collection of Indian art. Some of the collection went to the Natural History Museum and Kew Gardens. (See http://www.theguardian.com/artandde-sign/2003/sep/25/heritage.art)

[76] *The Pall Mall Gazette* (London, England), Friday, August 1, 1879; Issue 4506.

for founding an Indian Institute at the University of Oxford.[77] The ceremony, 'with full Masonic honours', of laying a memorial stone in the new Indian Institute in Oxford was carried out by the Prince of Wales on 2 May 1883.[78] The Institute, designed by Basil Champneys, was built on a prime site next to Bodleian building.[79] Sir Edward was naturally one of the distinguished guests at the founding ceremony and became one of the three trustees.[80] Lecture rooms only were ready for use when the Indian Institute opened in October 1884. The library, museum and reading room were all unfinished but by April 1885, with gifts of books and artefacts from India it was fully operational and in celebration, a conversazione was arranged, to which the Secretary of State for India was invited as well as Sir Edward and other dignitaries.[81]

At the beginning of the same year, the Northbrook Indian Club was formed, with premises near Whitehall, under the presidency of Lord Northbrook (a previous Viceroy of India), with the purpose of fostering closer relations between English and Indian gentlemen. Sir Edward was a natural candidate for membership and was one of those at a Saturday evening banquet in February, given by the Club at Westminster Town Hall in honour of the Marquis of Ripon, who had been heavily involved in the establishment of the Oxford Indian Institute.[82]

---

[77] *The Pall Mall Gazette* (London, England), Thursday, April 3, 1879; Issue 4404

[78] *Jackson's Oxford Journal* (Oxford, England), Saturday, April 28, 1883; Issue 6789.

[79] *Journal of the Royal Asiatic Society* (London, England), [Date Unknown]; pg. XXXI

[80] *Journal of the Royal Asiatic Society* (London, England), [Date Unknown]; pg. XXXI

[81] *Jackson's Oxford Journal* (Oxford, England), Saturday, April 18, 1885; Issue 6891.

[82] *The Morning Post* (London, England), Monday, February 23, 1885; pg. 3; Issue 35155. *19th Century British Library Newspapers: Part II.*

Sir Edward's interest in Indian affairs spread to an interest in other countries described as being in the Far East and he earned genuine respect for his compassionate views. In 1883, he was privileged with an invitation to 'A Siamese investiture: 'unique in this country'. It took place in London and was an honour given to 'the Envoy Extraordinary of the King of Siam'. Sir Edward was one of only a small number of British people present.[83]

Poor Relief

Among other matters where Sir Edward's contribution in Parliament was frequently prominent were issues of social reform, reform of working practices and law and order. Very early after being returned to Parliament as Member for Lanarkshire, he supported miners in seeking to obtain a Royal Commission to enquire into the length of hours worked by men and boys in the mines and the method used in determining the value of a miner's work, which at that time relied on weighing what a miner had extracted.[84]

In 1866, Sir Edward was one of three Scottish MPs who brought in a petition and bill relating to Glasgow Houses of Refuge.[85] He was one of three MPs again in 1872 bringing in a bill (the Poor Law (Scotland) Bill) providing for the improvement and better administration of the laws relating to the relief of the poor in Scotland.[86] The following year, though, he demonstrated unexpected opposition in voting against the

---

[83] *Glasgow Herald* (Glasgow, Scotland), Tuesday, November 27, 1883; Issue 284

[84] *Birmingham Daily Post* (Birmingham, England), Friday, July 22, 1859; Issue 422.

[85] *The Caledonian Mercury* (Edinburgh, Scotland), Monday, February 19, 1866; Issue 23912.

[86] *The Pall Mall Gazette* (London, England), Friday, March 22, 1872; Issue 2217

same Bill at the second reading. In moving the rejection of the Bill, Sir Edward explained that he did so...

>...because it contained alterations on the Bill of last year, which it was only natural Scotch members and their constituents should ask time to consider and as the Bill in its present shape had been in the hands of members only a week such opportunity had not been afforded. Moreover there was a suspicion that there was some secret understanding between Mr Crauford [the MP who moved the second reading] and the Lord Advocate, and that the bill then before the House was simply "a pilot balloon sent up to see which way the wind blew...[87]

It is clear that Sir Edward was not afraid to stand up for what he considered correct. On this occasion, although he supported most of the provisions of the bill, he disagreed with some of the new proposals regarding the amalgamation of parishes pointing out that some of those proposed, especially in Glasgow, would be unmanageably large.[88] In this, he had support from other Members and the Bill was thrown out.

A year later in 1874, Sir Edward introduced a deputation comprising a large number of MPs to Sir Stafford Northcote, the Chancellor of the Exchequer. The deputation was concerned with an issue of harmonisation with practice in England. As on other occasions, with his experience of practice on both sides of the border, Sir Edward was well placed to make a valuable contribution. This time, the issue concerned the funding for the poor with mental health problems ('Scotch lunatic paupers', as they were described). Sir Edward found the less favourable

---

[87] *Daily News* (London, England), Thursday, February 27, 1873; Issue 8374.
[88] *The Aberdeen Journal* (Aberdeen, Scotland), Wednesday, March 5, 1873; Issue 6530.

funding in Scotland unacceptable, particularly as the system for managing such people was in many ways better in Scotland (under the Board of Lunacy) than in England.[89]

Justice, the police and law and order

From an English point of view, the Scottish judicial system had many flaws and needed reform. In 1867, Sir Edward proposed in the House of Commons that the Court of Sessions in Scotland should be made more accountable. He had already put in work on a methodical system for Scottish Judicial Statistics and a fair means of assessing the amount of work performed by the judges and officials of the Court of Sessions and appreciation was recorded for this.[90] A commission was set up - The Scotch Law Commission - which had as its purpose the reform of the Scottish judicial system. However, Sir Edward and other Members who had already worked on reform were deliberately excluded and the commissioners included men whose preference was to maintain the status quo. There was considerable disquiet in some quarters that the commission would be self-defeating,[91] with the outcome that a new Royal Commission was established and Sir Edward was one of those who '... consented to act as Commissioners for inquiring into matters relating to the Courts of Law in Scotland.'[92]

In the burghs around Glasgow, the repeated attempts to extend the city's boundaries caused much debate. Related to this was the administration of the police and as boundaries were adjusted, so the administrative control of the police had to change. In this context, in 1873, Sir Edward introduced

---

[89] *The Dundee Courier & Argus* (Dundee, Scotland), Thursday, May 07, 1874; Issue 6483. *19th Century British Library Newspapers: Part II.*

[90] *Glasgow Herald* (Glasgow, Scotland), Monday, December 9, 1867; Issue 8714

[91] *Daily News* (London, England), Friday, October 30, 1868; Issue 7019.

[92] *The Aberdeen Journal* (Aberdeen, Scotland), Wednesday, November 25, 1868; Issue 6307.

a Bill to amend the General Police and Improvement (Scotland) Acts.[93]

Sir Edward had some involvement in penal reform in Scotland, contributing to the Bill to amend the Acts for the Administration of Prisons in Scotland,[94] which sought to divide the county in terms of prison administration and so reduce costs.[95] He also sought, when possible, to have Scottish matters relating to prisons debated in Parliament at the same time as such matters in England.[96]

Roads and railways

Sir Edward often involved himself in matters relating to the improvements to communication systems. Many roads (such as they were) carried tolls when Sir Edward first began representing Lanarkshire and the railways were in their infancy. In 1861, he brought in a bill for the construction of tramways in Scotland[97] and was on a select committee enquiring into Scottish roads and bridges.[98] In 1865, he supported the promoters of the Roads and Bridges (Scotland) Bill, the purpose of which was to better regulate turnpike roads and abolish tolls,[99] and in 1877, he brought in a bill 'to

---

[93] *Glasgow Herald* (Glasgow, Scotland), Saturday, June 21, 1873; Issue 10446

[94] *The Morning Post* (London, England), Monday, June 08, 1868; pg. 3; Issue 29483

[95] *Glasgow Herald* (Glasgow, Scotland), Wednesday, June 10, 1868; Issue 8872

[96] *The Leeds Mercury* (Leeds, England), Tuesday, July 11, 1876; Issue 11935

[97] *Glasgow Herald* (Glasgow, Scotland), Saturday, February 16, 1861; Issue 6584.

[98] *The Morning Post* (London, England), Saturday, June 01, 1861; pg. 2; Issue 27286. *19th Century British Library Newspapers: Part II.*

[99] *The Dundee Courier & Argus* (Dundee, Scotland), Friday, April 28, 1865; Issue 3658. *19th Century British Library Newspapers: Part II.*

amend the law in regard to the management and maintenance of roads and bridges in Scotland'.[100]

He had a particular interest in the development of railways in Scotland, and personally sought to bring in bills for railways in his part of Scotland, notably the Douglas and Dolphinton Railway and the Glasgow and South Western Railway.[101] With another Scottish MP, he brought in a Bill related to the expansion of the North British Railway.[102] However, he also involved himself in railway development all over the United Kingdom. He spoke in Parliament on a bill regarding a new railway to Brighton[103] and was on the select committee for ensuring the completion of new railways, with powers to scrutinise relevant officials, papers and records.[104] He chaired a committee relevant to a Welsh railway[105] and another on the Great Eastern Railway (Finance) (Recommitted) Bill.[106] He was one of the 'Court of Referees' regarding the development of the Midland Railway.[107]

Sale of Alcohol

Sir Edward was concerned, as were many others in positions of authority, at the detrimental effects of high levels of alcohol

---

[100] *The Pall Mall Gazette* (London, England), Tuesday, February 20, 1877; Issue 3746.

[101] *The Caledonian Mercury* (Edinburgh, Scotland), Monday, February 13, 1865; Issue 23595

[102] *The Caledonian Mercury* (Edinburgh, Scotland), Monday, February 19, 1866; Issue 23912.

[103] *The Morning Post* (London, England), Wednesday, February 17, 1864; pg. 2; Issue 28134. *19th Century British Library Newspapers: Part II.*

[104] *The Standard* (London, England), Tuesday, April 30, 1867; pg. 2; Issue 13332. *19th Century British Library Newspapers: Part II*

[105] *The Wrexham Advertiser, Denbighshire, Flintshire, Shropshire, Cheshire & North Wales Register* (Wrexham, Wales), Saturday, May 11, 1867; pg. 4; Issue 734. *19th Century British Library Newspapers: Part II.*

[106] *Daily News* (London, England), Thursday, July 25, 1867; Issue 6622.

[107] *Birmingham Daily Post* (Birmingham, England), Tuesday, April 30, 1872; Issue 4302.

consumption in Scotland. In 1858, he had a meeting with a deputation of Scottish licenced victuallers at the Home Office regarding licencing issues, where the possible assimilation of the laws of the two countries was among the topics discussed[108] and, in 1861, he was one of those enquiring into the operation of public houses in Scotland.[109]

By 1874, harmonisation of relevant laws in England and Scotland had plainly not taken place as various licensing acts had been passed which did not affect Scotland. Due to the fact that 'the consumption of spirits in Scotland had lately increased to a most alarming extent' it was felt 'desirable that some check should be imposed upon it.'[110] This was debated in the Spirituous Liquors (Scotland) Bill and a complicated method of control – the 'Gottenburg system' was proposed for trial, whereby 'the sale of spirits was placed completely under the control of the local authorities'. Sir Edward, 'while admitting that the system had many good points, freely criticised its details and expressed an apprehension that they would not all work satisfactorily. He was, however, in favour of trying the experiment.'[111]

Smaller concerns

Sir Edward also involved himself in a wide range of other issues. In 1859, he was one of a deputation of Scotch county members in a meeting at the Foreign Office on the guano

---

[108] *Glasgow Herald* (Glasgow, Scotland), Wednesday, February 10, 1858; Issue 5879.

[109] *The Caledonian Mercury* (Edinburgh, Scotland), Friday, July 12, 1861; Issue 22398

[110] *The Morning Post* (London, England), Thursday, May 21, 1874; pg. 4; Issue 31791. *19th Century British Library Newspapers: Part II.*

[111] *The Morning Post* (London, England), Thursday, May 21, 1874; pg. 4; Issue 31791. *19th Century British Library Newspapers: Part II.*

trade.[112] In 1864, he argued in parliament on the importance of Scottish banks issuing their own notes.[113] In 1868 he was at the War Office, as part of deputation, on the subject of barrack accommodation in Glasgow[114] and in the same year involved in the preparation of the Weights and Measures (Scotland) Bill.[115] 1873 saw him nominated onto a Select Committee dealing with the Cape of Good Hope and Zanzibar mail.[116]

He seems also to have become more and more involved in the committees that regulated the functioning of Parliament itself. So, 1873 saw him nominated to a Select Committee on Standing Orders, probably as chairman.[117] In 1874, he was nominated to the Select Committee on the Parliamentary Elections (Returning Officers) Bill[118] as well as to the Select Committee on Privileges, headed by Disraeli, to investigate the question of privilege.[119] In 1878, he was again nominated to the Select Committee on Standing Orders,[120] as he was in 1884[121] and 1885.[122]

---

[112] *Daily News* (London, England), Saturday, March 12, 1859; Issue 4002
[113] *Glasgow Herald* (Glasgow, Scotland), Monday, May 2, 1864; Issue 7586.
[114] *Glasgow Herald* (Glasgow, Scotland), Saturday, May 9, 1868; Issue 8845
[115] *Glasgow Herald* (Glasgow, Scotland), Monday, May 18, 1868; Issue 8852.
[116] *Daily News* (London, England), Tuesday, June 24, 1873; Issue 8474.
[117] *The Morning Post* (London, England), Monday, March 23, 1874; pg. 2; Issue 31740. *19th Century British Library Newspapers: Part II.*
[118] *The Pall Mall Gazette* (London, England), Tuesday, May 5, 1874; Issue 2875.
[119] *The Leeds Mercury* (Leeds, England), Saturday, March 28, 1874; Issue 11221
[120] *The Leeds Mercury* (Leeds, England), Saturday, January 19, 1878; Issue 12411.
[121] *The Morning Post* (London, England), Monday, February 11, 1884; pg. 4; Issue 34831. *19th Century British Library Newspapers: Part II.*
[122] *The Morning Post* (London, England), Saturday, February 21, 1885; pg. 4; Issue 35154. *19th Century British Library Newspapers: Part II.*

Charitable deeds

As an aristocrat, a land and property owner in East London and a Member of Parliament, Sir Edward contributed to various causes in the capital. In 1860, a public subscription fund was opened and Sir Edward became one of a committee to determine a memorial to the late Henry Hallam for his service to the Historical Literature of England.[123] In 1874, he was one of a deputation at the Foreign Office to ask the Earl of Derby, Secretary of State for Foreign Affairs, to make provision for family of the late Dr Livingstone.[124]

In 1885, Sir Edward was one of a long list of patrons for some 'Grand Amateur Theatricals' in aid of the Gordon Memorial Hospital, Port Said. There was to be a series of performances at the Olympic Theatre, London. One of plays to be performed was Cox and Box and Sir Edward will have smiled at the memory of the New Year theatricals in 1871 at the 'Theatre Royal' in Ottershaw when his children were small.[125]

In 1886, during the same weekend as a mass meeting of the unemployed on Hackney Downs, Sir Edward donated £25 (about £2250)[126] being described as one of the principal donors, to the Lord Mayor's Fund for the Unemployed in London.[127]

---

[123] *The Morning Post* (London, England), Wednesday, March 14, 1860; pg. [1]; Issue 26907. *19th Century British Library Newspapers: Part II*, Classified ads

[124] *The York Herald* (York, England), Monday, April 27, 1874; pg. 2; Issue 5371. *19th Century British Library Newspapers: Part II*.

[125] *The Morning Post* (London, England), Wednesday, May 13, 1885; pg. [1]; Issue 35223. *19th Century British Library Newspapers: Part II*, Classified ads

[126] www.measuringworth.com, retail price index, 2014 equivalent

[127] *Daily News* (London, England), Monday, February 22, 1886; Issue 12439

In particular, Sir Edward contributed over many years to the London Hospital in Whitechapel. Since this hospital was the chief receiving house for accidents in the metropolis[128] and since Sir Edward (as Lord of the Manor of Stepney) owned much property in the East End of London, it would have been an important cause to him.

In 1860, in an advertisement for the hospital's annual dinner, Sir Edward is listed as one of 'stewards for 120th anniversary' and as such was one of those selling tickets at one guinea each.[129] In 1864, he was 'one of a large number of noblemen and gentlemen consenting to act as stewards for the laying of the foundation stone ceremony of the new West Wing at the London Hospital on its 124th anniversary by the Prince of Wales.[130] In 1866, he was listed both as steward and contributor to an appeal for the London Hospital 'to meet the increasing expenditure of the charity[131] and again in 1868, he was one of stewards for the annual dinner in May.[132]

In 1873, there was a special appeal for £100,000 to build a new wing and for maintenance of the hospital and Sir Edward was listed among the early donors, having given £100 (about £7,500)[133], which was not among most generous (there were some of £1000 and £5000) but it was more than many gave.[134]

---

[128] *The Morning Post* (London, England), Thursday, May 05, 1864; pg. [1]; Issue 28201. *19th Century British Library Newspapers: Part II.*

[129] *The Morning Post* (London, England), Thursday, April 26, 1860; pg. [1]; Issue 26944, Classified ads

[130] *The Morning Post* (London, England), Thursday, May 05, 1864; pg. [1]; Issue 28201. *19th Century British Library Newspapers: Part II.*

[131] *The Morning Post* (London, England), Thursday, August 09, 1866; pg. [1]; Issue 28911. *19th Century British Library Newspapers: Part II.*

[132] *The Pall Mall Gazette* (London, England), Saturday, April 4, 1868; Issue 983 (and other papers)

[133] www.measuringworth.com, retail price index, 2014 equivalent

[134] *The Morning Post* (London, England), Saturday, March 29, 1873; pg. [1]; Issue 31433. *19th Century British Library Newspapers: Part II.*

In 1878, there was another appeal at the London Hospital. It was an urgent appeal, made at the Mansion House on 4 April, for a maintenance fund of £25,000 a year for five years and annual donations were sought over that time period. Details were given in a classified advertisement:

> The London Hospital contains 790 beds. It is the only large general hospital for one million persons, chiefly of the poorest classes. The accidents alone admitted into this institution are more numerous than those at any three other Metropolitan Hospitals combined. Its In-patients received last year were 6825, by far the highest number at any hospital in the country. The income from endowments is less that £14,000 a year. The (Unavoidable) Expenditure is £44,000 a year. Owing to the poverty of the districts surrounding the Institution, the deficiency can only be met by the liberality of the general public. The present appeal to obtain a maintenance fund for the next five years (no part of it is needed for buildings) is therefore earnestly pressed upon the attention of the benevolent.[135]

With his title and his wealth, some of which was derived from the 'poorest classes' served by the hospital, Sir Edward would have been very aware that he was one of the 'benevolent' being targeted. He was on the first list of subscribers,[136] having made a donation of £100 but it was 'in one sum' (one of the highest such donations) rather than a subscription over five years to ensure continuity of income – but, as if to temper this, Sir Edward also served on the appeal committee.[137]

---

[135] *The Standard* (London, England), Thursday, April 11, 1878; pg. [1]; Issue 16760. 19th Century British Library Newspapers; Part II, Classified ads
[136] *The Standard* (London, England), Thursday, April 18, 1878; pg. [1]; Issue 16766. *19th Century British Library Newspapers: Part II.*
[137] *The Standard* (London, England), Thursday, April 18, 1878; pg. [1]; Issue 16766. *19th Century British Library Newspapers: Part II.*

His interests in East London will also have encouraged Sir Edward to buy into the New River Company.[138] This was an artificial waterway, dating from 1613, and flowing through areas where he held property. Its purpose was to bring fresh drinking water to London from the River Lea and other springs.

Protecting the interests of landlords

Sir Edward's stewardship of the lands he had unexpectedly inherited led him to support some measures which sat uncomfortably with his forward-looking liberal views. While working hard in various ways to improve the lives of those less fortunate than himself, he believed unquestioningly in the hierarchy of classes and their different roles in society. Having become an aristocrat, therefore, he had no choice but to do his part to protect the interests of the landed class and he made it his business to understand the intricacies of Scottish law as it regarded landlords.

In 1865 he was appointed to a select committee on the valuation of lands and heritages in Scotland.[139] In 1870, he objected to a proposed method of valuing land[140] and therefore found himself one of those selected to be on the Committee to consider the Valuation of Lands and Assessment Bill.[141] In 1873, together with the Conservatives, he urged retention of the Law of Hypothec (a law protecting a landlord's investment

---

138 London Electoral Register, 1888, Search.ancestry.co.uk/Browse/Print_d. aspx/c6d2c0ec9ba5831f787de66d6035b383/493094727.jpg, accessed 12.10.12

139 *Daily News* (London, England), Thursday, March 9, 1865; Issue 5878

140 *Glasgow Herald* (Glasgow, Scotland), Thursday, May 5, 1870; Issue 9466

141 *The Dundee Courier & Argus* (Dundee, Scotland), Sunday, May 15, 1870; Issue 5238. *19th Century British Library Newspapers: Part II.*

in his land)[142] in the Hypothec Abolition Bill.[143] When it came to the vote on abolition, Sir Edward was teller for the noes – and the bill was comfortably defeated – so protecting the interests of the landed classes.[144]

He also supported the (established) Church of Scotland in opposing the Church Rates Abolition (Scotland) Bill. Its purpose was to prevent the enforcement of church rates by legal process, which was comparable to the situation already prevailing in England. Those who opposed, including Sir Edward, said it would ' improperly deprive the Church of its property' while the proposers said it would 'allay a good deal of irritation among those who were compelled to contribute to a Church to which they did not belong.'[145]

Sir Edward's life in London was certainly busy, both socially and politically and would have been fulfilling enough for many aristocrats of the time. Sir Edward, though, had another public life and responsibilities hundreds of miles away and further commitments a short journey away in Ottershaw.

---

[142] This was a Scottish law regarding the prior claim of a landlord for his rent over the crop and stock of a tenant farmer. Its purpose was to protect the landlord against the tenant taking all the proceeds of land in event of the landlord having invested in the tenant to enable him to raise a crop or stock.
[143] *Glasgow Herald* (Glasgow, Scotland), Friday, June 27, 1873; Issue 10451
[144] *The Aberdeen Journal* (Aberdeen, Scotland), Wednesday, July 2, 1873; Issue 6546.
[145] *Glasgow Herald* (Glasgow, Scotland), Thursday, July 6, 1871; Issue 9832.

Chapter 7

Ottershaw life

Ottershaw Park, Sir Edward's second seat

In 1859, two years after their marriage, Sir Edward and Lady Colebrooke bought 'the distinguished and highly valuable residential property known as Ottershaw Park',[1] near Chertsey in Surrey. The house was a Regency period mansion in Palladian style and had been enlarged and improved by previous owners.[2]

The house they bought (which was demolished in 1910) was substantially the same as when painted by John Hassell in 1824 and the sale particulars of 1859 give a vivid and detailed description of the property. It was a gracious and elegant dwelling, combining the benefits of country living with the convenience of the proximity of the railway for travelling the twenty two miles to and from London. It was described as being in the 'picturesque village of Chertsey' (although it was actually two miles distant), and two miles from the Woking, Chertsey and Addlestone stations on the South Western Railway. It was 'a gentleman's establishment upon a moderate scale', though was grand, by any standards. It

---

[1] *Ottershaw Park, sale details, 1859.* The sale particulars, from which this description is extracted, gave much detail about the mansion and estate.
[2] Athersuch, John, *An Illustrated History of Ottershaw Park Estate, 1761-2011*, Peacock Press, Hebdon Bridge, 2010

Ottershaw Park by John Hassell, 1824
Reproduced by permission of Surrey History Centre

included extensive parkland and ornamental woodlands with drives and walks.

It had two lodge entrances, the principal one from Chertsey (at the end of Coach Road) and the other from the road to Woking (the present Wey Farm entrance). There was a large porte-cochère to the mansion, leading to a large entrance hall. The library, which had a screen of ionic columns at each end, opened off the hall and led, through folding doors of plate glass, to a Music Room and then to the conservatory with an arcade of columns and arches and ornamental iron work. A double flight of steps then led to the pleasure grounds. Also on the ground floor was a gentleman's morning room, which led to the orangery and 'water closets appropriately situated', 'a magnificent dining room, 41ft by 18ft with Corinthian pilasters at each end, ...an elegant drawing room of octagonal form, with a domed ceiling, enriched cornice and Japanese columns; the whole decorated with unique taste in the Chinese style'.

The North Lodge (the Chertsey Lodge) of Ottershaw
Park, from the 1859 sale particulars
Reproduced by permission of Chertsey Museum

The porte-cochère, Ottershaw Park, from the 1859 sale
particulars
Reproduced by permission of Chertsey Museum

On the first floor was the principal bedroom with dressing room adjoining, seven other bedrooms, two dressing rooms, a housemaid's closet, and two water closets. On the top floor were six more bedrooms, some adapted for nurseries or servants' rooms. In the basement was a large housekeeper's room, a bedroom, butler's pantry, under butler's room, men servants' bedrooms, a strong room with iron door, lobby, and servants' hall. There were also wine and beer cellars, coal vaults, several water closets etc. etc.[3]

The mansion had one highly individual feature in that the kitchen was joined to the house by a passage but was quite separate from the main house. With other services for the house, it was in a small building to the north of the mansion – an inconvenience that Sir Edward soon remedied. This building was styled like a gothic chapel and was referred to using ecclesiastical terminology – although there is no evidence of it ever having been a church. It was:

> ...in the capricious form of a small monastic confine, in Gothic style. It was surmounted by a lofty tower, clock etc, and partly encompassed by an iron railing; the body of the building or nave [was] an excellent kitchen, lighted by a large mullioned window; adjoining is a bake house, pantry etc. The chancel: a neat dairy with painted windows.'[4]

The estate was a self-contained community, with a home farm producing food for the house and the estate. It included farm land, both arable and pasture where Sir Edward grazed his mixed herd of 34 Ayrshire and Alderney cattle.[5] There were also plantations suitable for game shooting.

---

[3] Sale details, 1859
[4] Sale details, 1859
[5] *The Examiner* (London, England), Saturday, December 2, 1865; Issue 3018.

The 'gothic chapel', Ottershaw Park, from the 1859 sale particulars
Reproduced by permission of Chertsey Museum

The Bailiff's House, cottages for employees and other buildings provided for the various services necessary for the running of such a community. They including stabling, a laundry and gun room and a 'meal house, tool house and fowls fattening house; drying house, slaughter house and boiling house; piggeries, bullock lodges, with twenty seven stalls; hay and straw houses, double barn, ...' turnip house, enclosed yards, with lodges for stock; cart and implement houses, workshop, small barn, cow house and yard; cart horse stabling, harness and chaff houses, granaries and lofts, ... kitchen gardens ... three vineries...forcing houses... small dairy, dog's kennel, venison house &c.'[6] – in short, everything necessary to support a substantial mansion and those who lived and worked in it as well as those on the adjoining estate.

---

[6] Sale details, 1859

Sir Edward took a real interest in the practices on his estates and shared new ideas between Ottershaw and Abington. One such occasion was when disease broke out among his cattle in Ottershaw. Instead of treating them all in 'cow-doctor fashion with stimulants' most were 'treated more gently with mashes of oat and barley meal'. The result was that those treated with 'mashes' survived but the nine treated conventionally all died. His experiment showed that the 'gentler' method was more successful and he wrote to the press to advocate it when disease broke out some time later in and around his estates in Scotland.[7]

Sir Edward made some changes to the mansion. He had the west wing conservatory demolished and rebuilt the east wing, which had been an orangery, to accommodate the kitchen and later the laundry, both of which were previously located in the 'gothic chapel'. He also had alterations made to the roof and attic. His architect was the Scot William Burn, who had a practice in Mayfair, near to the Colebrookes' London house, and an established reputation in country house work.[8]

Ottershaw Park was one of several estates owned by minor aristocrats and gentry near Chertsey and by the time Sir Edward and Lady Colebrooke purchased it, it comprised approximately 420 acres. The first mention of the local community by the name of Ottershaw was in the mid nineteenth century, around the time that the Colebrookes bought the estate, until when 'Ottershaw' referred only to the Ottershaw Park estate.

It was situated among a natural landscape of heathland. Since the soil in the area was poor, agriculture was difficult and supported only small hamlets. Of these, close to the estate were Chertsey Lane End and Brox and a short distance away

---

[7] *The Examiner* (London, England), Saturday, December 2, 1865; Issue 3018.
[8] Athersuch, p41

A garden view of Ottershaw Park, from the 1859 sale particulars
Reproduced by permission of Chertsey Museum

was the hamlet of Spratts. In the mid nineteenth century, however, improving agricultural techniques had led to much of the local land around these hamlets being turned into nurseries supplying the Covent Garden market.

Ottershaw Park was to become Sir Edward's second 'seat'. With his responsibilities as a Member of Parliament for a Scottish constituency, Sir Edward's time needed to be divided between Lanarkshire and London. Ottershaw was bought as a healthy family home, away from the disease, noise and other hazards of London but conveniently accessible from Westminster for Sir Edward.

Sir Edward's works in Ottershaw

In his time, the local community was not even large enough to be described as a village and Sir Edward could easily have buried himself on his estate and had nothing to do with local people. However, the Colebrookes clearly liked Ottershaw and their affection for the place grew into a sense of caring duty towards local people. During the twenty four years that Sir Edward owned Ottershaw Park, he was instrumental in the construction of four buildings in the local community: the church, which he paid for in its entirety and for which he also provided an initial endowment to provide an income of £100 (approximately £62,000)[9] a year for the incumbent;[10] the vicarage, which was demolished for housing in 1983, after several changes of use;[11] the village's first school (now converted into houses) and the Working Men's Club, the name of which was changed to Ottershaw Social Club in 1962[12] and which continues to thrive today, in the original building.

The Church and vicarage

Sir Edward must have begun thinking of building an estate church shortly after becoming the owner of Ottershaw Park in 1859, while he and Lady Colebrooke were still grieving for their son, Henry, three months after his death on 1 May 1859, at the age of six months. The loss of his heir would have been a shattering blow to Sir Edward, then aged 46, and Lady Colebrooke, aged 36. They did not know at that point that they would have more sons and Sir Edward would have seen Henry's death as a tragic repetition of the circumstance of his own generation when his eldest brother died in infancy.

---

[9] www.measuringwealth.com, average earnings, 2014 equivalent

[10] Brush, Pamela, *Christ Church Ottershaw, History and Guide*, Ottershaw, 2004, p5

[11] Barker, David M and Jocelyn L, *A Chertsey Camera*, Addlestone, 1992, p59

[12] Stratton, H J M, *Ottershaw Through the Ages*, H J M Stratton, 1990, p3

Christ Church, Ottershaw, c.1875
Reproduced by permission of Chertsey Museum

Christ Church, Ottershaw, interior, c.1875
Reproduced by permission of Chertsey Museum

Sir Edward engaged George Gilbert Scott,[13] probably then the best known architect, to design his church. Scott was the most prolific architect in the mid-nineteenth century and ran the largest architectural office of the time with around thirty assistants.[14]

It is likely that the church was originally intended as a memorial to the Colebrookes' dead son and by choosing a great architect with a national reputation, Sir Edward made it clear that he wanted to offer the best possible memorial to Henry. Although there is no record that the church was intended as a memorial church, the imagery in it and the four original windows (almost certainly from the workshops of Clayton and Bell[15])[16] strongly suggest this and an unobtrusive inscription at the base of the font bearing the child's initials and date of death would seem to confirm it.

If a memorial to Henry Colebrooke was the primary motivation for building a church on the Ottershaw Park estate, it can be

---

[13] Nikolaus Pevsner in *The Buildings of England, Surrey* thought Christ Church was designed by an assistant of Scott. He may have taken this view because it seemed unlikely to him that such an eminent architect would himself have had any interest in such a small and insignificant location. Neither English Heritage nor the Royal Institute of British Architects subscribe to this view but it has been perpetuated, probably because of Pevsner's high architectural standing. The present author believes there is much evidence that was not available to Pevsner to show that this view is probably incorrect. There are several reasons to believe that Scott himself was involved in the building of Christ Church. Moreover, all architects used assistants to 'work up' their designs, so technical input from an assistant was not unusual.

[14] Scott, Sir George Gilbert, *Personal and Professional Recollections*, originally published 1879, new edition, ed. Stamp, G, 1995, Introduction

[15] Clayton and Bell was a prolific manufacturer of stained glass in the second half of the nineteenth century. Their work was characterised by excellence in designs and high quality in manufacture. They worked extensively for George Gilbert Scott

[16] Eberhard, Richard, http://www.stainedglassrecords.org/Ch.asp?ChId=19824, 'stylistic attribution', and private correspondence with Alan Brooks, architectural and stained glass historian, July 2013

The font, Christ Church, Ottershaw

readily understood why it was so important to Sir Edward and Lady Colebrooke that it should be on estate ground, why an eminent architect was chosen and why the building was richly decorated.

It is more than likely that Scott, who was, at the time, preoccupied to the point of obsession with the 'Battle of the Styles'[17] over the building of the Government Offices in Whitehall, actually wanted to design the Colebrooke church himself as a personal favour and tribute to his faithful friend, Sir Edward Colebrooke. Sir Edward had supported him loyally, along with the Yorkshire MP, Edward Akroyd, who had already had a magnificent church built by Scott in his home town of

---

[17] The fierce debate, taken extremely seriously in the highest circles, as to whether the new offices to be built in Whitehall should be in Classical or Gothic style.

The base of the font, Christ Church, Ottershaw, showing the dedication to Henry Colebrooke. It reads: 'To the glory of God and in Memory of H.C. May 1ˢᵗ 1859'.

Halifax. They were both in a small band of MPs who staunchly supported Scott during the Battle of the Styles, on which Scott perceived his reputation to depend. As Scott wrote in his autobiography, they '...stuck nobly by me'.[18] Scott was indebted to Sir Edward for supporting Scott's own preferred Gothic style for the Government Offices[19] and for making his support so public, through a parliamentary speech (recorded in Hansard), in 1859:

> **SIR EDWARD COLEBROOKE** said, he was himself somewhat favourable to the Palladian style, but he thought they should not lose sight of the fact that the House had before it a design in most excellent taste, and he hoped the House would not throw away the chance of having such a handsome building raised, without knowing upon what they were likely to fall back after rejecting it. He trusted they would not recur to the plan which obtained the first premium, which he thought most objectionable. He understood that the noble Lord at the head of the Government on a former occasion instanced in favour of the Italian style a number of edifices raised in this metropolis. Was the National Gallery among those edifices? He referred to that

---

[18] Scott, p.184
[19] Scott, p.184

building to show that they were not always sure of securing a good building by adopting the Italian style. He had noticed with great pleasure how much Mr. Scott's design had been improved from the first drawing by being rendered more simple. He was quite willing to agree to the present Vote on the condition that it was to be clearly understood that nothing would be done to commit the House or the Government to any particular design in place of that one.[20]

Sir Edward and George Gilbert Scott were, quite remarkably, also possibly related[21] but would, in any case, have become well acquainted as a result of Sir Edward's support. Scott would undoubtedly have known of the tragic loss of the Colebrookes' infant Henry. It is therefore quite probable that there was a special bond, even affection, between the two men. It is therefore not as unlikely as it may initially seem that Scott himself, rather than an assistant, was indeed the architect of Christ Church, Ottershaw. The polychrome brickwork of the walls and window arches is typical of Scott's later work[22] and Christ Church is one of only four polychrome churches designed by Scott (none of the other three being attributed to 'an assistant').

The church building boom

In the 1860s there was something of an expectation that those with the means to do so would contribute to the church-building boom that followed the revelations of the 1851 census. The report on the census had shown that the percentage of people in England and Wales over the age of ten going to church was only 47-54%. Though astonishing by today's standards, this was considered worryingly low and the report stressed the extent of

---

[20] http://hansard.millbanksystems.com/commons/1859/aug/04/supply-civil-service-estimates#S3V0155P0_18590804_HOC_42, accessed 28.12.2012
[21] Scott, p3
[22] Cole, D, *The Work of Sir Gilbert Scott*, London, 1980, p.57

non-attendance,[23] particularly among the working classes. This sent such shock-waves through the ruling classes that the provision of huge numbers of new churches was considered imperative. Indeed, at a time of growing republicanism, it was considered that the provision of churches was a means of influencing workers[24] and the decade 1860-1870 saw the greatest number of new churches ever built in Britain. It seems likely, therefore, that very late in the planning of his estate memorial church, Sir Edward decided to open the church to the local community. The land on which the church had already been built (two roods and twenty seven perches[25]) was made over to the Ecclesiastical Commissioners 'for a new church and churchyard' just two weeks before its consecration.[26] Having decided to welcome local people into his church, he wanted to make it accessible so, of the 220 seats, 120 were, from the outset, to be for local people and free of pew rents.[27] In fact, Sir Edward managed never to charge any pew rents at all.

The church was consecrated by the Bishop of Winchester with the name Christ Church, Ottershaw and Brox on Thursday 19 May 1864, having cost about £4,000 – (as much as £2.5 million at 2014 rates),[28] and perhaps double the cost of a basic church. A collection was taken at the consecration and 'the sum collected at the offertory, which is to form the nucleus of a parsonage fund, was £1702 [£137,000][29].'[30] This was

---

[23] 'The 1851 religious census' in *The Victorian*, March 2011, p15

[24] Brown, C, 'How religious was Victorian England' in *Did Urbanisation Secularize Britain?*, Urban History Yearbook, 1988, p247

[25] Rood = ¼ acre, perch = 1/160 acre; total area 2480.5 sq yds

[26] Christ Church Ottershaw, Church Records, Deeds and Consecration papers, conveyance dated 5 May 1864

[27] Until well into the twentieth century, it was common to make a charge for using pews (pew rents) as principal means of generating church income. This tended to have the effect of emphasising social status within a parish.

[28] www.measuringworth.com, average earnings, 2014 equivalent

[29] www.measuringworth.com, retail price index, 2014 equivalent

[30] *The Times*, Monday 23 May 1864, issue 24879, p.6, col.D

a very considerable amount of money and suggests numerous very wealthy people were at the consecration.

Christ Church was (and remains) 'a remarkably pretty church',[31] according to the consecration report in *The Times*. The style was early English and it was built of brick with stone facings and it had a shingled spire. Sir Edward was a religious man and by building the church on the highest point of his land, at the top of the only hill on his estate, he made sure his church was as close to God as possible – something that was of great importance at the time. It also created a familiar land-mark for the local community and an easily seen visual reminder of God. The fact that Christ Church was planned as an estate church meant, though, that it was oddly sited in rela-tion to the community that it was belatedly intended to serve. It also meant that it was apparently not originally planned to have a vicarage. Frequently the two were designed together by the same architect but in the case of Christ Church, the fund for a vicarage was begun only at the consecration service. It seems that Sir Edward had no thoughts to pay the full costs of the vicarage himself. In the event, it was designed by an unknown architect and was not ready until two years after the consecration. Moreover, there was also no incumbent until June 1865 – more than a year after the consecration. All these indicators add weight to the conclusion that the idea to open the church to local people came late in its planning and that Sir Edward's original intention was simply for a lovely private and very personal memorial chapel, not needing a full-time incumbent or a vicarage.

Plans changed though and the vicarage was built alongside the church on land also given by Sir Edward but otherwise it was only partly funded, if at all, by Sir Edward. It was completed in 1866 (as the building itself announced). It was

---

[31] *The Times*, Monday 23 May 1864, issue 24879, p.6, col.D

Ottershaw Vicarage, c1914
Reproduced by permission of Chertsey Museum

a large building with 'ten bedrooms, stabling and a coach house',[32] its size, at the time, considered appropriate for a minister of the church.

Sir Edward went to considerable personal trouble to ensure the long-term viability of the church, providing an initial endowment towards the living of the perpetual curate and augmenting this through 'the consent by the Governors of the Bounty of Queen Anne[33] to accept the sum of £2200...as an augmentation to the above benefice'.[34] The deed for this is

---

[32] Barker, p59

[33] Due to his divorce disputes, King Henry VIII suspended the payment of 'annates' (the first year's revenues from an ecclesiastical benefice) to the Pope in 1532 and kept them for the Crown. In 1703, Queen Anne established a fund (Queen Anne's Bounty) to receive and use this 'confiscated' money for the relief of poor clergy, thereby supplementing their income.

[34] Deed of 1875, Surrey History Centre. The Wrotham Park archive also contains the consent by the Governors of Queen Anne's Bounty to accept the sum of £2200 as an augmentation of the Ottershaw benefice.

dated 13 January 1875 and its purpose was to produce an additional annual income for the incumbent.

As well as his financial commitment in building the church he also involved himself in the running of the church. The first Vestry Meeting was convened in January 1866 to elect Churchwardens and Sir Edward was elected one of the two Churchwardens, retaining this office until 1887, four years after he sold Ottershaw Park. After the first, Vestry Meetings were held at Easter and Sir Edward is recorded as attending all the meetings during his tenure as Churchwarden, even after he sold the estate in 1883, except for 1878 and 1879 for which there are no records of meetings.

As Churchwarden, Sir Edward gave his time, often working at a level of involvement much lower than would have been the case in his public life. At the Easter Tuesday Vestry Meeting in 1874, for instance, the meeting agreed to increase the insurance premium on the church and Sir Edward '...undertook to call at the Insurance Office, and arrange this'[35] and at the meeting in 1876, problems were raised regarding the flues and smoke and '...it ended in Sir Edw Colebrooke offering to see the manufacturer on the question & to get him to send someone down to examine the condition of the furnace.'[36]

As the founder of the Church, Sir Edward held the patronage (or advowson) and selected the first three incumbents.[37] When he sold the Ottershaw Park estate in 1883, he retained a piece of land extending to one rood and twenty perches, which he gave to the church (detailed in a conveyance dated 1884) for an extension to the Churchyard.[38] This additional land for the

---

[35] The *Christ Church Ottershaw Minute Book*, 7.4.1874
[36] The *Christ Church Ottershaw Minute Book*, 7.5.1876
[37] Brush, p11
[38] Christ Church Ottershaw, Church Records, Deeds and Consecration papers, conveyance dated 18 June 1884

churchyard was clearly a matter of great importance to Sir Edward as a letter from him during the sale of Ottershaw Park, dated 3 August 1883, reads: 'I should like to be satisfied that there is no mistake with regard to the piece of land that is reserved to be given for the churchyard'.[39]

Relations with Addlestone

At consecration, Christ Church was within the parish of Addlestone so was not responsible for the souls of the people of Ottershaw. It seems that the change from estate church to village church had happened too late for spiritual responsibilities to have been amended in time for the consecration. However, this situation changed nine months later. *The London Gazette* of 7 February 1865 reported:

> ...the assignment of a district chapelry to the consecrated church called 'Christ Church', situate at Ottershaw in the new parish of Addlestone, in the county of Surrey and in the diocese of Winchester.'[40]

The church was now charged with the care of souls in Ottershaw and Brox but it remained subservient to the parish of Addlestone and the incumbent was a perpetual curate not a vicar. The shape of the chapelry, according to the minutely detailed description in *The London Gazette* shows that Christ Church was primarily an estate church as it included the whole

---

[39] Wrotham Park archive (Stepney Manor correspondence). It seems that Ottershaw Park was managed throughout the Colebrooke ownership by the Stepney Manor Office, the address of which was Drapers Hall, 28 Austin Friars, London EC. The Wrotham Park archive holds numerous items relevant to Ottershaw Park, including deeds, indentures of conveyance and correspondence. Among these are a number of letters relating to the sale agreement including an additional endowment to the church and the conveyance of the further piece of land.

[40] *The London Gazette*, 7.2.1865, p583

of the Ottershaw Park estate with, additionally, the hamlets of Ottershaw and Brox, both of which were just outside the estate. An apparently arbitrary boundary through the eastern part of the community truncated the chapelry, leaving the hamlet of Spratts in the parish of Addlestone.

Although Christ Church was consecrated in 1864 and had its chapelry defined the following year, Ottershaw did not achieve the status of a parish until 1871. The Vestry minutes for the first few years show disagreement approaching animosity between Ottershaw and Addlestone that was resolved only by Sir Edward's personal intervention. Whilst a chapelry, all fees for marriages, baptisms etc had to be paid to the Vicar of Addlestone but the parish of Addlestone, while taking the fees, saw no reason to pay Ottershaw anything towards upkeep – indeed for a period in 1868, Addlestone Vestry simply did not respond to letters written from Ottershaw. Matters came to

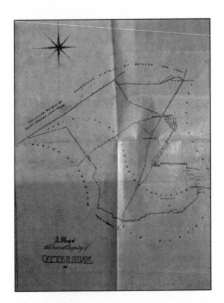

Map of the District Chapelry of Ottershaw, 1865
Courtesy of Christ Church, Ottershaw

a head in 1871 when Sir Edward, tired of being subject to ecclesiastical bureaucracy and with the support of the Bishop, wrote a trenchant ultimatum to the Vicar of Addlestone with '...a compensation of 100 guineas paid jointly by Sir Edward Colebrooke & Rev J R Oldham; by which act and agreement Ottershaw had become an independent Parish and Vicarage.'[41]

This saw Ottershaw gain its independence from Addlestone with the right to retain the fees it earned. Even with this, the absence of pew rents meant Christ Church ran a deficit for several years and Sir Edward and the Vicar paid the church's debts in 1873 and in subsequent years.[42]

The school

The subject of a new Infants' School was discussed and approved at the first Vestry Meeting. The new Church of England school was to replace a dame school, run by a member of the local gentry[43] and became Sir Edward's third benevolent involvement in Ottershaw. In 1869, he gave a parcel of land, valued at £50 (nearly £4,000),[44] on the edge of his estate, a little south of the church and vicarage on the road to Woking. It was not the most convenient location for the nearby hamlets and necessitated quite a long walk to school. He also contributed another £200 but the rest of the building costs were paid by the other four rate-payers of Ottershaw, from a School Building Fund (£1081), a grant from the Surrey Church Association

---

[41] The *Christ Church Ottershaw Minute Book*, 29.4.1871
[42] The *Christ Church Ottershaw Minute Book*, 21.4.1873
[43] *School Building Form*, National Archives, Kew, ED/103/110/43, p807. A reference is included in this document regarding the Dame school: 'The School was built by Mrs Gosling before there was a church at Ottershaw and has been chiefly maintained and managed by her. Mrs Gosling now intends to turn this school into cottages and is a promoter of the proposed new school.'
[44] www.measuringwealth.com, retail price index, 2014 equivalent

(£50) and a grant from the Privy Council (£204) making altogether £1335.[45] The school became a Board School following the Education Act of 1870 and the introduction of compulsory elementary education. An item in the *Glasgow Herald* at the time of the Education Act in England stated that, in country areas, the Boards of Management of the new Board Schools were to be elected by vestries. Given his parliamentary involvement it is not surprising that Ottershaw, under Sir Edward's guidance, was well abreast of legal requirements.[46]

The school (The Ottershaw National School, School No 15498) - 'a daily school for Boys, Girls and Infants' - opened in

Ottershaw Church of England School, c1910
Reproduced by permission of Chertsey Museum

---

[45] The *Christ Church Ottershaw Minute Book*, 18.4.1870
[46] *Glasgow Herald* (Glasgow, Scotland), Friday, February 18, 1870; Issue 9401

1870. It was almost certainly the work of an architect working for the County School Board and provided a school room for primary education with a headmaster's house. The documents for the founding of the school show Sir Edward as one of the 'chief promoters' and a manager of the school, along with the vicar. The school, for about 120 boys and girls, was intended for '...the instruction of the children of the labouring poor in the said district of Ottershaw...', which then had a population of about 130 families, '...the labouring portion of which are chiefly employed as Farm and Nursery Garden labourers'.[47]

From the beginning, the school was plagued by problems of attendance which impacted the standard of education achieved – Sir Edward did not find in Ottershaw the same enthusiasm for self-improvement that he found in Abington. The distance of the walk to school became a reason for absence in inclement weather. Additionally, the various activities of an agricultural community, such as the acorn harvest and furze gathering, also caused absences. Despite the generally low standard at the school, though, Sir Edward involved himself devotedly in its management and provided a present at Christmas for each child in the first few years. The Colebrookes also allowed the grounds of Ottershaw Park to be used for picnics to mark the end of the summer term.[48]

Working Men's Club

Sir Edward's last benevolent gesture was the building of the Working Men's Club. The need for a place to meet socially was apparent soon after the building of the church and the Rev J R Oldham, perpetual curate, allowed the use of his cottage, near the church. It became known as Vicarage Cottage and the Working Men's Club and Reading Room was begun

---

[47] *School Building Form*, National Archives, Kew, ED/103/110/43, p807
[48] *School Log Book for Christ Church, Church of England School, Ottershaw*, Surrey History Centre, CC1127/1/1-2, 3.1.1872

here in 1875.[49] By 1883, the building was too small and an alternative site was sought. At the first subscribers' meeting in 1883, the project was sponsored by landowners who pledged sums of money towards a purpose-built club building. Of these, Sir Edward was in the forefront and was elected the first President.[50] Land was purchased for the building in 1886 and local architect Theophilus Allen was contracted to design the building. The purpose-built club building opened in 1887, four years after the Colebrookes had sold Ottershaw Park.

Contemporary reports show that the Colebrookes spent considerable amounts of time in Ottershaw during the 1860s

The Working Mens' Club purpose-built premises (Ottershaw Social Club), 1912
Reproduced by permission of Chertsey Museum

---

[49] Brush, p10
[50] *Working Men's Club Minutes and Accounts Book,* Surrey History Centre, ref 6895/1,

and into the mid-1870s. Living in Ottershaw for extended periods allowed them to participate in the social life of Surrey. In 1866, the Meet of The Surrey Union hunt (foxhunting) was at Ottershaw Park on 15 December 1866,[51] as it was again in January of 1868.[52] Whether either Sir Edward or Lady Colebrooke joined the hunt is not mentioned.

In 1878, the fête of the Weybridge Branch of the Girls Friendly Society was held at Ottershaw Park with a special service in the church.[53] Sir Edward was also President of the Literary Institution in Guildford Street, Chertsey. This was an organisation with a subscription membership, open from 10.00am to 10.00pm, which had a reading room available for members' use, a recreation room and a good library of 2000 volumes.[54]

Sir Edward was listed as a magistrate in Middlesex and Surrey. As such, he was called upon to chair a special sessions in Chertsey on Saturday 18 December 1869, regarding an 'affray with poachers and keepers in Windsor Park'. A gamekeeper had been shot and the prisoners, who had been brought from custody in jail, were charged with poaching and attempting to commit murder. They were '...committed to take their trial at the March assizes and the magistrates refused to take bail.'[55]

Sir Edward, along with Mr Albert Savory, owner of the nearby estate Potters Park and the other churchwarden at Christ Church, supported the inhabitants of Ottershaw in retaining

---

[51] *Bell's Life in London and Sporting Chronicle* (London, England), Saturday, December 15, 1866; pg. 5; Issue 2,330

[52] *The Pall Mall Gazette* (London, England), Saturday, January 25, 1868; Issue 923

[53] Log books for Christ Church C/E School, Ottershaw,1870-2005, Surrey History Centre, ref CC1127/1/1-2

[54] Stratton, M, Collected notes, fragment, provided by Hannah Lane

[55] *The Morning Post* (London, England), Monday, December 20, 1869; p.5; Issue 29963.

allotments in the village. In 1875, there was an application by the trustees of the allotments to the Charity Commissioners for permission to sell the lands.

> ...this aroused much opposition in the village leading to the formation of the Chertsey Poor's Allotments Protection Association. Their cause was supported by Sir Edward Colebrooke and Mr Albert Savory, who staked out ¼ acre plots at all three sites of the allotments; by 1879 67 plots had been rented...The allotments were very important for augmenting low wages; nursery stock was cultivated at weekends and sold to the larger local nurseries.[56]

The Colebrookes spent less and less time in Ottershaw as the family grew up. Their town house in Mayfair became their home in the south, from where the delights of London were easily accessible. They visited Ottershaw sometimes for short visits but by the 1880s, by which time their youngest child was a young adult (and by which time London was much cleaner than in the 1850s), they had no need for it. Ottershaw Park had served its purpose well and Sir Edward had been generous to the local community. He sold the estate in 1883 but continued as Churchwarden and manager of the school until 1886, travelling from London to attend to parish business[57], when his health permitted.[58]

---

[56] Stratton, p13

[57] Brush, p8

[58] Sir Edward continued to deal with the Stepney Manor Office over property matters while recuperating in Cannes in the south of France in 1883-4.

Chapter 8

Lanarkshire life: MP for Lanarkshire 1857–68

General election of 1859

In 1859, following the collapse of the Conservative government, elections were announced with Sir Edward standing
again for Lanarkshire.[1] He was returned without opposition
on 3 May but his acceptance speech was given in his absence
by a political colleague:

> 'Sir Edward Colebrooke having been called to London the
> previous day in consequence of a family bereavement, on
> his being declared duly elected, Mr Alex. Graham, Capellie,
> stepped forward, and, in name of the honourable member,
> returned thanks to the electors. ...[2]

Sir Edward and Lady Colebrooke's infant son and heir had
died three days earlier on 1 May at their home at 37 South
Street, London. This personal tragedy seems to have led to
a rapid reappraisal of Colebrooke family life and they sought
somewhere healthier than London where they might raise their
family. By August 1859, they had bought Ottershaw Park in

---

[1] *Glasgow Herald* (Glasgow, Scotland), Saturday, April 9, 1859; Issue 6102.
[2] *Caledonian Mercury* (Edinburgh, Scotland), Wednesday, May 4, 1859;
Issue 21717.

Surrey – close enough to London to travel to and from Parliament on a daily basis but where the air was fresh and clean. He did not forget his supporters in Lanark though and just two months after buying Ottershaw Park, he was back in Lanark, where he gave a lengthy speech, thanking his electors for their support through what had been a personally difficult time for him.

He spelled out his position and was duly thanked, for which he:

> ...returned thanks for the manner in which they had expressed their confidence in him. He felt most deeply the responsibility of his position as the representative of this great county, and he assured them that no exertions would be wanting on his part to discharge his most important duties in the most satisfactory way.[3]

In another speech a few days later,[4] he explained that he sought to contribute as well as he could from his own interests and knowledge rather than grappling with many topics. These included his views on India which were related to his own family and background.

None the less, he went on to contribute to several committees, enquiries and public deeds that were probably not first among his interests. So, for example, he was nominated to serve on a select committee for the Leith Harbour and Docks Bill, with the 'power to send for persons, papers and records'[5]. He was also one of a deputation that secured an interview at the Home

---

[3] *Daily News* (London, England), Saturday, October 22, 1859; Issue 4194.
[4] *Glasgow Herald* (Glasgow, Scotland), Thursday, October 27, 1859; Issue 6174.
[5] *The Morning Post* (London, England), Saturday, June 16, 1860; pg. 2; Issue 26988.

Office on Saturday 16 March 1861, on the subject of the Prisons Act (Scotland).[6] In August, at a special meeting of the Police Committee for county of Lanark, he was charged with the inspection of police buildings.[7]

An Englishman in Scottish politics

As an Englishman in Scottish politics, Sir Edward was in a unique position – which he well understood himself – to contribute to the harmonisation of Scottish and English law and practices. In many areas of public life, England and Scotland had different systems and it was increasingly felt that these differences should be reduced. With his knowledge of English law and politics from family connections and from his time as MP for Taunton, and his increasing understanding of Scottish practices, he was able to make suggestions and recommendations that were recognised as wise and which were respected. So, for instance, he lent his support to the Faculty of Medicine at the University of Glasgow in their bid for harmonisation with England in that they should not have to provide information relating to a death without a fee.[8] In this context, he presented a number of petitions to Parliament from Lanarkshire, as well as several other counties, requesting a repeal of the challenged compulsory clause in the Registration of Deaths Act.[9]

---

[6] *The Caledonian Mercury* (Edinburgh, Scotland), Tuesday, March 19, 1861; Issue 22301.

[7] *Glasgow Herald* (Glasgow, Scotland), Saturday, August 10, 1861; Issue 6733.

[8] *Glasgow Herald* (Glasgow, Scotland), Tuesday, November 15, 1859; Issue 6190.

[9] *Glasgow Herald* (Glasgow, Scotland), Monday, March 26, 1860; Issue 6303.

In 1865, Sir Edward prepared to fight another General Election for the Lanarkshire seat. Under 'Election news: Lanarkshire', the *Caledonian Mercury* wrote:

> Sir Edward Colebrooke has issued an address to the electors of Lanarkshire in which he says he will again offer himself for election, and, alluding to his votes and labours in Parliament, mentions the County Registration Act, of which he is the author, and which among other good results will probably save Sir Edward and the county the trouble of a contested election.[10]

A few days later, though, it was hinted that Baillie Cochrane (from whom Sir Edward gained the constituency in 1857) might try to win back the seat:

> In the county we do not think Sir Edward Colebrooke will meet with any opposition although we have heard it hinted that owing to the opposition Mr Baillie Cochrane is to get for Honiton he may prefer measuring swords with Sir Edward for this county.[11]

Baillie Cochrane evidently thought better of fighting his popular neighbour, leading to comment from the *Glasgow Herald*, which was so antagonistic at the time of Sir Edward's first election:

> Some have the great good luck to find no rival in their line; and hence they are not required to make ruinous sacrifices, or to pass with martyr spirit through the process of "heckling" for the good of the country. Our own county

---

[10] *The Caledonian Mercury* (Edinburgh, Scotland), Saturday, June 17, 1865; Issue 23703.
[11] *The Caledonian Mercury* (Edinburgh, Scotland), Monday, June 26, 1865; Issue 23710

Member is one of these fortunate gentlemen; but it may be said he has fairly earned his repose, for he fought a good fight at the last election.

It then helpfully stated: 'Sir Edward Colebrooke is moderately liberal in his opinions' and with grudging praise added '...and has proved himself upon the whole an intelligent and capable Member of Parliament.'[12] The election required Sir Edward to be in Scotland earlier in the summer than usual, holding electioneering meetings between 11 and 14 July in the Town Halls of Lanark and Hamilton and in the Merchant's Hall, Hutcheson Street, Glasgow.

He was re-elected, unopposed, on show of hands and gave a comprehensive acceptance speech, thanking the voters for their support and outlining his personal policies and beliefs. He reminded voters that he did not blindly follow his Party's line, saying he had stood alone and voted independently on matters of principle and would do so again. He was particularly concerned about electoral reform both with respect to seats '...unworthily held by small and corrupt burghs,' and also regarding the view that the large constituency of Lanarkshire should be better represented. He undertook to fight for another Member of Parliament for the county.[13]

A public life

As a local dignitary with, from the early 1860s, a 'seat' in Lanarkshire, Sir Edward had a full and public social calendar. On 30 March 1863, when Lord Palmerston was installed as Lord Rector of the University of Glasgow, Sir Edward gave

---

[12] *Glasgow Herald* (Glasgow, Scotland), Tuesday, July 4, 1865; Issue 7953
[13] *Glasgow Herald* (Glasgow, Scotland), Monday, July 17, 1865; Issue 7964.

one of the toasts[14] at the banquet for more than 800 people in Glasgow City Hall that was 'one of the most brilliant ever in the West of Scotland.'[15] Until around late 1863, it seems that Lady Colebrooke seldom accompanied Sir Edward, very likely because their growing young family demanded her time elsewhere. A record of Lady Colebrooke being with her husband is dated September 1863, when a small company of Lanarkshire's elite, including Lord Belhaven, the Lord Lieutenant of the county, and Lady Belhaven gathered at the home of the Sheriff of the county.[16]

As the local landowner, Sir Edward held the patronage of the church in Crawfordjohn, so was a key figure in the religious life of the area. On 8 November 1866, the *Glasgow Herald* illustrated this in reporting the ordination of the new incumbent at Crawfordjohn Church:

> ... the Presbytery of Lanark met in Crawfordjohn Church for the purpose of ordaining the Rev James Cowan to the pastoral charge of Crawfordjohn parish...Sir Edward Colebrooke, Bart., M.P., the patron, afterwards entertained the Presbytery at his own mansion at Abington. This is a very harmonious settlement, and, from the known ability and character of the presentee, is likely to reflect great credit on the patron.[17]

[14] *Glasgow Herald* (Glasgow, Scotland), Tuesday, March 31, 1863; Issue 7245

[15] *Glasgow Herald* (Glasgow, Scotland), Monday, March 16, 1863; Issue 7232.

[16] *Glasgow Herald* (Glasgow, Scotland), Tuesday, September 29, 1863; Issue 7401

[17] *Glasgow Herald* (Glasgow, Scotland), Saturday, November 10, 1866; Issue 8377.

Sir Edward and Scottish Agriculture

From early in his acquaintance with his estates, Sir Edward took an interest in the welfare of his tenant farmers, preparing the way for an involvement at a practical level that was to earn him genuine respect and popularity among those whose lives depended on his management of the Colebrooke lands. He also interested himself in the agriculture that was fundamental to the communities in the rural parts of the county. He became knowledgeable and encouraged and celebrated the success of farmers and others who made their living from agriculture.

The first week of September saw the annual Abington Show, which had been established prior to the time of Sir Edward's inheritance. Sir Edward became President of the Abington Agricultural Society, providing prizes at the show and presiding at the dinner afterwards, recorded to have been held in 1862 in the Abington Inn.[18] The Abington Show was a substantial affair, drawing together the parishes of Crawford, Crawfordjohn, Lamington, Wiston and Roberton to exhibit their stock, with prizes given by local landowners, and wealthy farmers.[19] Additionally, '...a great many athletic sports took place during the afternoon; and altogether it was a high festival day at Abington village.'[20]

Sir Edward was also prominent in his support of the Biggar Cattle Show, organised by the Biggar Farmer's Club[21] and, in common with other members of the gentry in the area, provided prizes at other local agricultural shows. In the press notice of the Cattle Show of the Old Monkland Barony, Bothwell and

---

[18] *The Hamilton Advertiser*, 6 September 1862, p3
[19] Reid, Thomas, *A History of the Parish of Crawfordjohn, Upper Ward of Lanarkshire, 1153-1928*, Turnbull & Spears, Edinburgh, 1928, p103
[20] *The Hamilton Advertiser*, 6 September 1862, p3
[21] *The Hamilton Advertiser*, 30 August 1862, p3

Cadder Farming Society at Bailieston on Friday June 5th 1857, it was announced that Sir Edward Colebrooke would award a silver medal and jointly provide prize money of £3.0.0 for the best cow in milk at the show.[22] This medal, regularly awarded by Sir Edward from then on, was to become one of the annual awards at this particular show.[23] He took a particular interest in dairy farming: at the Lanarkshire Farmers' Society Annual Show of Farm Stock and Dairy Produce on Friday 28 May 1858, he awarded a silver medal for the first prize 'in Class V, Ayrshire cows in milk, in pairs, bred by the exhibitor, and never out of their possession';[24] at the Glasgow Agricultural Society's Show in June 1860, he presented a medal to the breeder of the best of all Ayrshire cows[25] and at the East Kilbride Open Show, also in June 1860, he presented a silver medal for the cow... showing the most breeding[26] - another award that was to become a regular feature of that particular show. In 1868, Sir Edward presented a silver medal for the Ayrshire breed at

Agricultural award medal presented by Sir Edward Colebrooke
Courtesy of ebay, 11.1.14

---

[22] *Glasgow Herald* (Glasgow, Scotland), Friday, May 8, 1857; Issue 5760, Classified ads
[23] *Glasgow Herald* (Glasgow, Scotland), Saturday, June 4, 1859; Issue 6150.
[24] *Glasgow Herald* (Glasgow, Scotland), Monday, May 10, 1858; Issue 5917
[25] *Glasgow Herald* (Glasgow, Scotland), Monday, May 28, 1860; Issue 6357
[26] *Glasgow Herald* (Glasgow, Scotland), Saturday, June 16, 1860; Issue 6374.

the Upper Ward of Lanarkshire Agricultural Association's show of farm stock and dairy produce for the 'best animal, male or female, of the cow kind'(!)[27]

Sir Edward also interested and involved himself in fish farming. According to a report of 1882, he worked with the Dodgers' Angling Club in 1855 to introduce grayling (salmon *salmo thymallus*) to the River Clyde.

> Thirty years ago there was not a grayling in all Scotland... about 1855...Mr Andrews, now our senior member, at that time president of the West of Scotland Angling Club suggested to the Club to attempt on a sufficient scale the acclimatisation of the grayling in the Clyde, a river which appeared, as it has proved, eminently suited for the trial. The Club entered heartily into the proposal, voted the necessary money and appointed a small committee to assist Mr Anderson in carrying it out. The aid of Sir Edward Colebrooke, the member for the county, was also enlisted, and he took much interest in the scheme, allowing the Club to select suitable ground on his property for their breeding establishment, and giving the help of his head keeper...' [Attempts to stock several other Scottish rivers apparently failed] 'In the Clyde alone success has been complete.'[28]

He had strong views regarding fishing and, in 1860, in the interests of preserving fish stocks, with his neighbour and recent political opponent, Alexander Baillie Cochrane, he proposed a bill against fishing with nets for trout and other freshwater fish in Scottish waters.[29]

---

[27] *Glasgow Herald* (Glasgow, Scotland), Wednesday, July 8, 1868; Issue 8896.

[28] *Glasgow Herald* (Glasgow, Scotland), Monday, December 25, 1882; Issue 3077.

[29] *Glasgow Herald* (Glasgow, Scotland), Monday, April 16, 1860; Issue 6321.

In due course, Sir Edward rose to hold office in agricultural organisations. So, in 1861, he became Vice President of the Glasgow Agricultural Society[30] for which, in 1862, he chaired the dinner for upwards of 80 gentlemen at the Society's tenth annual show on 11 June at the Tontine Hotel, Glasgow[31]– at which, in his speech, he showed knowledge of and commitment to high standards in agriculture.[32] By 1863, he was patron of the Upper Ward Horticultural Society, President of the Abington Agricultural Society[33] and 'one of the nine worthy patrons (noblemen, MPs and gentlemen) of the Glasgow Veterinary College'.[34] In January 1866 and subsequent years, he was elected as an Extraordinary Director of the Highland and Agricultural Society.[35]

In 1865, Lanarkshire was seriously affected by 'cattle plague' and in September, Sir Edward chaired a meeting of Justices of the Peace in the County Buildings, Lanark to discuss a Privy Council order relating to the disease.[36] A month later, at another meeting of Lanarkshire Justices, due to the continuation of the disease, he took the drastic action of proposing the exclusion of livestock from local fairs and markets.[37] By late November, Sir Edward was at Petersham Park, Surrey – perhaps Ottershaw Park had been let for the winter - but cattle plague in Lanarkshire continued to occupy his thoughts. He wrote to *The Times*, demonstrating his agricultural knowledge

---

[30] *Glasgow Herald* (Glasgow, Scotland), Monday, February 11, 1861; Issue 6579.
[31] *Glasgow Herald* (Glasgow, Scotland), Friday, June 6, 1862; Issue 6990.
[32] *Glasgow Herald* (Glasgow, Scotland), Thursday, June 12, 1862; Issue 6995.
[33] *Upper Ward Almanac and Handbook*, 1863, R Wood, Lanark
[34] *Glasgow Herald* (Glasgow, Scotland), Monday, June 15, 1863; Issue 7310
[35] *The Dundee Courier & Argus* (Dundee, Scotland), Friday, January 05, 1866; Issue 3874.
[36] *Glasgow Herald* (Glasgow, Scotland), Friday, September 8, 1865; Issue 8010
[37] *The Caledonian Mercury* (Edinburgh, Scotland), Wednesday, October 18, 1865; Issue 23808.

and his comments led to further interest and comment in both general and specialist newspapers. He advocated a good diet and careful and generous feeding, attributing the recovery of many of his own stock from cattle plague to such careful feeding.[38] He referred to the occasion when the disease had broken out among his Ottershaw herd and how those on a special dietary regime had survived.[39]

Support for working people

Sir Edward contributed to efforts at educational improvement on his estate, giving lectures himself on occasions. In the small village of Abington, there were well supported and highly successful initiatives at adult education. In March 1859:

> ...a highly interesting and successful course of lectures on popular and scientific subjects, delivered in the village schoolroom here, during the winter months, was brought to a close .... The introductory lecture was delivered by Sir Edward Colebrooke, Bart., M.P. – Subject "The Study of History".

There were eight other lectures, concluding with one given by the teacher at the Abington school. '...Throughout, the lectures have been well attended, and have afforded much important and interesting information, as well as mental recreation, to the villagers of Abington and others in the surrounding district....'[40]

---

[38] *The Derby Mercury* (Derby, England), Wednesday, November 29, 1865; Issue 6973

[39] *The Examiner* (London, England), Saturday, December 2, 1865; Issue 3018.

[40] *Glasgow Herald* (Glasgow, Scotland), Thursday, March 24, 1859; Issue 6088.

Sir Edward considered the work he carried out in various areas of education as among the most important work he did and interpreted his interests and obligations broadly. In September 1860, with many other notable people, he attended the Social Science Congress meeting of working men, the objective of which was furthering education among working people[41] and in 1861, he was requested by the Presbytery of Hamilton to present a petition to the House of Commons under the Parochial Schools Bill, regarding the salaries and pensions of schoolmasters.[42] In 1863, he was admitted as a member of the Scottish Meteorological Society at their meeting on 14 December.[43]

The Volunteer Movement[44]

Sir Edward was constant in his support for the Volunteer Movement. In 1859, he contributed to the fund, and was cheered for doing so, to form a force of rifle volunteers – the Shipping Volunteer Rifle Corps, whose purpose was to defend the interests of shipowners and employees should there be an invasion.[45] In 1860, he was elected a member of the Bothwell Company of the volunteer movement (numbered 56th in Lanarkshire).[46] In the same year, he was a member of a deputation to the Secretary of State for War to establish a school of

---

[41] *Glasgow Herald* (Glasgow, Scotland), Thursday, September 27, 1860; Issue 6462.

[42] *Glasgow Herald* (Glasgow, Scotland), Monday, July 1, 1861; Issue 6698.

[43] *The Caledonian Mercury* (Edinburgh, Scotland), Tuesday, December 15, 1863; Issue 23262

[44] The Volunteer Movement was a citizen army of part-time rifle, artillery and engineer corps, created as a popular movement in 1859, when a French invasion was feared. They formed local defence forces but many communities also had associated rifle clubs for the enjoyment of the sport of shooting.

[45] *Glasgow Herald* (Glasgow, Scotland), Saturday, November 26, 1859; Issue 6200.

[46] *Glasgow Herald* (Glasgow, Scotland), Monday, March 5, 1860; Issue 6285

musketry in Scotland.[47] In 1862, he attended a meeting in the House of Commons of those 'friendly' to the volunteer movement, to consider its position and what steps should be taken to give it permanency,[48] and in March 1868, as one of a deputation concerned with the volunteer movement, he sought better funding from the War Office.[49]

The division of the county

Sir Edward's knowledge of English political practice proved invaluable at the time of the Scotch Reform Bill, particularly with respect to the matter of having a second MP for his own constituency of Lanarkshire, then the largest of the Scottish constituencies. He gave a long speech on how it might be best to tackle Parliament to gain equal treatment with English counties[50] and expressed his concern that the Tories in England were opposed to an increase the number of Scottish MPs because they feared their Liberal views.[51] Eventually, however, the separation of the county into north and south divisions was agreed with Sir Edward standing as Liberal candidate for North Lanarkshire.[52]

Sir Edward addressed a meeting on 9 October in the County Hall, Hamilton, regarding his candidature for North Lanarkshire. The chairman spoke of his hope that Liberals

---

[47] *The Standard* (London, England), Friday, March 09, 1860; pg. 6; Issue 11099. *19th Century British Library Newspapers: Part II.*
[48] *The Caledonian Mercury* (Edinburgh, Scotland), Thursday, March 27, 1862; Issue 22619
[49] *Glasgow Herald* (Glasgow, Scotland), Friday, March 20, 1868; Issue 8802.
[50] *Glasgow Herald* (Glasgow, Scotland), Saturday, April 14, 1860; Issue 6320.
[51] *Glasgow Herald* (Glasgow, Scotland), Thursday, October 24, 1867; Issue 8675
[52] *Glasgow Herald* (Glasgow, Scotland), Monday, July 13, 1868; Issue 8900.

would be returned for both divisions and would be mutually supporting. Of Sir Edward he said:

> I am glad also of the opportunity of taking this chair, because it enables me to repeat once more the confidence which I feel in Sir Edward Colebrooke as our representative. Whether as a politician, a good Liberal, or a sound statesman, I think he is an honour and a credit to the county which returns him. (Cheers)

Sir Edward replied:

> ...I can assure you there was never any occasion on which I felt myself so much impressed, I may say, by a feeling of the responsibility of the task I have undertaken in endeavouring duly to represent the interests of this great community. And that feeling is not in the slightest degree allayed by the fact that to all appearances there is at present no opposition to my being returned as the favoured candidate of this great constituency.[53]

At a meeting in Airdrie to further his candidature on 13 October, further warm words were expressed about Sir Edward:

> The Hon. Baronet [has] represented the important county of Lanark for the last eleven years, with honour to himself and credit to the electors...It behoved the constituency of North Lanarkshire to send to Parliament a man of legislative experience and standing – and where could they find a more suitable representative than Sir Edward Colebrooke? (Applause)...he... [has] always professed Liberal principles and acted up to them. He was a man of progress, but not diverging into extreme measures. His courtesy, high position

---

[53] *Glasgow Herald* (Glasgow, Scotland), Saturday, October 10, 1868; Issue 8977

and standing [has] rendered him respected by all, and while maintaining with the utmost tenacity the principles he espoused, he was respected by members of his political party as well as by his political opponents. He made himself thoroughly conversant with the subjects which he took up. His opinions were heard on all occasions with deference, and exerted considerable influence on the legislature. (Cheers)

Out of these pre-election meetings, however, came other views that make Sir Edward seem surprisingly reactionary. He was, for instance, unwilling to put his name to restricting the labour of children aged under 12 to 10 hours a day as he thought would have no practical effect. He also did not think it was necessary to have a compulsory system of education. He thought the separation of males and females should continue in workhouses as, he claimed, the elderly generally preferred sleeping apart. He also said he opposed the ballot as he felt 'that the great body of electors would abhor a system of concealment'. Furthermore, outright support for Sir Edward was not universal. In particular, considerable feeling against him was to be found in places where he had opposed the area becoming a burgh.[54]

Throughout the meetings and debates on the possibility of a second MP for Lanarkshire, proposals continued to be raised regarding the extension of the boundaries of Glasgow so that the constituency coincided with the reality of the city. The Conservatives, who were in favour of changing the boundaries, complained that the Liberals – 'the natural friends of the poor' – had looked to protect their own political position while the Liberals' view was that the counties that had been 'rescued from the hands of the Conservatives' would once

---

[54] *Glasgow Herald* (Glasgow, Scotland), Wednesday, October 14, 1868; Issue 8980

more fall into political serfdom, or something equally dreadful, if the Parliamentary boundaries of Glasgow were extended a foot beyond their present limits. Extension of the burgh boundaries was plainly a potential danger to Liberal MPs like Sir Edward and he consistently opposed it.[55]

The result was the defeat of the Government proposal, with the effect that poorer men in the counties could vote while workmen in the burghs (urban areas) had to occupy a property of considerably higher rental value to have the same privilege. 'This unwarrantable distinction is entirely due to the fears and selfishness of the Liberal party – the friends *par excellence* of the working man,' claimed the Conservative-supporting *Glasgow Herald*.[56]

[55] *Glasgow Herald* (Glasgow, Scotland), Thursday, July 2, 1868; Issue 8891.
[56] *Glasgow Herald* (Glasgow, Scotland), Wednesday, October 14, 1868; Issue 8980

Chapter 9

Lanarkshire life: MP for North Lanarkshire 1868–1885

Sir Edward was elected to the new constituency of North Lanarkshire in November 1868. The long-wanted extra member been achieved by dividing Lanarkshire in half rather than by having second MP over the whole county. Sir Edward had not expected better representation to be achieved this way but was confident it would work. He would continue to serve his constituents in the northern division while another Liberal would represent in the southern division those he had previously represented. Sir Edward had been voted in on show of hands, unopposed. His welcome as Member for new division was reported in the *Glasgow Herald*, saying that his whole political life:

> ...had been characterised by moderation of sentiment, by calmness, considerateness, and solidity of judgement. On all great questions he had taken a prominent part, and he had so comported himself as to gain a high position in the House of Commons, and so reflect honour on the county that returned him. Parliament had seen fit to draw a territorial line across Lanarkshire, but Parliament could not divide the political heart of Lanarkshire.[1]

---

[1] *Glasgow Herald* (Glasgow, Scotland), Monday, November 23, 1868; Issue 9014

In his acceptance speech, Sir Edward alluded to all that needed to be done in exceptional times:

> These are no common times; they are days in which public opinion moves fast, in which great expectations will be raised as to the conduct of your representative, and in which exertions are required from a Member of Parliament which may well try the powers of a younger person than myself...[2]

A particular concern was all that needed to be done in the newly configured constituency following the widening of the franchise. There were many questions to address but especially '... the extension of a Christian education to all classes, and upon which the attention of the country is at present deeply fixed...' He stated his belief in the rightness of the unification of England and Ireland and was confident that this would be formalised by Parliament in due course:

> ...I have lived to see the downfall of many abuses, and it will be the triumph of my life to assist in passing a measure that shall bind the people of England and Ireland together in closer unity, and help further to consolidate the strength and resources of both countries...In assisting to bring about such a result, I shall not only be acting up to my own opinions, but I shall be truly and effectively representing the convictions of the public generally upon this matter'.[3]

---

[2] *Glasgow Herald* (Glasgow, Scotland), Monday, November 23, 1868; Issue 9014

[3] *Glasgow Herald* (Glasgow, Scotland), Monday, November 23, 1868; Issue 9014

Civic life

Just two months later, Lord Belhaven, the Lord Lieutenant of Lanarkshire, died. Sir Edward's appointment to the position was announced in the *London Gazette* of 29 January 1869:

> Whitehall, Jan 29. – The Queen has been pleased to appoint Sir Thomas Edward Colebrooke, Bart., to be lieutenant and sheriff-principal of the shire of Lanark, in the room of Robert Montgomery, Lord Belhaven, deceased.[4]

He was presented to Queen Victoria as Lord Lieutenant[5] of Lanarkshire at a levée on 5 March 1869.[6] Sir Edward was to hold this position until his death, meaning that his public profile, by then already high, became even greater. He was often the senior guest at civic events in Glasgow and elsewhere in Scotland and was involved in many causes. He was expected to take an interest in a wide variety of matters and to attend many functions, where, because of his position, he was usually called upon to propose one of the toasts or to respond to a toast. Absence from public occasions was a matter for comment. A flavour of his civic life can be gained from press reports...

'A gentlemen's club opened in Glasgow in 1869, in a new building that imitated the architecture of London clubs. Influential people joined, including Sir Edward....'[7] (He would have recognised that it would have been difficult and socially unacceptable for him not to join).

---

[4] *Daily News* (London, England), Saturday, January 30, 1869; Issue 7098.

[5] A uniquely British position, a Lord Lieutenant is the sovereign's representative in a county. It is now a largely ceremonial position although it formally held military authority.

[6] *The Morning Post* (London, England), Saturday, March 06, 1869; pg. 5; Issue 29716. *19th Century British Library Newspapers: Part II.*

[7] *Glasgow Herald* (Glasgow, Scotland), Friday, September 17, 1869; Issue 9269.

In October 1869, the Glasgow Autumn Circuit Court opened. This was a grand civic occasion with a procession headed by a body of police, a band, and a detachment of the 5th Fusiliers and a minister who said prayers. Sir Edward was an important attendee among the numerous dignitaries attending.[8]

In 1873, Glasgow held a week-long celebration of music – the Glasgow Music Festival. It was opened by a concert in City Hall, attended by her Royal Highness Princess Louise and her husband, the Marquis of Lorne. Sir Edward and Lady Colebrooke, together with Ginevra and Helen, were among the royal party, for whom a large box was specially erected.[9] They were also guests of the Lord Provost at a dinner at his residence, where they were introduced to the Princess.[10]

In 1876, he went to a dinner held by The British Association in Corporation Galleries, Glasgow,[11] an occasion where he would have felt comfortable in view if his own commitment to the union with Ireland. In November 1877, Sir Edward was one of the important guests on the platform when the Marquis of Hartington, Leader of the Liberal Party in the House of Commons, was presented with the Freedom of the City of Glasgow.[12]

In June 1885 in Govan, a suburb of Glasgow, Sir Edward attended a ceremony at which the new park was presented to the people of Govan. It was named Elder Park, after John

---

[8] *Glasgow Herald* (Glasgow, Scotland), Tuesday, October 5, 1869; Issue 9284

[9] *Glasgow Herald* (Glasgow, Scotland), Wednesday, November 5, 1873; Issue 10563.

[10] *The Colebrooke Letters*, 15.11.1873

[11] *The Belfast News-Letter* (Belfast, Ireland), Friday, September 15, 1876; Issue 19076

[12] *The Dundee Courier & Argus and Northern Warder* (Dundee, Scotland), Tuesday, November 06, 1877; Issue 7579.

Elder, a Clyde shipbuilder. The park had been given by his widow and it was Sir Edward's pleasant task to propose the toast to 'the donor of the park'.[13]

Combining civic and political life

It was often difficult for Sir Edward to determine in which capacity – Lord Lieutenant or Member of Parliament – he attended functions. In reality, on many occasions he attended in both capacities but if called on to propose a toast or respond to a toast related to parliament, his political role was predominant. A few examples illustrate this...

Commerce was fundamental to the health of the city of Glasgow and the 'Trades House of Glasgow'[14] was therefore an important institution. Sir Edward attended several of the annual dinners of the Trades House from 1869 onwards. In 1869, after the annual meeting, 150 gentlemen attended the annual dinner of the deacons and members in the Trades Hall. The deacon convenor presided and a toast was proposed to both Houses of Parliament. Sir Edward responded at some length, talking of the weighty challenges ahead with respect to reform, Ireland and education, especially for the House of Commons, 'where the burden of work was carried out'.[15] In 1875, Sir Edward is recorded as responding to a similar toast at the same occasion.[16]

---

[13] *Daily News* (London, England), Monday, June 29, 1885; Issue 12235

[14] The Trades House of Glasgow was formed in 1605 and comprised the various craft leaders under the leadership of the deacon convenor. It played an important part in the fostering of the trade and industry of the city. It also had and still has various charitable functions and still meets in the Trades Hall.

[15] *Glasgow Herald* (Glasgow, Scotland), Thursday, October 14, 1869; Issue 9292.

[16] *Glasgow Herald* (Glasgow, Scotland), Thursday, October 7, 1875; Issue 11164

In 1883, Sir Edward was appointed to the Grand Committee on Law, as was the Lord Advocate and other Scottish Members of Parliament.[17] He had been a magistrate (described as the 'resident justice') in Crawford and Crawfordjohn for many years and was to remain so for the rest of his life.[18]

In September 1885, Sir Edward went to the autumn meeting of the Iron and Steel Institute in Glasgow, which was held at the Corporation Galleries in Glasgow. The dinner afterwards was at Maclean's Hotel, where Sir Edward had the agreeable task of responding to the toast to the Houses of Parliament.[19]

Glasgow Municipal Extension Bill

In local politics, the issues of electoral reform and of the extension of boundaries of Glasgow were never far away. In the late 1860s, the area of particular discussion was Hillhead where the new university was being built. Many felt that that the inhabitants of Hillhead were already enjoying the benefits of the city as the city boundary was so close and that they should therefore be Glasgow taxpayers. Another and not infrequent view was that Sir Edward and other Liberals had engineered the non-extension of boundaries before the election for fear of gaining electors who would not vote for them but by 1869, Sir Edward was so secure that any such extension was unlikely to destabilise him.[20]

None the less, Sir Edward continued to oppose extension and in 1870, it was debated in a full House of Commons. While

---

[17] *Glasgow Herald* (Glasgow, Scotland), Friday, March 16, 1883; Issue 65
[18] *Upper Ward Almanac and Handbook*, various, R Wood, Lanark
[19] *Daily News* (London, England), Thursday, September 3, 1885; Issue 12292
[20] *Glasgow Herald* (Glasgow, Scotland), Friday, April 16, 1869; Issue 9138.

supporters of the scheme sounded lukewarm, Sir Edward and the Home Secretary argued forcibly against it, citing the opposition of several areas around Glasgow (Govan, Partick, Hillhead and Maryhill) whose inhabitants' chief concern was the implication that they would be paying rates to support the new city infrastructure. The issue at stake was that if the city boundaries were extended, more people would become taxpayers. Sir Edward and others opposed to extension felt too much agricultural land was being included. Sir Edward also opposed the extension as (with other Members) he felt it was inevitable that Parliamentary extension would follow – in other words the size of the burgh constituencies would be increased at the expense of the county constituencies.

The Glasgow Municipal Extension Bill was rejected[21] and, at celebratory dinners, numerous toasts were raised to Sir Edward, 'the leader of the onslaught on the Glasgow Municipal Extension Bill',[22] for his role in its defeat:

> To celebrate the defeat of the City Boundary Extension Bill, The Chairman proposed a toast to 'The House of Commons and Sir Edward Colebrooke, saying '...that among the Scotch members of the House of Commons, Sir Edward Colebrooke, the member for Lanarkshire, was distinguished as one of the most able and useful and his recent stand for the independence of the suburban districts - (hear, hear) – had earned for him the gratitude of the inhabitants. There was not one present but must have admired the manner in which Sir Edward Colebrooke led up his forces and defeated the great corporation of Glasgow, and by a grand flank movement overturned the great scheme that had been

---

[21] *Glasgow Herald* (Glasgow, Scotland), Friday, February 18, 1870; Issue 9401

[22] *Glasgow Herald* (Glasgow, Scotland), Wednesday, April 20, 1870; Issue 9453

prepared for enslaving the populous districts around. (Applause)[23]

Sir Edward was also involved in trying to correct the destabilising effect of faggot voting[24] and collected signatures against it to present in Parliament.[25]

General Election 1874

In 1874, the Liberal government seemingly having lost the trust of the country, a General Election was called and Sir Edward announced his intention of standing again for North Lanarkshire. He was the only candidate[26] but none the less embarked on a round of electioneering. At a meeting in Glasgow, he was introduced by the Chairman saying '...it was needless for him to remark upon the hon. candidate's consistency and sound judgement, for they had been amply proved during the 16 years he had represented Lanarkshire.' He was received with cheers and said he:

> ...was reminded that many of his old colleagues were disappearing from the public scene from time to time, and that his own strength and energy was not the same as when he entered upon the great duty of representing them in Parliament; and it was only the encouragement he had received and the forbearance of the constituencies that had induced him to come forward again and solicit from them that confidence which they had placed in him during four successive Parliaments.[27]

---

[23] *Glasgow Herald* (Glasgow, Scotland), Tuesday, April 26, 1870; Issue 9458.

[24] See note in Chapter 6

[25] *Glasgow Herald* (Glasgow, Scotland), Wednesday, March 23, 1870; Issue 9429.

[26] *The Dundee Courier & Argus* (Dundee, Scotland), Monday, January 26, 1874; Issue 6396. *19th Century British Library Newspapers: Part II*

[27] *Glasgow Herald* (Glasgow, Scotland), Saturday, January 31, 1874; Issue 10638.

On his re-election as MP for North Lanarkshire, Sir Edward spoke at the Glasgow suburb of Maryhill, already in the knowledge that Gladstone and the Liberals were going to be out of government and the Conservative Party under Benjamin Disraeli would be in power. Constituency elections were not all on the same day and Sir Edward explained that over the previous week he had been helping the South Lanarkshire candidate, Mr Hamilton, in canvassing. The *Glasgow Herald* reported Sir Edward's views at the meeting:

> During the four days that had elapsed since he was returned as their representative, a great change had taken place, and it now seemed likely that a Conservative Government would come into power. It would be for the first time for the last twenty-five years that the Conservative party had been in a position in which they would enjoy the opportunity of bringing forward measures with the prospect of having a majority to carry them. Now, the question before the country was not so much as to the shortcomings of Mr Gladstone as to the incoming of Mr Disraeli. He for one regarded that statesman with incurable distrust. He believed, however, that there was little cause for serious alarm as he believed the Liberal party would be strong enough to hold its own against any reactionary attempt on the part of the Tories. What they would chiefly have to guard against was legislation in the interest of one class, rather than in the interest of the whole community. In justice, however, to Mr Disraeli, he must say that his programme, so far as put before the public, was of the most meagre and inoffensive kind. There were to be no organic changes, no worrying of classes, no plundering, and, he supposed, no blundering. (A laugh.) He would watch with interest how the Tories were to dispose of the large surplus, and he felt considerable distrust on account of their foreign policy. He compared the policy of the Conservative Government with that of the Liberal party, and observed that, whatever might be their shortcomings, the present

Government stood well compared with any Conservative Government which had been in power for the last 50 years'.[28]

Burgh boundaries

The issue of the extension of burgh boundaries rumbled on with meetings continuing into 1875 in the various communities around Glasgow. In 1871, it had been proposed to extend the boundary to Partick – in view of the fate of the City Boundary Extension Bill eighteen months earlier, Sir Edward was astonished.[29] He remained opposed to such extensions of the burgh boundaries and, in 1871, he also opposed an increased water rate for Glasgow suburbs.[30] In March the following year, Sir Edward voted against the Municipal Extension Bill for Glasgow. There was a strong sense, though, that he did this more with an eye to his own position than out of conviction because he could lose votes in the county if he did not oppose it.[31]

Sir Edward's opposition was remembered more than a decade later in 1887, when he was no longer in parliament and when more electoral reforms had been carried through. The issue of amalgamating the smaller burghs into Glasgow was raised yet again at that time, with a Bill to include these communities into the city. The *Glasgow Herald* reported the comments of the Speaker of the House of Commons on the issue, addressing

---

[28] *Glasgow Herald* (Glasgow, Scotland), Tuesday, February 10, 1874; Issue 10646

[29] *Glasgow Herald* (Glasgow, Scotland), Tuesday, December 12, 1871; Issue 9968.

[30] *Glasgow Herald* (Glasgow, Scotland), Tuesday, October 3, 1871; Issue 9908.

[31] *Glasgow Herald* (Glasgow, Scotland), Saturday, March 23, 1872; Issue 10056.

how best to ensure that proper services could be extended to all. He recalled:

> '...the very strong opposition of Sir Edward Colebrooke to three bills on the ground that any addition to the city would change the county electorate. Now, however, the franchise in the burghs and the counties was the same...it was idle to talk of the legislation of 1835, 1870, 1875 or even 1879 as relevant to the question now...nowadays the better opinion was that small areas were disadvantageous, and that... the proper course in order to meet the demands for municipal governments was that the larger areas adjoining should swallow up the small.[32]

Even in so short a time, the extension of the franchise had changed political expedients and what Sir Edward had fought for so persistently was no longer relevant. In 1891, therefore, the City of Glasgow Act saw the city boundaries extended to the north, south and west of the city.

Education

The Endowed Schools and Hospitals (Scotland) Commission

Education remained Sir Edward's main interest throughout his political career. Probably his most important contribution to education in Scotland – certainly the issue on which he had the highest public profile - was as Chairman of the Endowed Schools and Hospitals (Scotland) Commission, to which he was appointed in 1872. Following Forster's education reforms in England and the introduction of compulsory elementary education in England in 1870, Parliament felt there was a need

---

[32] *Glasgow Herald* (Glasgow, Scotland), Saturday, February 19, 1887; Issue 43.

to investigate Scottish 'endowed' (privately funded) schools and associated institutions that offered an education to children who were in some way disadvantaged.

It was an important Commission[33] and the appointment was to take up a lot of Sir Edward's time with sittings over more than two years, involving a great deal of travelling around Scotland. 'Sir E is <u>very</u> busy with his Commission and flies backwards and forwards to Edinburgh,' wrote Lady Colebrooke in a letter.[34] A week in January 1873 illustrates how all-absorbing this was: he chaired a meeting in Edinburgh on Saturday 25 January 1873, when a detailed examination was made of Gordon's Hospital, Aberdeen.[35] He chaired another meeting just two days later, examining the management of Steell's Hospital in the town of Tranent (east of Edinburgh) as well as John Watson's Institution in Edinburgh.[36] Indeed, the *Aberdeen Journal* reported on 29 January 1873 that there were 'daily meetings last week' examining also Donaldson's Hospital and Trades Maiden Hospital (both in Edinburgh) and Schaw's Hospital in Prestonpans.[37]

The Commission reported and 'as a result of the labours of the Commissioners, valuable statistics were obtained in connection with the education endowments in Scotland, as well as

[33] Scrapbook, Lanark Local History Library, 1906, Ref:1906, p65
[34] *The Colebrooke Letters*, 12.11.72
[35] *The Dundee Courier & Argus* (Dundee, Scotland), Monday, January 27, 1873; Issue 6085. *19th Century British Library Newspapers: Part II.*
[36] *The Dundee Courier & Argus and Northern Warder* (Dundee, Scotland), Tuesday, January 28, 1873; Issue 6086. *19th Century British Library Newspapers: Part II.*
[37] *The Aberdeen Journal* (Aberdeen, Scotland), Wednesday, January 29, 1873; Issue 6525.

statistics on hospitals, elementary schools, secondary schools and universities.'[38]

However, Sir Edward's heavy involvement over the four years or so seems to have taken a toll on his health. Furthermore, the Government was apparently slow to act on its recommendations and there was a sense of frustration at matters not being addressed as urgently as the Commission anticipated. In September 1877, therefore, when Sir Edward chaired a meeting of the Executive Committee of the Association for Promoting Secondary Education in Scotland at the Marischal College, Aberdeen, educational endowments were among the matters discussed.[39] It was agreed to send a deputation in November to see the Lord Advocate[40] on the matter, at his chambers in Edinburgh. As it turned out, Sir Edward was unable to attend through illness and the Earl of Elgin instead tried to convince the Lord Advocate that the question of Scottish Educational Endowments should be dealt with immediately by the Government. He read a letter from Sir Edward reminding the Lord Advocate that the Association had brought this subject before the Home Secretary the previous year, and had been led to believe that the question would be dealt with immediately. The Lord Advocate assured the deputation that he 'would represent their wishes in the proper quarter, and hoped some action would be taken in the matter'[41] – scarcely a promise of prompt action. The welfare of disadvantaged children apparently had a low priority. None the less, writing in 1928, Thomas Reid noted that '...many of his suggestions

---

[38] Scrapbook, Lanark Local History Library, 1906, Ref:1906, p65

[39] *Aberdeen Weekly Journal* (Aberdeen, Scotland), Wednesday, September 26, 1877; Issue 7052

[40] The Lord Advocate was the chief legal adviser of the UK government and the Crown for Scottish legal matters.

[41] *Aberdeen Weekly Journal* (Aberdeen, Scotland), Tuesday, November 27, 1877; Issue 7105.

paved the way for thoroughly beneficial changes in our higher school system.[42]

It seems likely that the Catholic Church frustrated implementation of the recommendations that had been made: the *Glasgow Herald* reporting on educational trusts more than ten years later wrote:

> ... an investigation was made ... by a Royal Commission presided over by Sir Edward Colebrooke, ... and they came to the emphatic judgement that not only was the hospital system wasteful and extravagant, but that it was injurious in its effect upon the children who got what were called its benefits. It was a rather singular thing that when a system so contrary to what he might call the genius of Scottish education had been found in the experience of great corporations to be wanting, and had been condemned by the expression of opinion of an important and impartial tribunal such as the Royal Commission, that they should now at this eleventh hour find reverend seigniors who spoke in tones of mingled distress and anger at the sacrilege committed by a Royal Commission ...[43]

The outcome of 'Sir Edward's Commission' was evidently rather less than he would have hoped for. He may have found himself elected chairman as nobody else would take on what was probably a thankless task since it confronted entrenched attitudes. Whether or not that was the case, the main effect seems to have been to undermine Sir Edward's health.

---

[42] Reid, Thomas, *A History of the Parish of Crawfordjohn, Upper Ward of Lanarkshire, 1153-1928*, Turnbull & Spears, Edinburgh, 1928, p97
[43] *Glasgow Herald* (Glasgow, Scotland), Thursday, May 31, 1888; Issue 130.

Other educational concerns

There were numerous other educational concerns, at different levels, in which Sir Edward involved or committed himself. He was, for instance, appointed to the General Committee of the Clyde Industrial Training Ship for boys and attended the half-yearly inspection 'of this excellent and very popular institution' on 1 September 1870 with numerous other visitors.[44]

On 30 September 1874, in his capacity as both MP and Lord Lieutenant, Sir Edward and Lady Colebrooke were among the visitors to the Social Science Congress in Glasgow – a seven day event drawing together members of the Association of Social Sciences to share papers on topics such as new innovations, appliances and local improvements[45] and in 1877, in furtherance of his commitment to the advancement of knowledge, he was among a large gathering at a conversazione, given in Glasgow, by the Advocates' Society for those interested in the advancement of Social Science.[46]

In 1876, Sir Edward chaired an influential education meeting in Edinburgh. Having always believed that training in the Classics (Latin and Ancient Greek) was fundamental to a good education, it would have been personally satisfying for him to reach agreement at this meeting 'that measures ought to be taken forthwith for endeavouring to secure the continuance of classical teaching in the public schools',[47] a measure that he would have seen as an essential basis of a good education. At the same

---

[44] *Glasgow Herald* (Glasgow, Scotland), Friday, September 2, 1870; Issue 9569

[45] *The Morning Post* (London, England), Tuesday, September 29, 1874; pg. 7; Issue 31902. *19th Century British Library Newspapers: Part II.*

[46] *Aberdeen Weekly Journal* (Aberdeen, Scotland), Saturday, September 22, 1877; Issue 7049.

[47] *The Aberdeen Journal* (Aberdeen, Scotland), Wednesday, February 2, 1876; Issue 6682.

meeting, it was agreed to strengthen the support to secondary schools in the burghs. The same meeting also discussed the matter of endowed schools[48] – the education issue for which Sir Edward had been elected Commission chairman - and, concerned to keep the matter fresh, instructed the committee to keep before the Government the necessity of dealing with Scottish educational endowments.[49] This was at the time when the importance attached by the Government to this matter seemed to the members of the Endowed Schools Commission to be less than it should have been. Sir Edward was determined to use his position to keep up pressure on the Government for action.

In November of the same year, the Association for the Promotion of Secondary Education in Scotland met in Edinburgh, chaired by Sir Edward, and agreed to empower the committee to take steps to improve secondary schools in Scotland. Sir Edward proposed a higher rate (a property tax) to support secondary education and the *Aberdeen Weekly Journal*, perhaps surprisingly, reported '...a willingness throughout Lanarkshire to pay this higher rate to support secondary education, as envisaged and proposed by Sir Edward Colebrooke.[50]

Dean of Faculties of the University of Glasgow

Sir Edward's interest in and commitment to higher education was also recognised in 1869 when he was appointed Dean of Faculties of the University of Glasgow, a position he held

---

[48] 'Endowed schools' was the term used for independently maintained schools

[49] *Aberdeen Weekly Journal* (Aberdeen, Scotland), Wednesday, November 8, 1876; Issue 6722

[50] *Aberdeen Weekly Journal* (Aberdeen, Scotland), Saturday, September 22, 1877; Issue 7049.

until 1872. This was the largely honorary position of senior administrative officer but involved high profile public commitments. In October 1870, he attended a dinner given by the Principal and Professors for subscribers to the new university, so it seems certain that Sir Edward himself contributed to the striking new University of Glasgow buildings by Sir George Gilbert Scott.

The opening of the new session in the new buildings at Gilmore Hill was on 7 November 1870. Professor Lushington, the senior Professor in the university, gave the inaugural address and Sir Edward, as Dean of Faculties, gave thanks on behalf of the university to Professor Lushington for the address. He also gave a short speech, including a substantial and confident quote in Latin. Reflecting his own belief that education should be made as widely available as possible, he expressed also the need to continue subscriptions towards scholarships.[51] At the dinner in the evening, a toast was proposed to Sir Edward as Lord Lieutenant of the County mentioning '...his eminence as a statesman and ... the ability he brought to bear upon the discharge of his duties as Lord Lieutenant of the County'.[52] The following year, Sir Edward attended the Glasgow Scott Centenary banquet in City Hall, along with academics from Glasgow and Oxford University, where he was both one of the principal speakers and proposed a toast.[53]

Doctor of Laws

Benjamin Disraeli, then the leader of the Opposition, was elected to the position of Rector of the University of Glasgow

---

[51] *Glasgow Herald* (Glasgow, Scotland), Tuesday, November 8, 1870; Issue 9627
[52] *Glasgow Herald* (Glasgow, Scotland), Tuesday, November 8, 1870; Issue 9627
[53] *The Morning Post* (London, England), Wednesday, August 09, 1871; pg. 5; Issue 30473. *19th Century British Library Newspapers: Part II.*

in 1871. His visit to Glasgow to be installed as Rector in 1873 generated press interest at a national level. Disraeli gave an inaugural lecture and the university conferred an honorary degree of Doctor of Laws (LL.D) on him and on six other leading public figures including Sir Edward, in a ceremony that included 'capping and investing the recipients with their hoods as Doctors'.[54] It was a glamorous and prestigious occasion with all the leading gentlemen of the city invited to meet the honourable guest.[55]

In September 1876, Sir Edward's commitment to higher education took him to the Glasgow meeting of the British Association for the Advancement of Science.[56]

His known support of educational reform and improvement, referred to already, made it natural to seek his support in petitioning Parliament. An example of this followed the setting up of School Boards in England - following the Education Act of 1870 - when it was agreed to petition Parliament in favour of a Scottish Education bill. Sir Edward was the obvious choice to present the petition to parliament.[57]

Agriculture

Sir Edward continued to demonstrate his interest in and support for agriculture and agricultural development. In 1870, he attended the Hamilton Horticultural Society Third Annual Exhibition in Hamilton Town Hall. This society was already

---

[54] *The Leeds Mercury* (Leeds, England), Thursday, November 20, 1873; Issue 11112
[55] *The Aberdeen Journal* (Aberdeen, Scotland), Wednesday, November 19, 1873; Issue 6567.
[56] *Glasgow Herald* (Glasgow, Scotland), Friday, February 18, 1876; Issue 12079.
[57] *Glasgow Herald* (Glasgow, Scotland), Friday, June 29, 1883; Issue 155

flourishing and their exhibition had upwards of 1000 entries.[58] Sir Edward was keen to be seen to support such ventures.

At the 1874 Glasgow Agricultural Show, he was again reported to have awarded a silver medal for the 'best cow ... in the yard'. It was awarded to an animal that had already taken 11 firsts at former shows having 'all the marked features of an Ayrshire, being a cow of great substance, considerable breadth ... and a splendid milk vessel'(!)[59] The prizes continued annually and in 1883, Sir Edward provided a 'special prize'.[60]

At the Biggar Farmers' Club Show on Thursday 26 August 1875, there was great disappointment that there were no cattle or sheep due to an outbreak of foot and mouth disease. The disappointment, though, could not prevent the dinner being much enjoyed in the Biggar Corn Exchange. There were about sixty gentlemen present including the local MPs and a warm toast was proposed by the chairman, Sir G Graham Montgomery, MP for Peebleshire to Sir Edward, in his joint role as MP and Lord Lieutenant:

> ....it would be impossible to find one better calculated to fill the proud position as representative of Her Majesty... (I have noticed in the House of Commons) the great business habits, the great attention which Sir Edward ... always displayed and that his advice and assistance in Scotch matters was often looked up to by others...respond most heartily to the health of one who filled his high

[58] *Glasgow Herald* (Glasgow, Scotland), Monday, September 5, 1870; Issue 9571

[59] *Glasgow Herald* (Glasgow, Scotland), Thursday, May 7, 1874; Issue 10720.

[60] *Glasgow Herald* (Glasgow, Scotland), Thursday, May 3, 1883; Issue 106.

position in so creditable and so praiseworthy a manner. (Applause)[61]

The following decade saw several bad seasons and consequent depression in agriculture. In October 1877, Lady Colebrooke wrote in a letter:

> For years the poor Scotch have not had <u>such</u> a year! ...The flowers and vegetables were <u>so</u> backward that they were caught by the frost before they came out, and we could count the dishes of Peas, indeed almost the Peas we have had this Autumn. Mercifully <u>here</u> the farmers did not cut their Hay until after the Deluge, so it was got in pretty well here, but oh! the poor Corn! First some of it was frosted – but three weeks of <u>splendid</u> weather at the end of September and beginning of October ripened <u>some</u> and the farmers were getting it in as fast as possible, when frost and snow came, and last week as we were driving in a <u>fearful</u> snow storm, we saw people cutting right and left, and some of it was still green!![62]

The agricultural social round continued and by 1885 conditions had much improved. Sir Edward was at the Biggar Farmers Club Show dinner again, in his capacity as Lord Lieutenant of the county, but now no longer their MP. The Chairman proposed his health, saying in the 38 years when he had been their Member of Parliament, Sir Edward had gained the good esteem of both sides of House of Commons. 'He was a man whose views upon most subjects were sound and moderate...' Sir Edward, in replying, recalled '...the amount of cordial support he had received not only from those who furthered his election but from his political opponents...'. He also expressed

---

[61] *Glasgow Herald* (Glasgow, Scotland), Friday, August 27, 1875; Issue 11129
[62] *The Colebrooke Letters*, 23.10.1877

his hope that the success of the show indicated that bad seasons were at an end and congratulated the Biggar Farmers Club, commenting that they had never had a more successful show both in terms of stock and attendances.[63]

In 1883, Sir Edward contributed to an agricultural experiment in making silage that turned out to have far-reaching benefits for farming. The use of silage was very much at an early stage, at least in Scotland. From a traditional French technique, silage-making had recently been developed in the United States of America and it was now attracting interest in Britain. Sir Edward was in the vanguard of those experimenting with the technique in introducing it on two of his farms – one in Nether Abington and one in Kirkton. He paid the cost of the necessary silos while the tenant farmers paid the much lower costs of filling them, and he followed with interest the results of the experiments.[64]

The Volunteer movement

Sir Edward's enthusiastic support of the Volunteer movement remained strong as he always regarded the Volunteer corps as essential to the defence of the country. He held local office for the Volunteers for at least some of the time he was a civic dignitary in Lanarkshire, the *Glasgow Herald* reporting in 1885 that he had been re-elected Vice President (Lanarkshire) of the West of Scotland Rifle Association.[65]

He demonstrated his support in August 1874, when he took a party to a 'Sham Fight' on Lanark Moor. It was essentially a local occasion with the participants all volunteers from

---

[63] *Glasgow Herald* (Glasgow, Scotland), Friday, August 14, 1885; Issue 194.

[64] *Glasgow Herald* (Glasgow, Scotland), Friday, December 21, 1883; Issue 305.

[65] *Glasgow Herald* (Glasgow, Scotland), Thursday, December 10, 1885; Issue 295

Lanarkshire, including engineers, riflemen and administrative battalions.[66] The Colebrookes had hoped they would be joined for this by Mr W F Rawnsley, who had recently been tutor to the Colebrooke children, but were disappointed: 'We had planned so much to do with you. You were to ride at a Sham Fight with my husband at Lanark! You were to set off fireworks with us ... We are quite grieved not to have you.[67]

Sir Edward presented a cup for volley firing. It was presented in 1870 to the 1st Lanarkshire Rifle Volunteers at an annual concert and distribution of prizes in late January.[68] He also presented a Challenge Plate for volley firing, which was competed for throughout the West of Scotland. At the meeting in Irvine of the West of Scotland Artillery and Rifle Association in 1870, he was pleased that a higher score won it than in the previous year, showing improvement in firing in the intervening year.[69] At the meeting of the same association in Lanark in 1873, Sir Edward presented the trophy himself.[70] The 19th Lanark (Volunteer Rifles) seem to have been a particularly talented corps. In 1875, they won the trophy at the West of Scotland Rifle Association annual meeting on Lanark Muir,[71] as they had the previous year and in 1876, they were again the winners. Under the terms of the competition, being winners for the third year running meant they were able to keep the Challenge Plate permanently. Sir Edward generously provided

---

[66] *Glasgow Herald* (Glasgow, Scotland), Monday, August 10, 1874; Issue 10801.

[67] *The Colebrooke Letters*, 7.8.1874

[68] *Glasgow Herald* (Glasgow, Scotland), Saturday, January 29, 1870; Issue 9384.

[69] *Glasgow Herald* (Glasgow, Scotland), Monday, June 13, 1870; Issue 9499.

[70] *Glasgow Herald* (Glasgow, Scotland), Monday, June 9, 1873; Issue 10435.

[71] *Glasgow Herald* (Glasgow, Scotland), Monday, June 7, 1875; Issue 11059.

another trophy for the competition in subsequent years – a vase this time - and the terms of the competition were altered![72]

Sir Edward's pride in the local Volunteers was never greater than in 1869 and again in 1880 and 1887, when a Lanarkshire team won the prestigious China Cup[73] in a national competition held on Wimbledon Common and he had the great pleasure of formally presenting the cup to the team at Abington House. The 1869 event was described in some detail in the *Glasgow Herald*, which related that a special train left Glasgow 1.45pm. It took two hours to reach Abington, arriving at 3.45pm. It was met by a guard of honour and was preceded to Abington House by a band. There were congratulations, several photographs taken and upwards of 100 ladies and gentlemen sat down to a sumptuous dinner, provided by Sir Edward within a large marquee erected upon the lawn. The celebrations finished by 7.00 pm and the proud team returned to Glasgow by special train leaving Abington station at 7.30 pm.[74]

In 1887, Sir Edward and Lady Colebrooke, together with the young Colebrookes and distinguished guests, met the team at the entrance to their mansion, where, as on the previous occasions, Sir Edward made suitable proud remarks about the achievement of the team, some of whom were the same as eighteen years previously, when the county first won the trophy. As before, after the formal presentation, the cup was handed back to Sir Edward with the request that he, as Lord Lieutenant, should have custody of it for the year – a request

---

[72] *Glasgow Herald* (Glasgow, Scotland), Thursday, March 30, 1876; Issue 12114.

[73] The China Cup, according to the *Glasgow Herald*, was ...'a massive piece of plate....perhaps the largest piece of silver plate in the country'. It was made in Hong Kong and was originally presented by the volunteers of Shanghai. Lanark won it in 1869, 1880, 1887.

[74] *Glasgow Herald* (Glasgow, Scotland), Saturday, August 28, 1869; Issue 9252

Abington House, 1866
Courtesy of Biggar Museum Trust

which he accepted with great pleasure, as 'evidence of a distinguished prowess of the Lanarkshire team at the recent Wimbledon meeting'. Sir Edward commented that it was a matter of great pride for the county and for himself being charged with custody of the trophy for the third time.

Public relief

In November 1878, the City of Glasgow Bank failed with apparent suddenness. At a meeting convened by the Lord Provost in the Merchant's Hall, Sir Edward pledged £200 to a fund to relieve those who had fallen from relative affluence to poverty.[75] The effects of the bank collapse were so widespread

---

[75] *Aberdeen Weekly Journal* (Aberdeen, Scotland), Tuesday, November 5, 1878; Issue 7399.

that it began to be viewed as a national disaster and at a subsequent meeting Sir Edward encouraged others to give generously to a fund being set up. His proposal was carried and he was appointed to the committee charged with carrying out the fundraising.[76] Within a very short time, the fund exceeded £80,000.[77]

In January of the following year, as a result of industrial depression and a harsh winter, there was considerable distress among the poorer inhabitants of Glasgow. A central fund was set up for relief and Sir Edward was an early contributor. There were also local fundraising initiatives and it was reported that, following a public meeting of householders in Govan, Sir Edward insisted on supplementing his previous contribution with a cheque for a further £25.[78]

The Royal Visit

In the autumn of 1876, excitement in Glasgow ran very high as the city, prominently including Sir Edward, prepared for a visit from the Prince and Princess of Wales and their entourage. It was several years since their last visit to the city, when they had come for the laying of the foundation of the new university buildings on Gilmore Hill. The royal party would be stopping on their way back to London after a three week holiday at Dunrobin Castle as guests of the Duke of Sutherland. They were to stay the night before the visit at Blythswood in Renfrew, as guests of Colonel and Lady Campbell.[79] The day was to be an official holiday and the programme for their day visit was given

---

[76] *Aberdeen Weekly Journal* (Aberdeen, Scotland), Thursday, November 7, 1878; Issue 7401
[77] *The Morning Post* (London, England), Thursday, November 07, 1878; pg. 6; Issue 33186. *19th Century British Library Newspapers: Part II*
[78] *Glasgow Herald* (Glasgow, Scotland), Wednesday, January 8, 1879; Issue 12183.
[79] *Glasgow Herald* (Glasgow, Scotland), Tuesday, October 17, 1876; Issue 11486.

in detail in the local press on the preceding day. The Prince and Princess of Wales were to be accompanied by their eldest children, Prince Albert and Prince George as well as Prince John of Glucksburg and were expected to arrive by special train at the brand new St Enoch Square Station at ten minutes to eleven on the morning of Tuesday 17 October.

The day was reported at length by the *Glasgow Herald* and its report was taken up by numerous regional newspapers. The press were there in strength and the *Glasgow Herald* reported that many people had come out the evening before, despite drizzle and slush. 'For the most part they were representative of the class who have not been able to obtain tickets for any of the ceremonials of today, and who were therefore anxious to gratify their curiosity as far as possible in advance'.[80]

The city was lavishly decorated. Venetian masts, crowns and Prince of Wales feathers formed the principal features around St Enoch Square and buildings across the city were adorned with flags, bunting, streamers, banners and scrolls of drapery.[81] The special train steamed into the new station in St Enoch's Square, which opened for the first time for the royal visit, a few minutes before 11.00 am, to loud cheers. The Prince wore the uniform of a Colonel of the Sutherland and Caithness Volunteers, with a sprig of 'butcher broom',[82] a symbol of the Sutherland family in his glengarry bonnet.[83]

---

[80] *Glasgow Herald* (Glasgow, Scotland), Tuesday, October 17, 1876; Issue 11486

[81] *Glasgow Herald* (Glasgow, Scotland), Tuesday, October 17, 1876; Issue 11486

[82] Butchers Broom (Gaig-bhealaidh) is the plant badge of the Sutherland clan. Traditionally clans used plants as badges in order to recognise fellow clan members. Clansmen may wear a sprig of plant badge pinned behind the clan crest badge on a man's bonnet or a lady's sash-badge brooch. http://clanmurray.org/tartans.html (accessed 24.9.2013)

[83] A glengarry bonnet is a traditional Scottish cap which may be worn as part of Scottish military or civilian Highland dress.

Prince John was in the uniform of the Danish Life Guards and the children were in highland dress. The Prince and Princess were met from their Pullman car by the Lord Provost, Sir Edward (in full uniform as Lord Lieutenant), the Sheriff, and the magistrates (wearing their new and much-talked-of robes of office for the first time and attracting much attention), the chairman of the City Union and the Directors of the Glasgow and South-Western Railway Company. The prominence of railway personnel celebrated the new railway facilities and the general manager had travelled with the royal party from Renfrew but got off the train quickly when the train pulled into Glasgow, so as to be ready to welcome the royal party.

On the arrival of the Prince and Princess, Sir Edward shook hands second, after the Lord Provost. After introductions, the carriage procession set off to Glasgow Green for a review of the Volunteers. In the civic procession from St Enoch Square, Sir Edward was in the tenth carriage, ahead of the Lord Provost in the eleventh. The Prince and Princess were in the twelfth carriage, followed by the royal suite. 'It is almost impossible to convey any idea of the crowd it was so enormous. Several hundred thousand persons thronged Argyle Street' (the main thoroughfare) wrote the *Glasgow Herald*. The procession continued along London Street, at the end of which there was a grand triumphal arch erected over the entrance to Glasgow Green. It was made of wood but looked like marble and was crowned by the Prince of Wales feathers. There were three spans, the centre for carriages and the sides for pedestrians. It was decorated with the motto 'Ich dien' and with evergreens and flags including the Union Flag.

In the centre of the stand on Glasgow Green, a temporary apartment had been erected, decorated and furnished lavishly, for the use of the Princess and her suite. As soon as she was seated, the review of the Volunteers began, the Prince riding one of his own horses, which had been sent from London and other gentlemen of the royal party also on horseback. The royal party was attended by (among others) two Indian aides-de-camp of the 11th Prince of Wales Own Bengal Lancers, who attracted much attention in their unfamiliar uniforms.

After the review, there was a private lunch for about thirty guests, where Sir Edward and Lady Colebrooke were important guests, at the Lord Provost's mansion, after which, so that as many people as possible could catch a glimpse of the royal visitors, a circuitous route through the city was taken to George Square. Freemasons were prominent throughout the celebrations, accompanying the procession from lunch to the stone laying. It was estimated that over 7500 members of masonic lodges, were involved in the procession, with brass and fife bands and displaying far more than ever normally seen of the flags and paraphernalia of freemasonry. Indeed it caused some amusement among the crowds from those not familiar with the mysteries of the craft. The ceremonial was delayed as the masonic procession to George Square took much longer than planned. The royal party arrived at the Square in twilight at around 4.00pm, with Prince John now in the uniform of a past Grand Master. The Square had been decorated richly, at the expense of the Corporation of the City of Glasgow, in crimson and gold with shields and badges connected to the Prince of Wales. It was crammed with spectators: Sir Edward and Lady Colebrooke were among the 3000 guests on the platform.

The Lord Provost gave an address to the Prince, after which he presented him with a silver trowel. After responding to the address, the Prince ceremonially laid the foundation stone for the new post office and there followed 'the usual masonic ceremony' for the laying of the stone. When the foundation ceremony was over, the royal party returned to the station via

Buchanan Street for the train back to Renfrew, leaving at 5.25pm for dinner with Colonel Campbell at Blytheswood. Meanwhile, in Glasgow, from 7.00pm for an hour or so, there were illuminations and fireworks all over the city, including some on tramcars. The evening saw masonic dinners in the city, while the Prince and Princess, their duty done, took a special train to Kilmarnock, where their carriages were attached to the ordinary limited-stop mail train, leaving at 10.00 pm for the return to Windsor. The newspapers could not refrain from commenting that it would have been better if the royal party had stayed on into the evening.

It had indeed been a brief visit - just a few hours - to the West of Scotland but the city had gone to enormous lengths and huge expense to welcome the royal visitors. The opinion of the press was that, apart from the squares, decoration was less than on their previous visit. However, the press felt this was made up for by the enthusiastic reception from spectators and that the Prince and Princess must have been 'highly gratified' by their reception.

In truth, though, the royal visitors would have had better memories of the day if the unreliable Glasgow weather had not presented its worst. Autumn gales had stripped leaves from trees and flowers from gardens and the day had started grey. It drizzled early and the rain was drenching by time of the Review. It dampened flags and necessitated more protection on the carriages than planned, to the disappointment of those who had waited in the rain. The streets were muddy and spectators were bedraggled with some up to their ankles in mud. The drizzling rain and heavy haar (mist) obscured views and generally spoiled the spectacle. It did not deter the crowds though and there was much loyal cheering, with people collected in every conceivable situation, from the pavements to the chimney tops. The crowd broke through barriers at one point and rushed after the procession, whereupon the military charged several times among the advancing crowds causing some people to be crushed while others scrambled to get away.[84,85]

Sir Edward, as Lord Lieutenant, other dignitaries and the Corporation of the City of Glasgow who paid for the grand spectacle must have had a taste of disappointment at the end of the day since the perhaps reluctantly-made royal visit had not only been short but tarnished by the bad weather - the one ingredient of the day that was beyond their control.

Sir Edward Colebrooke by George Richmond, 1877
From the collection at Wrotham Park

[84] *Glasgow Herald* (Glasgow, Scotland), Wednesday, October 18, 1876; Issue 11487.
[85] *The Belfast News-Letter* (Belfast, Ireland), Wednesday, October 18, 1876; Issue 19104.

Re-igniting the fire of Scottish Liberalism

In 1877, with a Conservative government in power since 1874, it was of politically pressing importance to Sir Edward to be working towards the Liberals regaining power at the next General Election. The local Liberals began to increase their Party meetings and welcomed Lord Hartington, Leader of the Liberal Party in the House of Commons, to a meeting at Glasgow City Hall with the Liberals of West and South West Scotland. It was followed by a dinner, presided over by Sir Edward,[86] who said the visit would 'bring about a fresh epoch in the annals of the Liberal Party in Scotland'.[87] There was a recognition of the need of '...working to overcome losses of the last election...due to over-confidence and insufficient organisation'.[88] Numbers of supporters were growing fast and there was a new willingness to overcome personal differences in working together towards the same end.[89]

In the wake of Lord Hartington's visit, various local Liberal Associations sprang up. In August 1878, for instance, there was a meeting at Coatbridge, where it was decided to form a Liberal Association for the parish of Old Monkland.[90] It was in a letter read to this meeting that Sir Edward first intimated his intention to seek re-election for North Lanarkshire at the next election. In 1880, the Govanhill Liberal Association was

---

[86] *Daily News* (London, England), Monday, October 22, 1877; Issue 9829.

[87] *The Dundee Courier & Argus* (Dundee, Scotland), Thursday, November 08, 1877; Issue 7581

[88] *The Sheffield & Rotherham Independent* (Sheffield, England), Thursday, November 08, 1877; pg. 3; Issue 5881. *19th Century British Library Newspapers: Part II.*

[89] *The Dundee Courier & Argus* (Dundee, Scotland), Thursday, November 08, 1877; Issue 7581

[90] *The Leeds Mercury* (Leeds, England), Wednesday, August 14, 1878; Issue 12588

formed with Sir Edward becoming the first President and speaking at the inaugural meeting.[91]

At the beginning of December 1879, William Ewart Gladstone himself, leader of the Liberal Party and shadow Prime Minister, came to Scotland and Sir Edward was naturally one of the dignitaries expected to accompany Gladstone in Glasgow. Regrettably, he was 'unavoidably prevented' from doing this but he was none the less warmly acknowledged when 'three cheers were given for Sir Edward, in which Mr Gladstone heartily joined'.[92]

1880 General Election

In January 1880, after six years of a Conservative government, there was a feeling that a General Election would be called soon. Sir Edward spoke at a meeting in Coatbridge where he shared his views on a variety of issues. He described himself as having been a moderate Liberal all his life and unlikely, in his old age, to change his opinions. He referred to the Anti-Corn Law Bill and the Household Suffrage Bill, saying that he had had reservations about both but that he was now reassured. He looked forward to the extension of suffrage to the working classes so they could work with the middle classes and made the commitment that, if a Liberal government was voted in at the next election, this would be one of first issues dealt with.

Sir Edward distrusted Disraeli and was critical of much Conservative foreign policy. He condemned the war in South Africa (the Anglo-Zulu War) as an act of aggression, saying 'the Zulus were a friendly tribe'. Supporting an enquiry into

---

[91] *Glasgow Herald* (Glasgow, Scotland), Friday, January 30, 1880; Issue 12515.
[92] *The Morning Post* (London, England), Monday, December 08, 1879; pg. 0; Issue 33525.

the hanging of Afghans in Kabul by orders of the British General, he said the shocking acts that had been carried out in Afghanistan were a matter of shame and he questioned the right of the British to be there. His stated belief was that the Liberals were needed for humane progress to take place. His views met with approval and the meeting ended with vote of thanks to and confidence in Sir Edward,[93] as did a similar meeting of New Monkland constituents in Airdrie.[94]

In April 1880, the Liberals, under William Gladstone, returned to government and Sir Edward was returned unopposed.[95] During this Parliament, in addition to constituency responsibilities, duties as Lord Lieutenant and involvement in various agricultural and horticultural societies, Sir Edward's public work was wide-ranging. He continued as the local 'justice' for Crawford and Crawfordjohn; he was Commissioner of Supply and Commissioner for General Purposes (dealing with property and income taxes); he was on the County Road Board of the Upper Ward of Lanarkshire; he was President of the Upper Ward of Lanarkshire Association, President of the Edinburgh Upperward Association (an association for those from the Upper Ward of Lanarkshire living in or near Edinburgh), on the Police Committee and Chairman of the School Board.[96]

1885 General Election

A few months before the 1880 General Election, the suburban burghs of Glasgow were looking for the creation of another parliamentary seat out of part of Lanarkshire and part of Renfrewshire. It was clear that there was insufficient time to

[93] *Glasgow Herald* (Glasgow, Scotland), Wednesday, January 28, 1880; Issue 12513.
[94] *Glasgow Herald* (Glasgow, Scotland), Monday, March 22, 1880; Issue 70.
[95] *Glasgow Herald* (Glasgow, Scotland), Wednesday, April 7, 1880; Issue 84
[96] *Upper Ward Almanac and Handbook*, 1883, 1884, 1885, 1886, 1887

carry this through for the election that same year but, none the less, Sir Edward was asked to make representations for another Scottish seat.[97] The petitioning came to fruition in readiness for the General Election five years later when North Lanarkshire was divided.

As late as 1884, Sir Edward attended a franchise meeting in Partick, where it was argued that Lanarkshire should have greater representation. No county in Scotland would benefit more (it was claimed), Lanark being the largest county in Scotland. Compared to comparable constituencies, the view was that Lanarkshire should already have three or four members. The 1832 reforms had added about half million voters and those of 1868 about a million more. The bill then before Parliament would add a further two million with the implication that Lanarkshire should have three or four Members of Parliament to represent its people. Sir Edward's cordial welcome to the Partick meeting was reported in the *Glasgow Herald*:

'...now for nearly 30 years [he] had so faithfully and with such general respect and admiration, represented this county in Parliament, ... who in the House of Commons had won a position of authority not accorded to many private members...They welcomed one who sustained the honourable but arduous duty of representing in the House of Commons a larger constituency than was represented by any other single member from any part of the United Kingdom or Ireland. Sir Edward was the only member representing one thirty second of the counties of Scotland.[98]

---

[97] *The Sheffield & Rotherham Independent* (Sheffield, England), Tuesday, February 17, 1880; pg. 3; Issue 7928. *19th Century British Library Newspapers: Part II.*

[98] *Glasgow Herald* (Glasgow, Scotland), Wednesday, September 24, 1884; Issue 229.

Retirement

It was expected that Sir Edward would stand again for parliament following the Redistribution Bill of 1884, which was to increase parliamentary representation for the people of Lanarkshire. Even before the new constituency was created, however, Sir Edward felt it was time for him to step down from politics and signified his intention to retire from active public life. 'It was stated in Glasgow yesterday afternoon that Sir Edward Colebrooke, Liberal, has intimated that he will not seek re-election to Parliament at the next general election,' wrote the *Dundee Courier and Argus*. 'There will, therefore, be a vacancy in North Lanarkshire.'[99] He had had health problems and he very likely took these as a warning against the relentlessly busy lifestyle he had been obliged to lead for many decades. Lanarkshire without Sir Edward was difficult to contemplate: the Govan Liberals were unable to find a candidate and thought to ask Sir Edward to reconsider his decision to stand down, but after debate, decided against this.[100]

Sir Edward was kept working hard to the end of his last term in office. He was, for instance, asked to present the largest petition ever raised in Motherwell (more than one in four of inhabitants) against the disestablishment petition of fellow Liberal, Mr Dick Peddie,[101] the Member of Parliament for Kilmarnock Burghs.[102] He also assisted the local Liberals in

---

[99] *The Dundee Courier & Argus* (Dundee, Scotland), Saturday, March 01, 1884; Issue 9556and *The Pall Mall Gazette* (London, England),Saturday, March 1, 1884; Issue 5924

[100] *Glasgow Herald* (Glasgow, Scotland), Thursday, August 6, 1885; Issue 187.

[101] *Glasgow Herald* (Glasgow, Scotland), Saturday, May 2, 1885; Issue 105.

[102] John Dick Peddie was elected on a disestablishment platform in the General Election of 1880. In 1884 he introduced a private members bill on disestablishment, although it never came to a vote. He lost his seat in 1885 and did not stand again.

their searches for candidates. At a meeting of the mid Lanark Liberals after the election, they minuted their thanks to Sir Edward for his advice and assistance in selecting a candidate for the General Election.[103]

Prioritising in public office

It was impossible for someone like Sir Edward, with several public roles and positions, to attend every event and occasion to which he was invited and he therefore sometimes had to decline invitations. In view of his high profile, these were often noted with disappointment in the press.

The Ninth Exhibition of the Works of Modern Artists opened on 31 January 1870 at the Glasgow Institute of the Fine Arts. The Lord Provost was in the Chair and was plainly disappointed that several of those invited, including Sir Edward, were not present. 'This meeting we expected would have been graced by the presence of several gentlemen who have not found it convenient to attend,' he said. 'I do not think it necessary to read their letters of apology. One of these is from the Lord Lieutenant of the County, Sir Edward Colebrooke'.[104]

Important though religious observance was to him, Sir Edward made apologies for not attending the Sabbath Observance Demonstration at Glasgow City Hall in August 1871.[105]

Many dignitaries were present in 1875 for the inauguration of the Broomhill Home, run by the Association for the Relief of Incurables. Sir Edward sent his apologies, which were mentioned by the Lord Provost (by then his neighbour and

---

[103] *Glasgow Herald* (Glasgow, Scotland), Monday, June 21, 1886; Issue 147.
[104] *Glasgow Herald* (Glasgow, Scotland), Tuesday, February 1, 1870; Issue 9386.
[105] *Glasgow Herald* (Glasgow, Scotland), Wednesday, August 30, 1871; Issue 9879.

one-time political adversary, Alexander Baillie Cochrane).[106]
In the same year, he sent a letter to the Woodilie Lunatic
Asylum, apologising for being unable to attend the opening as
he was 'indisposed'.[107]

He made apologies for not attending some Trades House
dinners and he seems often to have sent apologies for the St
Andrews Day banquet of the Glasgow Society possibly because
he was usually in London in November, when it was held,
or possibly because he felt it would be uncomfortable for an
Englishman to attend.

In 1885, he sent apologies for his absence from a meeting
in Glasgow on the defence of the Clyde – measures to defend
the river and its approaches.[108] By this time, Sir Edward
was looking forward to standing down from Parliament, was
coping with ill-health and was clearly intending to reduce his
public commitments.

---

[106] *Glasgow Herald* (Glasgow, Scotland), Thursday, October 7, 1875; Issue 11164

[107] *Glasgow Herald* (Glasgow, Scotland), Saturday, October 23, 1875; Issue 11178.

[108] *Glasgow Herald* (Glasgow, Scotland), Tuesday, June 2, 1885; Issue 131.

Photograph of Sir T Edward Colebrooke, 1883
Parliamentary Archives, PHO/11/2/28

Chapter 10
Twilight

Mr Gladstone, who has increased the peerage more than any other Minister of modern times, proposes to add...Sir Edward Colebrooke, one of the most influential Scotch members...[1]

So rumoured an Ipswich newspaper, drawing on a much-syndicated news item. It was anticipated that before the autumn session of parliament in 1884, Mr Gladstone would advise the Queen to give away half-a-dozen new coronets, of which 'that veteran old Scotch Liberal'[2] was to be one. Gladstone was anxious that it should be seen 'as one of those ordinary episodes in the life of a Ministry' but as all were 'staunch party men [who] may be relied on to give a solid vote for the Franchise Bill'[3] the general assumption was that loyal supporters had been chosen in order to increase the Ministerial minority in the Upper House.[4]

However, Sir Edward was never raised to the peerage. This may have been because, already suffering from repeated ill

---

[1] *The Ipswich Journal* (Ipswich, England), Saturday, August 2, 1884; Issue 8150.
[2] *Nottinghamshire Guardian* (London, England), Friday, August 01, 1884; pg. 6; Issue 2045.
[3] *Nottinghamshire Guardian* (London, England), Friday, August 01, 1884; pg. 6; Issue 2045.
[4] *Nottinghamshire Guardian* (London, England), Friday, August 01, 1884; pg. 6; Issue 2045.

health and determined to retire, he turned down the honour. (In February 1884, he paired with a Conservative member for parliamentary voting while he spent time in Cannes for his health.[5]) By the following year, though, he was being reported in the press as supporting the Liberal Unionist cause and it is likely that, as these tendencies became known in the autumn of 1884, political differences made him seem unreliable and that this led to the proposed peerage being withdrawn. This was hinted at in an Irish publication, which wrote: 'As to Sir Edward Colebrooke, he is a Whig of the worst type,' [although he was] 'one of the most influential Scotch members...' [6]. After much speculation and reporting in the press that Sir Edward would be honoured with a peerage, there was a silence as to why it did not happen.

Sir Edward had announced his intention to leave Parliament prior to the 1885 General Election. He had become known as loyal, serious, sincere, hard-working, dogged and totally without any wish for self-aggrandisement. He had been a 'rank and file' MP, never achieving any ministerial office in government. After his departure, a reporter gave him the following epitaph:

> His name conjures up the figure of a tall, venerable looking and weather-beaten politician... making, in a nearly empty House, a very dull speech on a night of weary debates. But he had a great deal more political capacity than he always put into his speeches and when he left the House of Commons, there was a distinct loss.... In him, Mr Gladstone loses another of his political associates.[7]

---

[5] *Glasgow Herald* (Glasgow, Scotland), Monday, February 18, 1884; Issue 42

[6] *Freeman's Journal and Daily Commercial Advertiser* (Dublin, Ireland), Friday, August 8, 18 84; Issue N/A.

[7] *Liverpool Mercury etc* (Liverpool, England), Wednesday, January 15, 1890; Issue 13111

This venerable man is caricatured in a 'Spy' cartoon that appeared in Vanity Fair magazine in 1885 – one of a large series of caricatures of statesmen. The cartoon caption described him as '...a grave and learned person, not given to humour, oratory or other trifles'.[8] His empty sleeve is highlighted – but unfortunately on the wrong side.

The cartoon caption should not be allowed to detract from the enormously important role Sir Edward played in Scottish politics. It was written of him: 'Of the various members that Lanarkshire sent to Parliament in the course of the last [nineteenth] century, none enjoyed the confidence of the electors over such a long period as did Sir Edward Colebrooke, Bart.'[9]

Vanity Fair cartoon of Sir Edward by 'Spy', 1885. His empty sleeve is highlighted but on the wrong side.
Courtesy of Biggar Museum Trust

---

[8] Vanity Fair, 28.2.1885, Statesman No 460
[9] Scrapbook, Lanark Local History Library, 1906, Ref:1906, Undated article, p65

Sir Edward began to spend more time at his London home and continued to attend the fashionable functions of the aristocracy in London when his health permitted. In June 1887, he and Lady Colebrooke were among the many guests at a garden party given at Lambeth Palace by the Archbishop of Canterbury and his wife. Queen Victoria herself was the principal guest, staying about an hour with her entourage.[10]

Whilst preparing to stand down from parliament, Sir Edward was also editing and preparing for publication a monumental work: *The Rise of the British Power in the East* by the late Scottish statesman, Mountstuart Elphinstone (1779-1859)[11] – for whose memorial he had had a key planning role in 1860. The book was eventually published in 1887 at the price of twenty six shillings.[12] Coincidentally, another biography appeared at the same time, which could explain why advertisements for Sir Edward's book were so numerous over several years among the classified advertisements, both anticipating the publication and afterwards. The only criticism of Sir Edward's work was that, with 553 pages, it was a little long. Reviews were generally very positive though: '...it would be difficult to find a more trustworthy or satisfactory guide to one of the most eventful periods of Anglo-Indian history than Elphinstone's posthumous volume...'[13] '...so carefully revised, so admirably annotated, and so thoroughly indexed.[14]

---

[10] *The Morning Post* (London, England), Monday, June 27, 1887; pg. 3; Issue 35887. *19th Century British Library Newspapers: Part II.*

[11] Mountstuart Elphinstone was a noted administrator in India. He became Governor of Bombay, where he improved the accessibility of education to Indians.

[12] *The Pall Mall Gazette* (London, England), Friday, February 29, 1884; Issue 5923

[13] *The Pall Mall Gazette* (London, England), Thursday, March 17, 1887; Issue 6864.

[14] *Glasgow Herald* (Glasgow, Scotland), Wednesday, June 1, 1887; Issue 130.

Sir Edward also travelled to Scotland when he could and continued to deal with local Scottish affairs. He was, after all, still Lord Lieutenant of Lanarkshire and enjoyed good relations with almost everyone from the local gentry to his tenant farmers, who looked to him for support.

The authorities of Partick had applied through Sir Edward for their new public park to be called Victoria Park, a request the Queen had granted. The park was publicly opened on the afternoon of Saturday 25 June 1887 in commemoration of the Queen's Golden Jubilee.[15]

The Irish Question and the Liberal Unionist

It was, though, unquestionably his attitude towards Ireland, then part of the United Kingdom, that most coloured Sir Edward's twilight years. His interest in and stance towards the Irish Question separated him from Liberal colleagues, especially Gladstone, in a way that would have been unimaginable just a few years earlier.

Sir Edward made known his views on Ireland and Irish issues as early as 1868. At a time of growing religious freedom in Great Britain, he questioned, with all Liberals, the justification of imposing an Established Church on a predominantly Catholic country. He foresaw that if this were done, the repression would cause unrest and disturbances would follow. At that time, his view was that the Churches of England and Scotland were, in general, causes for good but the Church of Ireland, representing a wealthy minority, operated against the welfare of the majority and should be disestablished.[16] His views changed somewhat over the following years.

---

[15] *Aberdeen Weekly Journal* (Aberdeen, Scotland), Thursday, May 19, 1887; Issue 10061.

[16] *Glasgow Herald* (Glasgow, Scotland), Saturday, October 10, 1868; Issue 8977

In 1885, the new parliament was hung. It was led by the Conservative Prime Minister, Lord Salisbury, but defeat came early - on the Queen's speech – and the Prime Minister resigned. The Liberals, under Gladstone, were in power again and in 1886, he proposed offering independence to Ireland, something that had been under consideration for some while and a move Sir Edward was very much against.

In December 1885 and no longer a Member of Parliament, Sir Edward had attended a meeting of the 'Mansion House committee', begun in 1881, for the defence of property in Ireland,[17] following which, he joined the Unionist Liberal Committee - a committee formed of Liberals from both Houses of Parliament, Chairmen of Liberal Associations and others. Its purpose was to maintain the legislative union. While the intention was not to split the Liberal party, such were the numbers who felt strongly on this issue that it was feared that there would be a large defection at an election. The intention of the committee, therefore, was to make the influence of Liberals opposed to the Irish proposals felt in time to avoid serious damage to the Liberal Party.

On 24 April 1886, Sir Edward wrote from his London home, to the Glasgow Junior Liberal Association:

> Sir,- In the extraordinary position in which the Liberal Party is placed by the proposed legislation of the Government, in regard to Ireland, I do not know where to turn for common action in public matters in our country. It is right I should say that I am thoroughly opposed to the measure before the country. Any attempt to sever the union of the kingdoms without taking security for the rights of the loyal minority in Ireland would, in my opinion, lead to

---

[17] *The Morning Post* (London, England), Saturday, December 19, 1885; pg. 3; Issue 35412. *19th Century British Library Newspapers: Part II.*

intolerable oppression, and the attempt to pass such a measure would be little less than a crime. I regard the intended securities as utterly illusory, and the measure itself as full of danger to the Empire.[18]

The Home Rule Bill was defeated in June, leading to Gladstone's resignation and a general election was called. So strong were Sir Edward's views against granting independence to Ireland that, having stood down from Parliament less than a year earlier, he was persuaded to stand as the Unionist candidate for North-East Lanarkshire.[19]

Lord Hartington, who was to become the leader of the new Liberal Unionists, visited Glasgow the same month and Sir Edward was one of those in the reception party when he arrived at the station.[20] He also chaired the meeting (as 'our old friend and former respected member') where Lord Hartington spoke at length condemning Gladstone's proposal on Ireland. He called on people, irrespective of their party to vote against it.[21] Lord Hartington's visit spearheaded similar meetings in the communities around Glasgow and a few days later, Sir Edward addressed a meeting in Airdrie, at which he spoke of his hopes that the Liberal Party would reunite once the issue had been resolved.[22] His view was, he said, that he felt the Home Rule Bill was conducive to separation. He added a personal note, saying that he had been planning to enjoy retirement but the issue was so serious that he could not stand by. He added though that it was painful to be now separated from so many old friends and from a leader (Gladstone) he

[18] *Glasgow Herald* (Glasgow, Scotland), Tuesday, April 27, 1886; Issue 100.
[19] *The Dundee Courier & Argus* (Dundee, Scotland), Thursday, June 24, 1886; Issue 10281. *19th Century British Library Newspapers: Part II.*
[20] *Glasgow Herald* (Glasgow, Scotland), Saturday, June 26, 1886; Issue 152.
[21] *Glasgow Herald* (Glasgow, Scotland), Saturday, June 26, 1886; Issue 152.
[22] *Glasgow Herald* (Glasgow, Scotland), Tuesday, June 29, 1886; Issue 154

had respected[23] but that many candidates were standing independently of their parties.

Gladstone was undaunted and went to the country with another General Election. When it came to voting, it transpired that the electors of Lanarkshire, in all three divisions, supported Gladstone's proposals. In the country at large, however, a Conservative government swept back to power, strengthened by their alliance with the Liberal Unionists.

Sir Edward's vote had been small (he lost by 279 votes[24]) but, despite his defeat, he continued to support the Unionists. At a meeting in Glasgow on 19 August, an Imperial Union Club was established, 'which would be open to all existing political parties who engage to maintain the integrity of the empire, the unity of the three kingdoms and the supremacy within the United Kingdom of the Imperial Parliament'.[25] A good number of distinguished men, including several MPs became members.[26]

After his defeat in July as Liberal Unionist candidate for North-East Lanarkshire, Sir Edward returned to London. He wrote from his London home, making his apologies for missing a Unionist meeting in Glasgow and thanking his supporters. He said too that he believed opinion was changing and that the Unionists would be proved right. In his absence, the meeting thanked Sir Edward for his patriotic and gallant conduct in coming forward.

---

[23] *Glasgow Herald* (Glasgow, Scotland), Saturday, July 3, 1886; Issue 158.

[24] *The Standard* (London, England), Thursday, July 08, 1886; Issue 19340. *19th Century British Library Newspapers: Part II*.

[25] *The Bristol Mercury and Daily Post* (Bristol, England), Friday, August 20, 1886; Issue 11940

[26] *The Bristol Mercury and Daily Post* (Bristol, England), Friday, August 20, 1886; Issue 11940

The meeting went on to discuss how some public mark of respect might be given to Sir Edward, not only for his important work in the prevailing national crisis but also for his long public service as Lord Lieutenant of the County and Member of Parliament. The unanimous view of the meeting was that Sir Edward should be asked to sit for his portrait, to be hung in the County Hall and a replica be made for presentation to Lady Colebrooke. The meeting appointed a committee to carry out the resolution and subscriptions limited to one guinea were invited.[27] The portrait was painted by Norman Macbeth, RSA and was presented to Lady Colebrooke in October 1886 at the meeting of the Commissioners of Supply in Lanark. It was subsequently transferred to the County Hall in Hamilton.[28] Sir Edward was prevented by illness from attending the presentation himself but sent a letter gratefully acknowledging the kindness of his friends and neighbours:

> More than fifty years have passed since I first came here a perfect stranger to you all. I have formed friendships that have lasted through life, and for a long time I have enjoyed the confidence of a great constituency. I have been permitted to take part not merely in the public affairs of the Empire, but in promoting as far as in my power, the local affairs of this great country…Though my active life is closed, I trust to be able to lend a helping hand as long as I am permitted to do so to anything that will advance the local and Imperial interests of this great country.'[29]

Irish Home Rule had dominated a turbulent political year: the Liberals had thrown out their leader's Bill in June and the Conservatives returned to power in July. Scottish Unionists began organising themselves. Sir Edward felt so strongly on the issue that retirement was put aside and by October, he was

---

[27] *Glasgow Herald* (Glasgow, Scotland), Thursday, July 15, 1886; Issue 168.
[28] In 2013, no trace could be found of this portrait
[29] Scrapbook, Lanark Local History Library, 1906, Ref:1906, p65

back in Glasgow to chair a meeting to form a West of Scotland Branch of the Liberal Association for the Maintenance of the Legislative Union between Great Britain and Ireland[30] and he was elected president. He went on to be elected president of similar associations elsewhere including the Liberal Unionists of the Central Division of Glasgow.

Concern was expressed that not only home rule for Ireland but also home rule for Scotland was being discussed, and serious efforts were being made to spread the home rule movement to Scotland.[31] Sir Edward was dismayed both at the disintegration of the Liberal Party to which he had dedicated himself for so long and at the prospect of home rule for both Ireland and Scotland. The *Glasgow Herald* described a meeting where he shared his views:

> At a meeting of Liberal Unionists for West Scotland last night, Sir Edward Colebrooke, who presided, said he was most anxious to see the reunion of the Liberal Party, but in the utterances of Mr Gladstone and his lieutenants he could find no approach to a principle on which they were likely to come to an agreement. On the contrary, there was a studious endeavour to extend the Home Rule movement, and in view of questions which might emerge, he urged the importance of the maintenance of their organisation.[32]

and the *Aberdeen Weekly Journal* quoted:

> It would be a sad day for Scotland if it took the advice of Mr Gladstone in his letter to a Glasgow gentleman that it

---

[30] *The Hampshire Advertiser* (Southampton, England), Saturday, October 23, 1886; pg. 3; Issue 4211. *19th Century British Library Newspapers: Part II*.

[31] *Aberdeen Weekly Journal* (Aberdeen, Scotland), Thursday, October 21, 1886; Issue 9889.

[32] *Glasgow Herald* (Glasgow, Scotland), Thursday, October 21, 1886; Issue 252.

should consider whether it should not have Home Rule for itself.[33]

It must have seemed to Sir Edward that everything for which he had worked so hard was beginning to disintegrate. He found it...

> ...no easy matter ...to oppose those with whom he had hitherto acted but the crisis was so unprecedented that he felt compelled to use every exertion within his power to avert the dangers that menaced the Empire from the Irish policy of Mr Gladstone.[34]

Many thought that Unionism would die out before long[35] but meetings continued. Sir Edward, sometimes through ill-health, was obliged to miss some meetings and was one of those sending his apologies when the radical Joseph Chamberlain[36] addressed a meeting of Liberal Unionists in Edinburgh in April 1887.[37]

At the end of July 1887, a huge gathering of 12,000 -14,000, met to hear Sir George Trevelyan[38] put the counter argument to Chamberlain and Liberal Unionists. Sir Edward was effectively

---

[33] *Aberdeen Weekly Journal* (Aberdeen, Scotland), Thursday, October 21, 1886; Issue 9889.

[34] Scrapbook, Lanark Local History Library, 1906, Ref:1906, p65

[35] *Glasgow Herald* (Glasgow, Scotland), Tuesday, December 21, 1886; Issue 304.

[36] Joseph Chamberlain, unusually for politicians of the time, was a self-man businessman, having not attended university. He made his career in Birmingham, entering Parliament as a radical Liberal at the age of forty and rising to prominence quickly. He resigned from Gladstone's third government in opposition to Irish home rule.

[37] *Birmingham Daily Post* (Birmingham, England), Saturday, April 16, 1887; Issue 8986.

[38] Sir George Trevelyan was a Liberal politician who broke with Gladstone over the 1886 Irish Home Rule Bill. He re-joined the party after amendments were made to the bill.

described as a Conservative at this meeting in Trevelyan's comment: 'I hope Sir Edward Colebrooke, the Lord Lieutenant of Lanarkshire, will be a good Whig again'. The beginnings of a movement to sever links between the Liberals and the Unionists was clear, the Liberals expressing strong views (referring to Catholics in Ireland and Nonconformists in Wales) that too many people were not properly represented as they were not members of the established church.[39]

Poor health

Sir Edward suffered increasingly from poor health. In January 1888, Lady Colebrooke wrote to Rawnsley:

> Sir Edward has been so ill for 5 weeks now, with a <u>very</u> bad attack of eczema that I have hardly had time to answer anything but business Letters (a good many, as I had <u>his</u> as well as my own business to transact!) ... I am thankful to say Sir E is better now, <u>one</u> of his nurses is going to depart, and I trust next week, if it keeps as mild as at present, he may get out.[40]

In August 1888, plans were well advanced for Queen Victoria's second visit to Glasgow, thirty nine years after her first visit.[41] She was to inaugurate the New Municipal Buildings and pay a state visit to the International Exhibition of Science, Art and Industry in the city. Amongst other dignitaries, she was to be presented to Sir Edward as Lord Lieutenant of Lanarkshire when she arrived at St Enoch's Station.[42] Disappointment will have been bitter, though: Sir Edward, who, as described by

---

[39] *Reynolds's Newspaper* (London, England), Sunday, July 31, 1887; Issue 1929.

[40] *The Colebrooke Letters*, 7.1.1888

[41] *The Standard* (London, England), Thursday, August 23, 1888; pg. 3; Issue 20006. *19th Century British Library Newspapers: Part II*

[42] *Glasgow Herald* (Glasgow, Scotland), Saturday, August 4, 1888; Issue 186

Lady Colebrooke, was making a slow recovery from illness, was not well enough to keep this important appointment and one of the Vice Lieutenants of the county had to stand in for him.[43]

In November 1888, as Lord Lieutenant, Sir Edward was able to recommend for appointment about forty new Justices of the Peace for Lanarkshire,[44] although there is no report of him being at any public function to mark these appointments. From this time on, the press reported many functions that Sir Edward missed due to ill health: the General Meeting of the Glasgow Trades House in October 1888;[45] a meeting in connection with the Glasgow and West of Scotland Branch of the Imperial Federation League, addressed by Lord Brassey (one of the men nominated for a peerage at the same time as Sir Edward);[46] a meeting in Aberdeen on the occasion of a visit by the Chancellor of the Exchequer, whose address was billed as an important speech on the political situation,[47] and a meeting under the auspices of the Scottish National Liberal Unionist Association in St Andrew's Hall, Glasgow, for an address by Joseph Chamberlain. (This last meeting would have been of particular importance to Sir Edward so he must indeed have been very unwell to have missed it.)

The fourth annual prize meeting of the Scottish Rifle Association took place at Darnley Ranges near Glasgow in June 1889. Amongst other trophies competed for as the

---

[43] *Glasgow Herald* (Glasgow, Scotland), Tuesday, August 14, 1888; Issue 194

[44] *Glasgow Herald* (Glasgow, Scotland), Thursday, November 1, 1888; Issue 262.

[45] *Glasgow Herald* (Glasgow, Scotland), Thursday, October 11, 1888; Issue 244

[46] *Glasgow Herald* (Glasgow, Scotland), Thursday, October 25, 1888; Issue 256.

[47] *Glasgow Herald* (Glasgow, Scotland), Wednesday, October 31, 1888; Issue 261.

'regular competition' was Sir Edward's challenge vase but there was no suggestion that he was present for the presentation to the second team of the 3rd Lanark Volunteers.[48] At around the same time, Sir Edward was reported to have subscribed £10 to the initial expenses of the Clyde Brigade Encampment at Irvine,[49] but, again, there is no hint that he was present.

Commitment to Unionism

Unionist support remained strong and Sir Edward's name was revered. In June 1889, there was a joint meeting of the Conservative and Liberal Unionist Associations of North East Lanarkshire for an address by William Whitelaw[50], during which Whitelaw said:

> This country had seen many men growing old in the service of the State. They had seen many men wearied with the fatigues of the Ministry, but there was no more highly prized or more greatly trusted service than that of the late candidate for the Division - Sir Edward Colebrooke - (cheers) who spent no less than 43 years of his life in the service of his country, gave 28 of these years not to North-East Lanarkshire but to a Division three times as large, of which North-East Lanarkshire formed a component part. Surely then he might have had great hesitation in accepting such a position as that which he now occupied. But there were many encouragements to a Unionist candidate. He believed that the ranks of Unionism were far from remaining

---

[48] *Glasgow Herald* (Glasgow, Scotland), Wednesday, June 12, 1889; Issue 140
[49] *Glasgow Herald* (Glasgow, Scotland), Thursday, June 20, 1889; Issue 147
[50] William Whitelaw was a Scottish Unionist politician who was elected Member of Parliament for Perth in 1892.

at the point at which they stood at the last election. They were very rapidly on the increase...[51]

At the beginning of December 1889, Sir Edward's health allowed him to leave home in London to chair a meeting of the West of Scotland Imperial Union Club, where they were to host as principal guest Mr A J Balfour, Chief Secretary for Ireland. Sir Edward, over cake and wine, proposed the health of Mr Balfour before the committees entertained him to lunch.[52] Sir Edward was cheered and everyone was pleased his health allowed him to be present that day and to see that he had lost none of the old fire within him.[53] He spoke of evils of long standing in Ireland and claimed that, since the Unionists had been formed four years previously and since the current [Conservative] Unionist government had been in office, much good had been done in Ireland.

Marriage of the Colebrooke heir

By this time, Sir Edward's son and heir, Edward Arthur, had married Alexandra Harriet, 7th daughter of the late General the Hon. Alfred Henry Paget MP and his wife Cecilia and a goddaughter of the Princess of Wales. The wedding took place at St Peter's Church, Vere Street, Marylebone on 7 June 1889 and the guests included royalty and members of the very highest levels of the aristocracy.

It seems to have been an oddly-timed wedding and quite possibly brought forward because of Sir Edward's ill health and

---

[51] *Glasgow Herald* (Glasgow, Scotland), Thursday, June 20, 1889; Issue 147.

[52] *Glasgow Herald* (Glasgow, Scotland), Saturday, November 30, 1889; Issue 287.

[53] *Glasgow Herald* (Glasgow, Scotland), Wednesday, December 4, 1889; Issue 290

fears for his future. It was certainly a 'fashionable' wedding but, as the bride's family were in deep mourning for her father, no invitations were issued and no reception was held.[54] Only the families of the bride and bridegroom gathered at Lady Paget's London residence in Queen Anne Street for a wedding breakfast, after which the newly married couple went no farther than Bushey Park for their honeymoon.[55]

[54] *Glasgow Herald* (Glasgow, Scotland), Tuesday, June 18, 1889; Issue 145
[55] *The Standard* (London, England), Tuesday, June 18, 1889; pg. 5; Issue 20262. *19th Century British Library Newspapers: Part II.*

Chapter 11

Epilogue

Sir Edward Colebrooke died on 11 January 1890 at his London home. He was 76.

He had been in Scotland only a month previously and was reported to have been in good health until early January, '... when bronchitis supervened and that combined with asthma brought his life somewhat suddenly to a termination on Saturday morning.[1] His family were all with him, except for Edward Arthur, his heir, who was in Monte Carlo. Ned's doctor refused to let him travel because he had influenza.

Sir Edward was buried in the churchyard of his church in Ottershaw:

> The remains of Sir Edward Colebrooke, Bart., were interred yesterday with the strictest privacy at Ottershaw, Woking, Surrey. The cortege left the deceased baronet's residence, 14 South Street, Park Lane, W., at 12 o'clock, only the near relations of the family in London and a few friends accompanying the remains. Amongst those present were Lady Colebrooke and three daughters, Mr Roland Colebrooke, Lord Hamilton, Mr Hozier, M.P., Captain

---

[1] *Aberdeen Weekly Journal* (Aberdeen, Scotland), Tuesday, January 14, 1890; Issue 10902.

Paget, Mr George Paget, Sir Henry Le Marchant, Mr
Francis Le Marchant, and Mr Mackenzie of Dolphinton,
Commissioner of the Scotch estates. Sir Edward Arthur
Colebrooke who has succeeded to the baronetcy was
strictly forbidden by his doctor at Monte Carlo to travel
to London for the funeral.[2]

There were numerous obituaries in both London and provincial papers, some simply a statement of his death but many,
including provincial English newspapers, generous in their
praise and compassion for a popular man:

> Sir Edward Colebrooke was well known and greatly liked
> both in the House of Commons and in society. His venerable
> figure was constantly to be seen, mounted on a very neat
> back, in Rotten Row, and both at their London house and
> at their Scotch seat – Abington – Sir Edward and Lady
> Colebrooke maintained a wide and genial hospitality.
> Sir Edward Colebrooke was a very wealthy man, owning
> considerable house property in London besides his Scotch
> estates. In politics he was a life-long Whig, and of late years
> had been a sturdy Unionist.[3]

and

> [He]…sat in the House of Commons as a Liberal for
> 38 years, …but he never made any show in public life, as he
> rarely spoke, but was content to steadily support his party
> leaders. He greatly liked and admired Mr Gladstone and it
> was only under great pressure that he joined the Unionists

[2] *Glasgow Herald* (Glasgow, Scotland), Thursday, January 16, 1890;
Issue 14, Births, Deaths, Marriages and Obituaries.
[3] *The Yorkshire Herald, and The York Herald* (York, England), Thursday,
January 16, 1890; Issue 12051. *19th Century British Library Newspapers:
Part II.*

in 1886 as, after resigning his seat ... in 1885, he had strenuously exerted himself to procure the election of the Liberal candidate. Sir Edward Colebrooke was an excellent landlord and he was very popular among all classes in Lanarkshire. He took an active part in county business for nearly half a century. His health had been failing for the last two years.[4]

and, under a heading "Partick"

The Provost further referred to the recent death of Sir Edward Colebrooke who, prior to the Redistribution of Seats Bill had represented the district of Lanarkshire in which the burgh of Partick was situated. Sir Edward had devoted a great deal of his time and attention to the

Lady Elizabeth Colebrooke
Courtesy of Christ Church, Ottershaw

---

[4] *Hampshire Telegraph and Sussex Chronicle etc* (Portsmouth, England), Saturday, January 25, 1890; Issue 5667.

interests of the burghs, and in their numerous conflicts with Glasgow had been their staunch friend having rendered valuable assistance in maintaining their independence. It was unanimously agreed to record a sense of the loss sustained by Sir Edward's death, and to communicate to the Dowager Lady Colebrooke an expression of respectful sympathy with her and her family in their sad bereavement.[5]

Lady Colebrooke survived her husband by six years and lived her final years in London, the Colebrooke seat of Abington having passed to Edward Arthur, 5th baronet Colebrooke on the death of Sir Edward. She died on 26 October 1896.

The question of a final resting place for Sir Edward and Lady Colebrooke presented a challenge. In general, the aristocracy were buried at the family seat. However, although he had given so much of himself to Lanarkshire, Sir Edward was not a Scot and Abington, was not 'home'. He had had no connection with his predecessors' seat in Chilham, so burial in the family vault there would have had no meaning. Towards the ends of their lives, London had become home. However, London churchyards were so full that those who died in London were increasingly transported on special trains for burial at the London necropolis at Brookwood in Surrey. The anonymity of this vast cemetery would have been unattractive to the Colebrookes while their own pretty little church in Ottershaw, with its own churchyard, provided by Sir Edward, offered an attractive final resting place at their much loved third home.

It is likely they negotiated their burial place when they sold the Ottershaw Park estate, so that, at the end of their busy and well-connected lives, they could be laid to rest in the peace of

---

[5] *Glasgow Herald* (Glasgow, Scotland), Saturday, February 1, 1890; Issue 28

The Colebrooke grave at Christ
Church, Ottershaw

the churchyard of their memorial church. Their grave is near
the front of the churchyard and is marked by a simple cross.
Their names, without titles or rank, are in small letters at the
base with a simple epitaph. It is no more ostentatious than
the other graves in the churchyard: in death as in life, they
were quiet about their deeds.

The dedications on the Colebrooke grave read:

Thomas Edward Colebrooke
Born 19th August 1813
Died 11th January 1890
"Blessed are the pure in heart for they shall see God"

Elizabeth Margaret Colebrooke
Born June 14th 1823
Died October 26th 1896
"For so he giveth his beloved sleep"

The windows in the nave of the Church are a splendid memorial to Sir Edward and Lady Colebrooke but these were installed by their children. They chose the very best to honour their parents by going to the studio of Charles Eamer Kempe - a proud memorial to a great man and his wife. The inscription (translated from the Latin) at the base of each window reads:

> Remember before God Thomas Edward Colebrooke
> 4th Baronet Founder of this Church and
> Elizabeth Margaret his wife AD
> 1900. Loved children to loved parents

The images in each window were carefully chosen and each is crowned by the Colebrooke crest, with the insertion of an open-palm hand to indicate the baronetcy.

The crest of the Colebrooke baronetcy, crowning each of the Colebrooke windows at Christ Church, Ottershaw

The church tower was built in 1885. With its bells, it was paid for by William Edward Gibb, who had bought Sheerwater Court in 1873.[6] The Gibbs were good friends of the Colebrookes, being mentioned in *The Colebrooke Letters*. The tower and bells were, though, a memorial not to the Colebrookes but to Gibb's father and in thanksgiving for his children.[7]

In reviewing Sir Edward Colebrooke's life, it is immediately apparent that it was very full and very busy. Any of his four lives could have been a full life for a wealthy, aristocratic land-owner. With his family, he lived in three different places and in each of those places he contributed more than most people do in one. In general, the Colebrooke year was neatly divided, with the same time of year being spent in the same place. So, when Parliament was in session, the family were, for the most part, in London, the census returns of 1861 and 1871 revealing that the family was living in Mayfair at those times. Clearly, however, the census records provide only a partial picture of the Colebrooke lives. When the Colebrooke children were young, the family was more often in Ottershaw, to benefit from the healthier air and environment. Even then though, Parliamentary duties often kept Sir Edward in London, while Lady Colebrooke and the children remained in Ottershaw. Lady Colebrooke's frequent absence from society events bears testimony to this arrangement.

Sir Edward was a personal friend of William Gladstone and a respected politician in Scotland – perhaps remarkable for an Englishman. He was also a good and respected landlord, and was undoubtedly much liked on his Lanarkshire lands.

---

[6] www.heritagewalks.org (accessed 2.7.2012)

[7] Brush, Pamela, *Christ Church Ottershaw: History and Guide*, original compiled by D C S David, 1989, revised and updated by Pamela J Brush, Ottershaw, 2004, p9

He built much of the modern village of Abington,[8] which stands as '...a memorial to this ...kind landlord who did all he could to improve the lot of his tenants'.[9] He established a school in the village of Abington many years before the passing of the Scottish Education Act in 1872[10] '...in the welfare of which he always maintained the greatest interest'.[11] He was personally involved in running his estates, adopting new techniques and improving methods used. Thomas Reid, writing in 1928 said: 'His memory is still ...revered in the Upper Ward as a firm friend, a considerate landlord, a wise and foreseeing politician.[12] For the most part, Sir Edward juggled his four lives with great skill, fulfilling his expected roles with competence, instilling confidence in his associates and colleagues in Lanark, London and Surrey and spending time with his family. Just occasionally, the demands on his time meant he was unable to satisfy everyone.

It is clear that there were three strong influences that dictated how Sir Edward Colebrooke lived his life. The first was his father; the second was the unexpectedness of his inheritance and the third was his efforts, almost desperate at times, to ensure that he left an heir to the baronetcy.

His father's scholarship and selflessness impressed itself upon Sir Edward at a young age and remained a potent influence on his interests and activities throughout his life. Initially, it looked as if he would follow in his father's footsteps in the

---

[8] Haddow, George, *Pictorial Guide to Upper Clydesdale*, Norman Hunter, Port Glasgow, 1907, p34

[9] Scrapbook, Lanark Local History Library, 1906, Ref:1906, p65

[10] Reid, Thomas, *A History of the Parish of Crawfordjohn, Upper Ward of Lanarkshire, 1153-1928*, Turnbull & Spears, Edinburgh, 1928, p97

[11] Haddow, George, *Pictorial Guide to Upper Clydesdale*, Norman Hunter, Port Glasgow, 1907, p38

[12] Reid, Thomas, *A History of the Parish of Crawfordjohn, Upper Ward of Lanarkshire, 1153-1928*, Turnbull & Spears, Edinburgh, 1928, p94

Indian Civil Service. As it turned out, he actually stayed in India only a few years and never returned, but his experiences, added to his father's example, became a powerful driver. It led him to painstakingly collate his father's papers, add a remarkably selfless commentary and publish the work in 1872, knowing it was unlikely ever to have more than a small readership. He joined the Royal Asiatic Society, founded by his father, and was a life-long member (his obituary in the Society's journal recorded that he had been a member for 54 years[13]), becoming a Vice President at an early age and President 1864-6, 1875-7 and 1881.[14] He frequently contributed to debates in Parliament on Indian affairs and offered views altogether more liberal than his contemporaries. He knew Hindi and he involved himself with other organisations and with people connected with India. Finally, in his private entertaining, he hosted parties and dinners where large numbers of 'Asiatics' were invited. He gained a reputation for knowing and understanding India and was called on to give advice. His father's habit of scholarship translated itself into tireless dedication to the places and causes that were important to him and, whilst never seeing himself as a scholar, he was known as a scholarly politician.

Sir Edward's title and wealth had come to him unexpectedly. He was not brought up to be an aristocrat or to inherit wealth or to lead the kind of life that came with a title, lands and money. He had to learn very fast about behaviour in society and about managing the large number of people, such as tenant farmers, who depended on him. He never forgot his gift of fortune and it led naturally to him having liberal views and a benevolent attitude. It also gave him the belief that his life should be dedicated to work and a constant effort to improve

---

[13] *Journal of the Royal Asiatic Society*, London, 1890, p498
[14] Wrotham Park archive

the lot of those who had been less fortunate than himself. Such a character, at his time, made him a natural Liberal politician and it was surely this that led him to decide to try to make a difference in Scotland, where his inherited lands were located and where Liberalism was strong.

Having inherited the Colebrooke baronetcy so unexpectedly, Sir Edward felt it part of his duty to ensure that, when his time was over, it passed satisfactorily to the next generation. There were, moreover, no nephews-in-waiting so it was imperative that his elder son was trained for the role. He saw this as a very weighty duty and was devastated when he lost his first son and heir. He was blessed with a second son (and indeed a third) but was faced with constant challenges in raising his heir. Both Edward Arthur and Roland suffered from poor health and there were several occasions when both of them might have died. Their delicate health led to the family winters in the south of France, desperate hurried trips to the boys' schools and the family having to live apart while the health of one or other of the boys demanded action over and above parliamentary, constituency and estate business – and indeed over anything else. It will have saddened Sir Edward and Lady Colebrooke, furthermore, that neither of their sons was particularly bright. The *Colebrooke Letters* make it clear that strenuous efforts were made on numerous occasions to try to ensure that Ned's studies kept abreast of expectations. Latin and Greek were then considered particularly important for a young man in Ned's position and they were subjects that Ned seemed to find particularly difficult. It will not have cheered Sir Edward to realise, as was very plain, that his daughters were considerably more talented academically than his heir.

Sir Edward and Lady Colebrooke's tremendous efforts with Ned were, initially at least, and in their lifetimes, successful since they lived to see their heir well married.

Sir Edward was a respected politician in Scotland where his principal political concerns related to the extension of the franchise and the improvement of education.

He supported the volunteer movement all his life and would have been pleased and proud to know of the continuing prowess of local men in Lanarkshire: the Sir Edward Colebrooke Challenge Vase, which was open to volunteer battalions throughout Great Britain, was won, just five months after his death, by a team of twelve men of the 3rd Lanark for the third time in succession. Under the rules of the competition, the 3rd Lanark were able to keep the cup as their property.[15]

In his benevolence, he was not unusual among wealthy people in the nineteenth century but he was exceptional in working so determinedly and for so long to improve life for his fellow men.

In some areas, such as the extension of the franchise, Sir Edward was forward-looking and even radical. In other spheres, he was more reactionary and a champion of the landed classes which he had joined so unexpectedly at the time of his inheritance. This led to moves to protect landed interests and his adoption of the Unionist mantle in an attempt to protect the landed minority in Ireland.

Ginevra, Helen and Roland led lives that were essentially middle class and much more 'ordinary' than the lives of their aristocratic parents. Edward Arthur, on inheriting the baronetcy and Mary, through marriage, led aristocratic lives.

Ginevra, the eldest of the Colebrooke children, married very shortly after her father's death, two days before her thirty third

---

[15] *The Dundee Courier & Argus* (Dundee, Scotland), Wednesday, June 11, 1890; Issue 11522. *19th Century British Library Newspapers: Part II.*

birthday, on 17 November 1890,[16] at the Church of the Assumption, Warwick Street, London. She married the Marchese Di Camugliano-Nichollini. It may be that she deliberately delayed her wedding so as not to leave her father in his final months as her marriage was to take her to Italy, the country to which her parents introduced her in her teens. However, the Marchese was a Catholic and the wedding took place in a Catholic church. Sir Edward distrusted Catholics (Lady Colebrooke had noted in 1875: '...Sir E does not like Catholics permanently in the House...'[17]) so it may be that she delayed the marriage so as not to incur her father's disapproval. The wedding was a very small affair. 'Owing to the illness of the Dowager Lady Colebrooke, the marriage was private, and only the nearest relations and the Italian Ambassador and members of the Embassy were present.'[18] The fact that Lady Colebrooke did not attend the marriage – despite poor health being given as the reason — adds weight to this possibility. Ginevra and her husband made their home in Florence at 16 Via del Fossi. The Marchese died on 30th January 1912 but no record has been found of her own death. They had no children.

On 17 December 1894, at St James Church, Piccadilly, Mary married Edmund Henry Byng,[19] Viscount Enfield, who became 6th Earl of Strafford on the death of his father, the 5th Earl. There are several references to the association of the Colebrookes and the Byng family from early in Sir Edward's career so Mary almost certainly met her future husband through family friendship. It was a quiet marriage, because her mother, the dowager Lady Colebrooke, was seriously ill at

[16] *The Morning Post* (London, England), Tuesday, October 21, 1890; pg. 5; Issue 36926. *19th Century British Library Newspapers: Part II*
[17] The Colebrooke Letters, 20.4.1875
[18] *The Morning Post* (London, England), Tuesday, November 18, 1890; Issue 36950. *19th Century British Library Newspapers: Part II.*
[19] *The Bristol Mercury and Post*, 18 December 1894, Issue 14541

the time. Mary's home after marriage was Wrotham Park in Hertfordshire and her husband played a key role as one of trustees of the Colebrooke estate in the unravelling of the Colebrooke fortunes after the bankruptcy of her brother, Lord Colebrooke. A number of Colebrooke family portraits were purchased by the 6th Earl of Strafford from his brother-in-law, and still hang at Wrotham Park.[20] They had two children. Mary died on 2 October 1951 and her husband died on 24 December following.[21]

Helen and Roland Colebrooke did not marry. Helen tried to make a career as an author and playwright, achieving some minor success with 'Winged Dreams' in 1909, and 'Fetters of the Past'. She also published an article entitled 'Poor Dick' for volume 45 of The Pall Mall Magazine in 1910 but had numerous other attempts turned down. The Wrotham Park archive holds several manuscripts for books and plays as well as letters from publishers and literary agents. She seems to have spent time on the south coast with references to Folkestone and Brighton in the Wrotham Park archive. However, she purchased and refurbished 35 Bruton Street, London in 1911.[22] She died on 21 January 1916. Roland was a socialite in Britain and America. He wrote a piece for the piano entitled 'The Wheel of Fortune' and died at the early age of 46 on 19 January 1910.[23]

On Sir Edward's death in 1890, Edward Arthur succeeded his father as 5th Baronet Colebrooke, with his seat of Abington House and the titles Hereditary Keeper of the Castle of Crawford and Lord of the Manor of Stepney. His assumption

---

[20] http://www.londonopenhouse.org/london/search/factsheet.asp?ftloh_id=8518, accessed 6.10.2013
[21] http://freepages.family.rootsweb.ancestry.com/~londonaye/colebrooke_family.htm
[22] Wrotham Park archive
[23] Unattributed obituary, pasted into the back of *The Colebrooke letters*

of his father's title had an inauspicious start as he was in Monte Carlo at the time, a circumstance which gave a foretaste of predilections that were to be his undoing only a few years later. He missed his father's funeral and the family will have been painfully reminded of Edward Arthur's earlier health problems and must have wondered how his health would continue to affect the fifth Baronet Colebrooke.

Abington House burned down in October 1898[24] and despite plans, it was never rebuilt. The Colebrookes moved to the smaller Glengonnar House nearby, on a temporary basis that became permanent.

Fire at Abington House (picture postcard of a painting, artist unknown)
Courtesy of Biggar Museum Trust

---

[24] Reid, Thomas, *A History of the Parish of Crawfordjohn, Upper Ward of Lanarkshire, 1153-1928*, Turnbull & Spears, Edinburgh, 1928, p94

Sir Edward Arthur's London home for a while was 19 Green Street, Park Lane, then the imposing Stratford House, Stratford Place[25] and later 5 St James's Square, London. He was created Baron Colebrooke of Stebunheath in 1906 and was lord-in-waiting to King Edward VII (1906-10), to King George V (1910-11) and permanent lord-in-waiting to King George V, 1924-36. He was appointed Master of the Robes to King Edward VIII and was Private Secretary to the Lord Lieutenant of Ireland. He was also Lord High Commissioner to the Church of Scotland (1906-7), made a Privy Counsellor in 1914 and created Knight Commander of the Royal Victorian Order in 1922 and Knight Grand Cross of the Royal Victorian Order (GCVO) in 1927. He was a Justice of the Peace and a Deputy-Lieutenant for Lanarkshire.[26]

At Glengonnar House, Lord Colebrooke entertained the Prince of Wales (later King George V) for a week in 1904. In 1906, King Edward VII made a five day private visit, for which local people made an enthusiastic public welcome with flags, bunting and other decorations.[27] According to a local source, it was the visit of the king that led to the financial ruin of Lord Colebrooke[28] although his own obituary spoke simply of unwise speculations.

Lord Colebrooke was declared bankrupt and the Abington estate passed to trustees, including his brother-in-law, Edmund Henry Byng (Lord Strafford), in 1907. The contents of Stratford House in London were auctioned in a spectacular

[25] Wrotham Park archive

[26] Newspaper cutting, unidentified newspaper, February 1939, Scrapbook, Lanark Local History Library, p012

[27] Reid, Thomas, *A History of the Parish of Crawfordjohn, Upper Ward of Lanarkshire, 1153-1928*, Turnbull & Spears, Edinburgh, 1928, p98

[28] Author in conversation with founder of the Biggar Museum Trust, March 2012

four-day sale in December 1908.[29] The Scottish estate was broken into lots and sold off from 1910. Glengonnar House and Gilkerscleugh House – a hunting lodge on the Colebrooke estate – were sold at auction in Edinburgh in 1911.[30] Just how much of his heritage Lord Colebrooke squandered his hinted at in a letter written from Abington by his wife, Alexandra, to her sister-in-law, Molly (Mary Colebrooke):

Dearest Molly
… Would you ask Edmund [Byng] if he would be kind enough to communicate with….at Kensington Palace. He says he knows of someone who would buy my pearls he thinks. It will be no harm trying. He wants to know where he can see them. I am so glad to think you will have the Hogarth.[31] It seemed sad to think of it going out of the family.
Yours affectionately
Alex[32]

A substantial part of the Colebrooke book collection from Abington was put up for sale in Edinburgh by the trustees as late as June 1923.[33]

Lord and Lady Colebrooke had a son and two daughters. Their son died in a motorcycle accident in 1921 so with Lord Colebrooke's death in 1939, both the baronetcy and the barony became extinct.[34]

Sir Edward Colebrooke had been prudent and careful in the stewardship of his inheritance. His heir was very different and

---

[29] Wrotham Park archive
[30] Sale particulars, Wrotham Park archive
[31] A painting
[32] Letter, Wrotham Park archive, dated 7 November but no year.
[33] Wrotham Park archive
[34] Pine, L G, *The New Extinct Peerage 1884-1971*, London, 1972, p81

it would have pained Sir Edward to know how quickly the Colebrooke fortunes were dissipated after his death. Edward Arthur seems to have been obsessed with social status – with which he was spectacularly successful - and with ostentation, for which even the very considerable Colebrooke wealth was insufficient to sustain his ambitious lifestyle.

The destruction of Abington House meant the loss of many family artefacts, presumably including family portraits for which records exist in the National Portrait Gallery but for most of which no trace has been found. The fire and the earlier sale of Ottershaw Park erased much of the evidence of Sir Edward Colebrooke's life and his heir's imprudence lost most of what remained. None the less, digitisation and the internet as well as the chance finding of *The Colebrooke Letters* have enabled the piecing together of the jigsaw that is this book in a way that would have been unimaginable to Sir Edward. They have also allowed a detailed appreciation of this essentially ordinary man, who in his hardworking quiet extraordinariness still offers an example of service that will not become dated with time.

Appendix

Works by Sir Edward Colebrooke

Edited **Essays** by Henry Thomas Colebrooke, 2 volumes, published 1837

Two Visits to the Crimea in the autumns of 1854 and 1855, published 1856

The life of Henry Thomas Colebrooke, published 1873

Life of the Honourable Mountstuart Elphinstone, Governor of Bombay, 3 volumes, published 1884

Small Holdings, date of publication unknown

The Creeds of India: An Historical Sketch a Lecture Delivered to the Uddingston Young Men's Mutual Improvement Association, October 9th 1979, privately printed in Scotland

Papers Respecting the Succession by Adoption of Sovereign Princes in India

Journal of the Royal Asiatic Society, numerous contributions including:

On Imperial and Other Titles, IX, p314
On the Proper Names of Muhammadans, XI, p171
Memoir of Mountstuart Elphinstone, XXVIII, p221

Edited works of **Hon. Mountstuart Elphinstone,** *The Rise of the British Power in the East*, published 1887

(Several of these have been digitised)

Bibliography

Athersuch, J, *An Illustrated History of Ottershaw Park Estate, 1761-2011*, Peacock Press, Hebdon Bridge, 2010

Barker, DM and JL, *A Chertsey Camera*, Addlestone, 1992

Brown, C, 'How religious was Victorian England' in *Did Urbanisation Secularize Britain?* Urban History Yearbook, 1988

Brush, PJ, *Christ Church Ottershaw: History and Guide*, original compiled by D C S David, 1989, revised and updated by Pamela J Brush, Ottershaw, 2004

Burke, *Sir B, A Genealogical and Heraldic Dictionary of the Peerage and Baronetage*, London, 1878

Cole, D, *The Work of Sir Gilbert Scott*, London, 1980

Colebrooke, TE, *The Life of Henry Thomas Colebrooke*, Trübner, London, 1873

Haddow, G, *Pictorial Guide to Upper Clydesdale*, Norman Hunter, Port Glasgow, 1907

Hamilton Herald, *Lanarkshire Illustrated*, 1903

Heald, H, (ed), *Chronicle of Britain and Ireland*, Chronicle Communications Ltd, Farnborough, 1992

Irving, GV and Murray, A, *The Upper Ward of Lanarkshire*, Vol 1, 1864, Thomas Murray & Son, Edinburgh

Journal of the Royal Asiatic Society, London, January 1890

Mair, R H (ed), *Debrett's Peerage, Baronetage, Knighthood and Companionage*, London, 1884

Murray-Fennell, M, 'Focus on a 19th century innovator', *Country Life*, 23 June 2010

Pevsner, N and Nairn, I, *The Buildings of England, Surrey*, Penguin, 1962

Pine, LG, *The New Extinct Peerage, 1884-1971*, London, 1972

Reid, T, *A History of the Parish of Crawfordjohn, Upper Ward of Lanarkshire, 1153-1928*, Turnbull & Spears, Edinburgh, 1928

Scott, Sir G G, *Personal and Professional Recollections*, originally published 1879, new edition, ed. Stamp, G, 1995

Stratton, HJM, *Ottershaw Through the Ages*, HJM Stratton, 1990

Survey of London, Vol 39, *The Grosvenor Estate in London*, Part 1 General History, Part II The Buildings, The Athlone Press, University of London for the GLC, 1977

Sutherland, M, *Sola Bona Quae Honesta: The Colebrooke Family 1650-1950*, Sawd Books, 1998

The London Gazette, 7.2.1865

The Pall Mall Gazette (London, England), Saturday, January 25, 1868; Issue 923

The Times, Monday 23 May 1864, issue 24879, p6, col D

The Victorian, March 2011, No 36

Upper Ward Almanac and Handbook, 1860, R Wood, Lanark

Yeates, P, *The Cree Nurserymen of Lanarkshire and Surrey*, Cree Family History Society, 1992

Documents

Biggar Museum Trust
　　Several pictures and maps

Chertsey Museum
　　Ottershaw Park sale details 1859, Chertsey Museum,
　　CHYMS.0135.3

Christ Church Ottershaw
　　The Christ Church Ottershaw Minute Book, 1866-1963
　　Map of the chapelry, 1865

Lanark Local History Library
　　Scrapbook, Lanark Local History Library, 1906
　　Scrapbook, Lanark Local History Library, 1939

Lane, Hannah
　　Stratton, M, Collected notes, fragment
　　Several maps

National Archive, Kew
　　School Building Application for Ottershaw National
　　School, ED/103/110/43, School No 15498, p807
　　Colebrooke, T E, Letter from Balaklava, 1854, PRO/
　　30/22/11F

National Portrait Gallery, card index

Parliamentary Archives
　　Parliamentary archives, ERM/10B/54

Surrey History Centre

Series OTT/2/- Church Establishment and Benefice 1865-1884

OTT/2/3, regarding perpetual curacy

OTT/2/4, Deed regarding augmentation of benefice, 1875

OTT/2/5, regarding discharging mortgage on parsonage

OTT/2/6, regarding further £33.6/8d added to £100 benefaction

CC1127/1/1-2, log books for Christ Church C/E School, Ottershaw,1870-2005

6895/1, Working Mens' Club Minutes and Accounts Book

GB/NNAF/F178598, Colebrooke, M E and others, *The Colebrooke Letters*, Surrey History Centre, Record Ref 7369, NRA cat ref NRA 3518 Surrey R O misc, 1870-1916

The Victorian Society

Litten, J W, *The works of the Scott family of architects in England and Abroad*, 1967

Royal Institute of British Architects, *Sir George Gilbert Scott: A history of his works based on published material*, 1957

Websites

http://freepages.family.rootsweb.ancestry.com/~londonaye/colebrooke_family.htm

http://www.exploringsurreyspast.otg.uk/GetRecord/SHCOL_7369#sthash.YIreF78P.dpuf

http://hansard.millbanksystems.com/commons/1859/aug/04/supply-civil-service-estimates#S3V0155P0_18590804_HOC_42

www.heritagewalks.org

http://www.stainedglassrecords.org/Ch.asp?ChId=19824

www.search.ancestry.co.

http://clanmurray.org/tartans.html

http://www.londonopenhouse.org/london/search/factsheet.asp?ftloh_id=8518, accessed 6.10.2013

http://freepages.family.rootsweb.ancestry.com/~londonaye/colebrooke_family.htm accessed 6.10.2013

http://eresources.rhul.ac.uk/kb/19th_Century_British_Library_Newspapers

www.measuringworth.com

Sources of images

Signature, title page

The Christ Church Ottershaw Minute Book, 1866-1963

Chapter 6

37/14 South Street, front of Nos 14-24 (even, right to left), c1931, *The Survey of London*, p24, picture c

37/14 South Street, back of Nos 6-14 (even, left to right), 1929, *The Survey of London*, p94, picture b

All unattributed images are from photographs taken by the author.

Lightning Source UK Ltd.
Milton Keynes UK
UKOW03f1106280314

229028UK00001B/3/P